Oldest Allies,
Guarded Friends

March 1, 1969. A quarter-century after Normandy, the newly-inaugurated Richard Nixon visits Paris. The start of a promising relationship between Charles de Gaulle and an American president, extraordinary in itself, is cut short by the General's decision to test his popularity with the French people, in the ill-fated referendum of the following month.

Oldest Allies, *Guarded Friends*

❖ ❖ ❖

The United States and France Since 1940

CHARLES G. COGAN

Foreword by
Stanley Hoffmann

PRAEGER

Westport, Connecticut
London

Library of Congress Cataloging-in-Publication Data

Cogan, Charles.
 Oldest allies, guarded friends : the United States and France
since 1940 / Charles G. Cogan; foreword by Stanley Hoffmann.
  p.   cm.
 Includes bibliographical references and index.
 ISBN 0–275–94868–4 (alk. paper).—ISBN 0–275–95116–2 (pbk.)
 1. United States—Foreign relations—France.   2. France—Foreign
relations—United States.   I. Title.
 E183.8.F8C58   1994
 327.73044—dc20   94–1150

British Library Cataloguing in Publication Data is available.

Library of Congress Catalog Card Number: 94–1150
ISBN: 0–275–94868–4
    0–275–95116–2 (pbk.)

First published in 1994

Praeger Publishers, 88 Post Road West, Westport, CT 06881
An imprint of Greenwood Publishing Group, Inc.

Printed in the United States of America

The paper used in this book complies with the
Permanent Paper Standard issued by the National
Information Standards Organization (Z39.48–1984).

10 9 8 7 6 5 4 3 2 1

Copyright Acknowledgments

The author and publisher gratefully acknowledge permission to reproduce the following
copyrighted material:

From *The Complete War Memoirs of Charles de Gaulle.* Copyright © 1955, 1956 and
1959 by Librairie Plon. Reprinted by permission of Georges Borchardt, Inc.

From *Years of Upheaval* by Henry Kissinger. Copyright © 1982 by Henry A. Kissinger.
By permission of Little, Brown and Company.

Contents

Foreword

Charles Cogan's well-informed, beautifully researched, and elegantly written account of a number of contests between France and the United States has two great merits. The first is that he emphasizes what lies behind many of these clashes: the confrontation of two universalisms, of two remarkably similar convictions that the values one's nation stands for are universal values; and the belief that there can therefore be no difference between the pursuit of the national interest and the quest of what is good for all. As Cogan points out, in the United States that belief dates to the American Revolution, that is, to the birth of the United States. In France, this belief begins with the French Revolution—late in France's long life—but it had, so to speak, been incubated throughout the eighteenth century by the various *philosophes* of the Enlightenment; in the nineteenth century French historians, especially Jules Michelet, often interpreted earlier French history as if it all had been meant to culminate in French universalism. The trouble lies, of course, in the difficulty that each of these universalisms has in accepting and acknowledging the other one. The United States, long a negligible player in the field of international relations, behaved, when it became a major actor, as if its benevolence and moral superiority were beyond doubt and challenge, and as if all other players were too selfish, small, or evil to be on the same ethical level with the United States. The French, while acknowledging the similarity of goals of the two revolutions and of their respective proclamations of human rights, have often suspected American behavior in world affairs of self-serving hypocrisy. They have sharply distinguished between universal values common to the two nations, on the one hand, and on the other, a cultural and political way of life that they accuse the Americans of wanting to spread universally and that contains many aspects that the French dislike.

Behind many of the misunderstandings and collisions Cogan analyzes, we find, on the American side, a mix of parochialism and *hubris*, and, on the French side, not one but two forms of cultural anti-Americanism. One, on the Right, dislikes the equalitarian and multicultural melting pot of the United States (France's melting pot is seen as hierarchical and based on the prevalence of a single model of integration through assimilation); it dislikes American mass culture, "excessive" social and geographical mobility, and a social ethos based on "savage" competition, the central role of money, individual success and profit, and the frenzied quest of what is new at the expense of tradition. Here, nostalgia for a feudal and a peasant past leads to distaste for democracy and capitalism. On the Left, there is another kind of anti-Americanism, which deplores American mistreatment of the "natives" and other minorities, the lack of social conscience of American capitalism both in the United States and abroad, and the manifestations of American imperialism abroad. The various French Catholic currents of thought and feelings have contributed to both forms of rejection.

What has sharpened the conflict is that these universalisms began to compete at a time when one was clearly ascending and the other was just as clearly in decline, a fact that fed American complacency (as well as exasperation) and French resentment (and determination to resist). This brings us to the other merit of this book: Even when the author disagrees with French positions, methods, and styles of negotiation, he shows that what appeared to many Americans—even in high places—as merely petulance, meanness, and childish obstinacy needs to be seen as a stubborn, not always wise or successful but certainly rational, defense of French interests and of a certain French conception of international order. Cogan explains the rationale behind French policies and shows their continuity.

A brilliant young French civil servant and strategist, Marisol Touraine, has recently written: 'France's position seems guided more by the concern for asserting what France is or should be than by any concern for reaching a given goal. In other words, it is a certain definition of international order which shapes French foreign policy, and France's perception of France's place in it.'[1] Hence, we see France's preoccupation with rank, highlighted by Cogan, especially after the calamitous debacle of 1940; also, France's determination no longer to be a mere follower of Britain, as in the 1930s, but to be treated as Britain's equal. And since Britain's strategy and perception of its interest were to be as close as possible to that of the United States, France's strategy had to be different, since the place of first lieutenant of the American colossus was already occupied. Nor was it a place the French craved, given their desire for independence, either for France or for a Europe in which France would lead. It is this quest for a breathing space, for a margin of maneuver, that gave rise to a third kind of anti-Americanism—an *antiaméricanisme d'Etat*, quite compatible with a desire to borrow a number of American variants of economic modernization (Charles de Gaulle's anti-Americanism), or with sympathy for American democracy and contributions to high culture (in François Mitterrand's case). De Gaulle's (or Michel Jobert's) battle against the "two hegemonies" never meant that they deemed the two hegemons "morally equivalent": France was firmly in the camp of the "free world." But the universe of values was one thing; the universe of power and interests was quite another. In his analysis of a number of cases involving France's relation to NATO and its determination to be a nuclear power, Charles Cogan has incisively and fairly characterized the antagonists' positions, and has treated their policies with care and respect.

It is difficult to predict how the Franco-American relationship will evolve. Paradoxically, the end of the Cold War should have led to a reduction of tensions: The "cage" in which French officials often felt they were being kept is no longer needed, and the United States is turning inward and is being criticized more often for its "withdrawal" than for its overbearing imperiousness. But even in the Gulf War, Mitterrand, much to America's annoyance, maintained a certain French "difference," and the GATT talks in 1993 brought out acute examples of French anti-Americanism of all three types. The fact that the post-Cold War world has turned out to be far less comfortable for France—less hospitable to the policy of self-assertion de Gaulle had symbolized—may make certain pragmatic accommodations easier, as in the case of NATO in 1993 when the United States allowed the European members to develop certain possibilities of strategic autonomy and the French accepted that the forces of the West European Union could be placed under NATO command. But the two competing foreign policies now advocated in France—the official one, of consolidating the European Union (as the best way of "containing" the new Germany), and the opposing quest for French national independence in a broader and looser Europe—both entail possible clashes with the United States, on a variety of issues, military, economic, and cultural.

Charles Cogan's book provides both an exemplary interpretation of past disagreements and a guide for understanding future ones. It combines academic scholarship and first-hand, practical experience, and it is attentive to nuances of policy as well as to the idiosyncracies of leaders—a fine achievement in every way.

Stanley Hoffmann

NOTE

1. In "La représentation de l'adversaire dans la politique extérieure française depuis 1981," *Revue française de science politique* 43 (October 1993), 808.

Preface

This work consists of a series of case studies on the relationship between the United States and France since World War II, beginning with the trouble that arose between Charles de Gaulle and Franklin Roosevelt after the French defeat in 1940. It is not a linear treatment of this relationship since the "great misunderstanding" of 1940, but rather reference is made, where necessary, to other events outside the study (for example Suez, Indochina, the Common Agricultural Policy) to establish some thread to the presentation.

The work begins with several observations of a general order on the French-American relationship, and some reflections on the political cultures and historical background. Then, after examining the deep trouble of the wartime period, which was not only between senior American officials and de Gaulle but also between the United States and France,[1] the work examines a series of episodes that serve as illustrations of the French-American relationship, and the difficulties of this relationship, in various areas: economic relations, approaches to strategy, decolonization, nuclear relations, and transatlantic relationships. Without being exhaustive, this account serves, rather, to illustrate the problems and the specific nature of the French-American relationship. The episodes are:

- The debate on the interim aid to France in late 1947 (economic chapter).
- The debate on the European Defense Community (EDC) and the failure of the EDC proposal in 1954 (defense case).
- The raid on Sakhiet-Sidi-Youssef in Tunisia in February 1958 and the Anglo-American good offices mission, which was the straw that broke the camel's back of the Fourth Republic (decolonization case).
- The debate on the Multilateral Force (MLF), the background of which lies parallel to the American refusal of nuclear "sharing' and the French quest for an atomic bomb,

which came to realization with the explosion at Reggane in 1960 (intended partly as a nuclear case).

- The "year of Europe" in 1973 when, after the launching of détente between the Soviet Union and the United States, the latter sought to define its relationship with Europe (case on the relations between the United States and Europe).

- The Euro-Corps, or Franco-German Corps, a dispute that began to unfold in 1990–92, revolving around the question of the independence of Europe's defense (post–Cold War case).

A final chapter delineates some of the lessons learned from these case studies, as well as some ways to approach the future.

Let me add a word about translation. Where French-language works have been translated into English, I have in virtually all cases used that translation. Otherwise, the translations are mine. In case of doubt, I have specified myself as the translator. The matter of Jean Lacouture's biography of Charles de Gaulle is somewhat special: His three-volume work was rendered into a two-volume work in English. Much of the second volume was either left out or truncated; accordingly, I have drawn from his French-language version of this volume, providing my own translation. For the rest of his work I have used the published translation. In addition, I have at times quoted from the French-language version of de Gaulle's war memoirs rather than the English translation when I used the appended documents, which are not included in the English text.

This book is adapted from a doctoral dissertation presented to the John F. Kennedy School of Government at Harvard University in 1992. I would like to thank in particular my thesis advisers, Professors Ernest May and Stanley Hoffmann, for their unfailing support and guidance, as well as Professor Samuel P. Huntington, director of the John M. Olin Institute for Strategic Studies at Harvard, where I have been conducting research and writing since 1991. Specifically, I wish to acknowledge the financial support of the Tracy B. Kittredge Foundation and the Olin Institute. Finally, in addition to the persons who graciously consented to be interviewed (including several officials knowledgeable on the Euro-Corps) and the exemplary archivists at the U.S. presidential libraries, I would like to thank my wife and my brother for their constant encouragement and support.

NOTE

1. Stanley Hoffmann, "The Man Who Would Be France," review of Jean Lacouture, *De Gaulle, vol. 1, The Rebel 1890–1944*, trans. Patrick O'Brian (London: Collins Harvill, 1990), in *The New Republic*, December 17, 1990, 36.

Oldest Allies,
Guarded Friends

❖ 1 ❖

Introduction

The French not only forget benefits received and injuries endured; they even come to dislike those to whom they are indebted, while ceasing to hate those who have done them harm. Diligence in returning good for good, and in exacting vengeance for evil, comes to be a sort of servitude which they do not readily accept.

La Rochefoucauld,
Maxims[1]

It seems to me that God, with an infinite skill and wisdom, is in the process of preparing the anglo-saxon race for a moment which is certainly coming. ... If I am not mistaken, this powerful race will burst out upon Mexico, upon Central America and South America, then on the islands in the sea, then upon Africa and beyond.

Rev. Josiah Strong,
Our Country[2]

MODELS

Trajectories

In the course of the nineteenth century, a moment of history took place in which the trajectories of France and the United States crossed: an ascending curve for the United States, a descending one for France. The crossing point could have been in approximately 1885, the year the Reverend Strong wrote the bombastic words cited above. Perhaps more symbolically, the moment could be situated around the Congress of Berlin in 1878, when Benjamin Disraeli, whose French was abominable, was persuaded to present his speech in English. That occasion could be taken as the beginning point of English as the language of diplomacy, replacing French. According to a biographer of Disraeli, Sarah Bradford, the prime minister was persuaded by the British ambassador in Berlin that the delegates would be disappointed if he spoke to them in French: "They know that they have in you the greatest living master of English rhetoric, and they are expecting that hearing your speech in English will be the intellectual delight of their lives."[3]

Obviously, to speak of rising and falling stars in a French-American context is an oversimplification. There were others in the firmament of 1878: England in the glory of its empire, Bismarck at the summit of his new Reich, the encroaching Russia of Tsar Alexander III, plus others. At the same time France had barely emerged from the constitutional morass that had followed defeat by the Prussians and the insurrection in Paris "where [the French] renewed the cycle of revolutions."[4]

Today the same actors, or nearly all of them, are still there, especially Great Britain, Germany, and the Soviet Union (now rebaptized Russia); it is therefore somewhat artificial to deal with French-American problems without taking into consideration the other countries playing in the same arena. In a certain sense Great Britain, Germany, and France have disputed the favors of the United States since the latter emerged as a superpower, and often the French-American game is superimposed by a chessboard of four or five players.

Nevertheless, in spite of these complications, and in spite of the differences in area, population, and system of society between the United States and France, the intention here is to address the relationship between these two countries— a relationship that turns in a particular way around the message. These are two countries (one could almost say *the* two countries) that are carriers of universalist messages that came out of their revolutions, and where the uniqueness of their nationality arises from those revolutions. The sentiment of the French, not always recognized by the Americans, of having something unique to say to the world is persistently evident. Too often the United States, from the fact of its superior size and because of its status of having "started from nothing" as a nation—and therefore belonging to all—has taken upon itself, and itself only, the "prerogative of the message."

For France the ancient superiority becomes the present inferiority—a sense of being permanently overwhelmed by the Anglo-Saxon world. A long history of rancor and mistrust stems from this. The oldest ally of the United States has become its touchiest friend as well as the Western country most determined in opposing American policy in Europe since World War II.

The term "atlantist" takes on the status of a code word resonating with the resentment that the French political class has retained, remembering the treatment that the United States inflicted on the Free French movement during World War II. The very term "Atlantic Charter," a revision which the Americans proposed in 1973 in all good faith, carries a bad connotation for the French: They were absent at the creation of the original "Atlantic Charter" between

Winston Churchill and Franklin Roosevelt on August 14, 1941 (which was understandable), but more important they were expressly excluded from the first anniversary celebration in 1942 by the bad humor of Franklin Roosevelt after the St. Pierre-Miquelon incident, even though the Free French movement, along with fourteen other countries, some of them governments-in- exile, had endorsed the charter on September 24, 1941!

As Alfred Grosser wrote, "the most acute transatlantic antagonisms were and still are those between the French and the Americans."[5] Unfortunately, in the political context and often in the personal context there is a mutual lack of regard, just under the skin, such as that shown by the anonymous general in the Pentagon who, exasperated after the French refusal of overflight of American planes at the time of the raid on Libya in 1986, declared to all and sundry that the French have never really fought well since Napoleon.

Today, according to Jacques Attali, the former guru-cum-pupil of François Mitterrand, it is the American star that is starting to decline. In his book *Lignes d'Horizon*,[6] Attali speaks of eight cities that he calls "hearts," which were, at successive moments in history, centers of markets and cultures, from which their influence radiated out to the milieu, which surrounds the heart, and farther out to the periphery, which represents the exploited regions. The most recent cities are London, which emerges toward 1750, Boston toward 1880, and New York toward 1930.[7]

We are now, according to Attali, at the end of a crisis—a long period of uncertainty and apparent regression. A crisis ends when a new market type becomes organized and thus a new heart establishes itself.[8]

Attali foresees the emergence of a "European space" and a "Pacific space," both of them rivals and both of them "two integrated spaces where the economic powers will replace the two military powers, both now in decline."[9] Along with these he envisages two quasi-hearts. For the European continent, "the region that extends from London to Milan"[10] seems the best placed to become the quasi-heart. For the Pacific, on the other hand, "power is shifting from one coast of the Pacific to the other" because of the "decline of the United States." Although "many still refuse to believe it,"[11] notes Attali, "everything seems to indicate that in this *Pacific Space*, economic power, in its most essential part, the mastery of massive investments that form industries, today resides in Japan."[12]

Rank

"Rank." Always "rank." The obsession with "rank." Before the Second World War, it was not talked about. It was not claimed because it was possessed. Then came the collapse of 1940. France was humiliated not because she was conquered but because the "collaboration" made of her a satellite of Germany, more precisely a nation of second rank.[13]

The whole matter of the Memorandum on the Directory in 1958 has to do with this obsession about rank. At that particular point, Charles de Gaulle, having just assumed power, was suddenly confronted by unilateral American actions in the Middle East, particularly in Lebanon and at Quemoy-Matsu.

In September 1958, in the wake of these crises, de Gaulle wrote to President Dwight D. Eisenhower to state that the North Atlantic Treaty Organization (NATO) did not satisfy either the security of the world or the security of France; in addition, "it seems necessary to France that a world-wide organization should be created and that it should include the United States, Great Britain and France."[14] By this means France sought a parity of consultation with Great Britain in dealings with the United States. However, the French seem habitually to think that more goes on between Great Britain and the United States than is actually the case. And partly because of this reality, but only partly, Eisenhower's response was studiously vague.

The question of rank was very much present in the Gulf Crisis of 1990–91. President Mitterrand stated that he was ready to assume the responsibility of involving France in an armed conflict against Iraq because France "must be worthy of its responsibility as a major power."[15] Is this by itself a compelling reason to go to war? Or again: "France is present. It must remain present. France is not a small country. It has a say. . . . France must be present before as well as in the aftermath of this conflict."[16]

The French preoccupation with rank, which, as Jacques Attali visualizes it, will gradually become focused on a greater European identity, comes from the fact that France had a population of 26.5 million in 1789,[17] well over twice that of Great Britain.[18] It also comes from the fact that a good part of Germany was only a scattering of mini-kingdoms and principalities until very late in modern history. In sum, it comes from the fact that, to borrow a phrase from General de Gaulle (uttered to Konrad Adenauer at their first meeting at de Gaulle's home at Colombey-les-Deux-Eglises in September 1958), "the French people had for centuries grown accustomed to think of their country as the mastodon of Europe."[19]

De Gaulle, initiated into history from childhood by his father (a teacher), was very conscious of how France lost what it had become accustomed to by the defeat in 1940. If today President Mitterrand is able to speak of the responsibilities of a great power, it is thanks in large measure to the determination of de Gaulle not to lose the privileges of a major power.

There is a dialectic here, created by the defeat of 1940, that remains operative: France has sought both rank, which implies participation, and independence, which often tends toward exclusion—the major theme being that all the while France must be allowed to express its "difference," or, as it is sometimes put, a "French specificity." It is this contradiction and the symbiosis of these drives that one must take into account when examining the meanderings and paradoxes of French foreign policy since World War II. Needing expiation after the collapse of 1940 France became the most difficult of the United States's Western partners as it sought—with success, thanks to the talents of its elites and of some of its leaders, especially de Gaulle—to reestablish its rank.

Once the rank was reestablished, through nuclear force and through the *trente glorieuses*—the thirty years of economic growth between 1950 and 1980—France has had to accommodate itself to the responsibilities of this rank. The interconnections are such that, in order to maintain it (in particular its active presence in the club of five veto-wielding powers in the United Nations Security Council), France is obliged from time to time to be a follower of the United States. This was the case in the Gulf War which, from a slightly different viewpoint, also represented the first application, posthumous, of the Memorandum of the Directory of 1958. De Gaulle proposes; Mitterrand disposes.

Quarrel

"Etre grand, c'est soutenir une grande querelle" (To be great is to sustain a great quarrel). These words appear at the beginning of the foreword of Charles de Gaulle's second book, *Le Fil de l'Epee* (*The Edge of the Sword*), first published in 1932.[20] They are attributed to Shakespeare in *Hamlet*, without a specific citation. However, they clearly refer to Hamlet's soliloquy in Act IV, scene iv:

> Rightly to be great
> Is not to stir without great argument,
> But greatly to find quarrel in a straw
> When honor's at the stake.[21]

"To be great is to sustain a great quarrel." This appears as a leitmotif in de Gaulle's thoughts. In his *War Memoirs* he speaks of a period following the publication of *The Edge of the Sword*, when he was transferred to Metz in 1937, and his absence from Paris deprived him "of the opportunities and contacts required for carrying on my great controversy" (*querelle*),[22] that is to say, his effort to convince his political and military superiors to equip the French Army with an armored strike force. At a later period, during World War II and again in the spring of 1958, de Gaulle's "quarrel" became a great and ferocious struggle to obtain power.

Jean Monnet, the man in the bowler hat,[23] appeared to be more in the dimensions of a Frenchman seen through foreign eyes, and more in keeping with the image of a complaisant France, than was the "great beanpole" who was General de Gaulle, the haughty and choleric man whose *képi* ("coiffure militaire rigide," or stiff military hat, as defined in *Le Petit Robert*) accentuated a temperament little given to compromise. Monnet, who was the antithesis of de Gaulle in the rebuilding of Europe after the war culminating in the synthesis of the 1970s (the European Council of member states *plus* the "supranational" Commission of Brussels), came up with this key word "quarrel," in describing the first definitive position on the political organization of Europe taken by de Gaulle as chief of state. It was in the general's press conference of September 5, 1960. Monnet said: ''Whatever reservations one might have about its content, one could not ignore this fresh launching of Europe to which de Gaulle had linked his own prestige. . . . I had sensed that the time was coming for a great European debate. I only hoped that it would not turn into a great dispute [*querelle*].''[24]

One could not better find what opposed the man who aspired ''to unite men, to solve the problems that divide them, and to persuade them to see their common interest,''[25] and the man who knew how to ''sustain a great quarrel.'' The former was so ''supranational'' that he worked for the British after the defeat of France in 1940 and even carried a British passport, in contrast with the latter, who worked virtually alone in Great Britain on behalf of his defeated country and took umbrage at any attempt by Britain to slight France.

Independence as a Quarrel

In the Gaullist context, ''independence was the great quarrel of France,'' according to Professor Maurice Vaïsse.[26] In the perspective of de Gaulle, Vaïsse maintains, this did not take the form of a drive toward hegemony but sprang from the past, from the history and culture of France. In his words, de Gaulle wanted to ''develop the national personality.''[27]

With, and because of, the defeat of 1940, independence constituted itself as a quarrel. De Gaulle never allowed himself to lower his guard with the powerful Anglo-Saxon countries that hemmed him in. Although not ordained in the heavens, a sort of permanent tension developed in the relations between the United States and France. On the other side of the Atlantic a disregard sprang up in the political class—the ''establishment''—toward the Gaullist movement, a movement described by the general himself in the following terms:

A taste for risk and adventure pushed to the pitch of art for art's sake, a contempt for the cowardly and indifferent, a tendency to melancholy and so to quarreling during the periods without danger, giving place to an ardent cohesion in action, a national pride sharpened to its extreme by their country's ill fortune and by contact with well-equipped allies, and, above all, a sovereign confidence in the strength and cunning of their own conspiracy—such were the psychological characteristics of this elite, which started from nothing and was to grow, gradually, until it drew after it the whole nation and the whole of the Empire.[28]

This description of the Gaullist movement recalls the phrase by Stanley Hoffmann, who found at the core of de Gaulle's thinking ''an element of mysticism that Americans did not appreciate.''[29] It is not hard to divine from the foregoing passage from de Gaulle's *War Memoirs* the profound antinomy between the psychological characteristics of Gaullism and the dominating outlook of Roosevelt, this scion of the East Coast establishment, surrounded for the most part by people from the same milieu.

Very quickly the Gaullists were described in official American correspondence as troublemakers, fanatics, and even "fascists" (fascism being the great scourge of the era, there was an inordinate fear that it could break out again, anywhere). The Gaullists were regarded with some justification as people little given to consensus or compromise. In brief, they were not "prudential," a term that appears several times in this study.

The very tall new French general, in his ignorance of the United States ("his knowledge of this enormous country had previously been limited and imperfect," wrote Jean Monnet of the time of the visit of de Gaulle to Harry Truman in 1946[30]), chose badly his representatives in America, although he did not have a large pool of talent, at least at the beginning, for selection.

Reliability and Independence

After World War II, when a triumphant United States tried to make a wounded France into a more reliable partner, it intruded on the French sense of independence. And when the French took steps to affirm their independence, rejecting multilateralism to the extent that they could, they became in American eyes less reliable partners.

The French (and many other Europeans) looked on reliability in a different way. For them the United States had to give Europe a feeling of security: an assurance of the long-term viability of the American commitment to defend the European continent. To Europeans the Americans did not always measure up: the doctrine of "flexible response" sometimes seemed to them a bowing out of responsibility. It raised doubts about the American resolve to wage nuclear war on the continent, if need be. However, from the American side of the Atlantic, this strategy seemed the only pragmatic way of checking a Soviet Union that was arriving at nuclear parity and had achieved conventional predominance.

The whole affair of the European Defense Community (EDC) and the Multilateral Force (MLF) stemmed from a perpetual and seemingly inescapable dilemma: how to bring about European unity and at the same time assure Europe's defense—without offending the sensibilities of the French regarding their independence.

For the French the dilemma posed itself in another way: how to avoid the snares of multilateralism and "supranationality," and thus assure their independence, without falling into isolation. In this France was well placed in its geography: it is hard for the "country of the center" to fall into isolation. It is difficult to create a defense structure for Europe without France.

The reliability sought by the United States conflicted with the full independence for which the French were striving. There were differing perspectives between the new imperium across the Atlantic and the oldest nation in Europe. The Americans, without so saying and sometimes without so thinking, conceived partnership, however reasonably and pragmatically articulated, as under their sponsorship. As "leader" of the imperium constituted by the "free world," the United States quite naturally looked upon its partners ultimately as countries that would follow along. This did not mean that the United States necessarily considered them satellites.

France, as the most ancient nation in Europe, has tended to regard the nation-state as the basic entity of civilization. Moreover, having experienced the highs and lows, from supreme conquests to unspeakable abasements, the French have developed, especially as an outcome of World War II, an advanced, even extreme, sense of national independence. This having been said, however, the French sense of independence, at least in the twentieth century, never became dangerous and wild à la Germany, only annoying.

This concept of national independence is often expressed, in keeping with the French tradition, in abstract terms. Jean Laloy, in his book on Yalta, described the French state of mind at the time of that conference in February 1945:

The view from Paris: Europe must prepare itself to become one day "the arbiter between the two camps, Soviet and Anglo-Saxon." France, while concluding the "necessary alliances," must succeed in grouping together "the states which border on the Rhine, the Alps, the Pyrenees" in order to prevent another Reich from being able once again to threaten her. The implementation of these very broad views led France to try to weaken what remained of Germany as much as possible and to pursue in the immediate postwar period a policy equidistant from the "two camps" but, for that very reason, very far removed from reality.[31]

Laloy puts his finger on what was, and what remains, a sort of surreal quality to French foreign policy since World War II.

Long after Yalta, French nuclear policy, developed magisterially by de Gaulle as a guarantee of a place at the table among the great powers, still retains, in its highest level of abstraction, a sort of unreal quality in terms of its application to the world of reality: war is something prepared for not to be won but prevented.

This is not to say that the French nuclear capability does not amount to much; far from it. Rather, it is out of place operationally in a superpower world and just possibly irrelevant as a weapon. This is one reason why the French have always sought to keep an aura of uncertainty about this nuclear arm. This French national weapon, justified from the outset as giving "sanctuary" to French territory, is, thirty years later, coming increasingly into contradiction with the building of a united Europe. The discordance between the Community spirit, at the head of which has been the French-German tandem, and the French nuclear deterrent is all too obvious. And it is not only the Americans who find fault with a French exclusiveness that is quite removed from the idea of partnership.

POLITICAL CULTURES

I call attention to these events, Sire, because I believe in what History teaches. And that which is being made before our eyes plunges its roots in the past more than ever.[32]

In the relations between nations there are specific problems, unique particularities, special redolences. This enters the realm of the national spirit, an elusive but nonetheless palpable notion.

It is not startling, and yet it says everything: the American political culture is at the opposite pole of that of France. In a declaration published on December 11, 1990,[33] behind which was a movement inspired by Jacques Delors called "Démocratie 2000," twelve socialist deputies from different factions warned that representative democracy in France was facing dangers and appealed for a "Republican morality" that brings with it, among other things, "the superiority of fraternity over egoism." They perceived "a crisis with the French model, born with the Republic," whose great principles were

the affirmation of the State as against corporatism, the sovereignty of the law—the expression of the general will—the representation of the citizens by those they elect, the equilibrium of powers, notably of the political vis-à-vis the economic, the role of the parties and the trade unions as privileged intermediaries, and vectors of conflicts.

Today, continued the manifesto, French society "has become stuck in a progressive 'americanization' of behavior and of the way of life: the exaltation of individual success, the scorn of failure, the ignoring of those who are excluded, the pauperization of the State, the omnipotence of television . . . the rise of pressure groups, the mixing of individual demands with the general interest . . . and finally, the increasing shrinkage of the realm of the political."

Apart from a general French reflex of criticizing that which comes from the Anglo-Saxon, and especially American, world, there are few better descriptions of how many Frenchmen see America as the antithesis of their own tradition, especially contained in the phrase "the exaltation of individual success"—a notion that encounters broad disapproval in several currents of French thought, beginning with the left.

The historian François Furet has noted that the idea that "the happiness of the individual [should] become the goal of society, and that the social [aspect] is the sum of all these individual happinesses,"[34] meets with disapproval not only in the traditional left but also in French counterrevolutionary thought, especially Catholic. Having the individual as the basis for the social realm is considered "the disguising of egoisms," which leads to a twofold deterioration, political and moral—political by a sort of anarchy and moral by hedonism. This is the result of obedience having been suppressed by individualism.

The concept of society as a market where the individual lives for himself and his own happiness, and for that of those close to him, where the state intrudes as little as possible into civil society—in short, the model of American-style liberalism (in the European sense of the term liberal)—has never been to the liking of a majority of Frenchmen. Furet sums it up in speaking of "modern individualism, with its inevitable civic deficit, which contains the moral detour that it introduces: the absence of the common good. This is a real and great problem, evident for the last two hundred years."

One finds in France even today a moralism that has a Catholic tint to it, whether it comes out of a religious or a republican environment. Few things are less to the taste of the French than the Calvinistic notion that considers trade, and the profit one derives from trade, as a good in itself. Robespierre heaped public scorn on the mercantilism of the British. This taboo goes back to the Catholic past of France, however repudiated and scorned it is. François Mitterrand is a reflection of this Catholic and rural past of a majority of Frenchmen, with his objurgations against "money which corrupts, money which kills." The fact that Mitterrand's considerable holdings are largely in land (some gifted) excuses them or causes them to be ignored. They are not the result of commerce.

The manifesto of "Démocratie 2000" recalls the speech of Jean Jaurès, with its overtones of the morality of the French left in the nineteenth century, before the National Assembly on December 20, 1911:

We only see [in the Americans] men of billions, of business, of the obsession with money. We would say [however] that there are certain indications . . . that [some] enlightened [American] billionaires . . . are seeking, before their death, more noble sustenance for their thought, for their soul. . . . Whence comes this reawakening of idealism, which is not on the surface because it digs below the period of the dollar, the mercantile period, to the deepest sources of English and American life, down to the soul of the puritans who were seized with the enthusiasm of the Biblical prophets and who dreamed in their own fashion of a society of liberty and justice.[35]

On a number of occasions during the history of the United States, the dream of the Puritans, mentioned by Jaurès, of a society of liberty and justice has turned into a nightmare: slavery, the rotten fruit present in the Constitution itself, a stain that tortured the American mind until the outbreak of the Civil War seventy-five years later; the ravages of the industrialization that followed, the epoch of the robber barons and the "mauve decade," present in the speech of Jaurès cited above; the denial of civil rights to blacks that did not end until the 1960s; and more recently, the transformation of urban ghettos into combat zones at the approach of the twenty-first century.

Thus is the varied moral landscape in the United States. These contrasts are revealed in Alexis de Tocqueville's *On Democracy in America*, the second part of which seems to contradict the first, according to Pierre Birnbaum in an article in *Le Monde*.[36] The first part of *On Democracy in America* was published in 1835. Three years earlier de Tocqueville had returned from his visit to America; Birnbaum described his state of mind upon returning: "He needed to return, to find France again, to reflect on the contradictory history of these two societies charged with resolving, the one and the other, this "universal" and "lasting" fact which is the equality of conditions." For de Tocqueville, Birnbaum noted, the problem was

to avoid the manifold forms of despotism that democracy itself can spawn, that of a too-powerful State dominating a myriad of isolated and helpless individuals, also that of an administration that is too centralized, and finally that of the unchecked domination of a majority that has little respect for the rights of minorities.

According to Birnbaum, the key observation of de Tocqueville in the first part of *On Democracy in America* was that "the Americans fought by means of liberty the individualism to which equality gave birth, and they conquered it." It is these "multiple liberties," according to Birnbaum,

that check both an often intolerant Jacobinism as well as various forms of Bonapartism. This is why de Tocqueville is attentive to the virtues of decentralization resulting from a "weak" government, American-style . . . [where there are] juries that themselves are associated with decision making, and also a pluralist press that stimulates discussion and debate.

This "weak" government of America rests on the federal system which serves as a shield against the all-invading centralized state. This is very different from the French model, where even the language elevates the word "state" by capitalizing it. When the French system centralizes it centralizes everything, following a tradition that long predates the Revolution, as de Tocqueville points out in "The Ancien Régime and the Revolution."

Even in the first part of *On Democracy in America*, Birnbaum observed, de Tocqueville drew attention to what he termed "the question of the blacks, in the sense that this population remains as though outside the benefits of democracy." However, it is particularly in the second volume, published in 1840, that de Tocqueville became more pessimistic about the risks facing a democratic society. He perceived an "administrative centralization . . . at present almost consubstantial with the establishment of a democracy within which individuals are tempted to draw in upon themselves, more concerned with their own happiness and not that of their fellow citizens."

According to Birnbaum, the second volume of *On Democracy in America* almost contradicts the first. Thus de Tocqueville, in the final analysis, perceives what Furet calls the "civic deficit" of Anglo-Saxon democracy, and this criticism has lost none of its pertinence to this day.

America is a "contractual" and "horizontal" society, to borrow the words of François Furet, different from the more "vertical" and "aristocratic" societies of Europe: in the United States, "one does not drag one's pedigree behind him." (One recalls the famous phrase of Lincoln: "I am not a descendant; I am an ancestor.") Furet presents the image of an immigrant, carrying nothing but his own native intelligence, who arrives variously at Wall Street, at the City in London, or at the Bourse in Paris. A priori he will have more success in New York than in London or Paris "because in the United States he will encounter less resistances."

France, a vertical society, is constructed of political compartments. In this sense Pierre Laval was a traitor two times over. He betrayed France to Germany following the defeat in 1940 and, in going from the left to the right, he betrayed the workers of Aubervilliers who had given him their support when he began his political career in the elections of 1919. America, a society of weaker ideological convictions, has much less rigid political compartments, though this has become less so in the very recent past. America is essentially a society of equality of rights:

[It] is not an absolute democracy where the majority always decides; it is a constitutional democracy where constitutional rights constrain what the majority can do . . . [because] the majority sometimes utilizes its power through its elected representatives to crush the individual liberties of those less numerous or despised.[37]

This equality of rights ultimately cannot be legislated, except for rare constitutional amendments which are subject to ratification by majorities in three-quarters of the states. The arbiter of the equality of rights is the Supreme Court. All are created equal. Everyone has a right to life, liberty, and the pursuit of happiness. But in this sometimes frantic pursuit, it turns out that there are some who are left by the wayside. Furet sums it up: "America is a market like a jungle, an absolute market in the literal sense of the term, but arbitered by strict rules of law. If these are transgressed, one goes to jail. France is not really a market because the State is everywhere, and at the same time there are not strict rules of law."

France, again according to the words of Furet, is "legicentrist . . . the whole French democratic tradition, such as was founded by the Revolution, is legicentrist. There is nothing above the sovereignty of the people." Even the rights of man (civil rights) are prescribed by the legislators. The result

is an extraordinary weakness in the national juridical culture. No one discusses the foundation of the law. These things are thought of in terms of legitimacy. The Monarchy, the Ancien Régime serve as great symbolic figures. This is striking in relation to the American example, where the Constitution takes on the character of a Sacred Arch. There is no other date but 1787. In France there is a sort of postrevolutionary culture which has inherited from the Revolution a formidable uncertainty concerning the law.

According to Furet, conceptually and philosophically,

it is a sort of extension of the revolutionary phenomenon to the absurd whereby there are never laws, there is never a formal guarantee of universal procedure that regulates civic existence. . . . The rupture of the universalism of the law . . . [which took place in] [17]89 is so strong in our country and in our political civilization that it has lasted for decades and decades, for centuries and centuries. Look at the extent to which the juridification of political life is weak. One discovers this today in, for example, the stock market problem.[38] There is no law.

By contrast, and again according to Furet, America is a country that is juris-prudential and "prudential." States Furet: "The Anglo-Saxons have . . . a pru-dential culture. It functions by a segmentation of the law." The Supreme Court, an emanation of the concept of "separation of powers" ("checks and bal-ances") from French liberal thought, that is from Montesquieu, has set itself as defender of the rights of man, beyond the spirit and sometimes beyond the tolerance of the average man.

On the other hand, in France civil rights are prescribed by laws, which are made by Parliament. Political culture is thought of in terms of "legitimacy." This goes back to the revolutionary experience of the tabula rasa, on which Furet reflects in the following terms:

How is it that the French—and this does not exist in the United States, where there is no aristocracy, no monarchy, no Catholic church—how is it that the French were seized with this almost insane ambition to say that ten centuries, fourteen centuries do not matter at all. The social contract, the body politic is going to be remade: the tabula rasa. For thirty years I have been studying this, and it is more obscure than ever.

Furet adds that the problem with the French is that they think it is simple.

Furet almost arrives at an answer when he says, "The rejection of history by the French Revolution is explained by its history." That is to say, by that which preceded it: the century of the Enlightenment and the birth in the salons of Paris of French rationalism, with its quality of abstraction, which perforce lent itself readily to a mind-set of tabula rasa.

In the course of its long night of revolution (1789–99), France oscillated between a flowering of the rights of man, thus of the individual (Phenomenon 1789), and a sort of upside-down absolutism, a heritage, in a way, of the ancien régime. The second tendency, Jacobin dictatorship, gradually gained the ascen-dancy, under the banner of *la volonté générale*, or the general will—following the legacy of Jean-Jacques Rousseau, and a handful of men, frequently changing in composition, ruled the country in a bloody dictatorship (Phenomenon 1793). And because of this absolutist, monarchist past, scorned though it was, the French mentality could adapt to a centralized and unitary state of the Jacobin, and later Bonapartist, style.

France emerged from its revolutionary ordeal profoundly divided. Of all the countries of Europe, as a result of its Revolution, France was mentally in a state of civil war for more than a century and a half afterward. There have been attempts to surmount or suppress these divisions by a sort of sublimation con-tained in the notion of *la volonté générale*, which each political grouping, but especially the left, has sought to co-opt. Particularly for the republicans (with a small "r"), the key word is "faction": these "factions" who refuse to submit to the general will represented by the Republic; or worse still, those "leagues" (and here we encounter the anticlerical term *moines ligueurs*, or "agitator monks") who plot and bestir themselves outside the parliamentary arena.

It is precisely this fascination with the "general will" of Rousseau that leads the French to think in terms of "legitimacy"—as an alternative and superior to "constitutionality." The next chapter in this study deals with the fierce struggle among the French people in the name of legitimacy that broke out in the wake of the collapse of the French Army in 1940. From each side, from de Gaulle and from Pétain, there is an aspect of the tabula rasa. For Vichy a constitution is destroyed by a vote of parliament, and those in power proceed to govern without a new constitution but with a presumed "legitimacy." From London the tall rebel general (temporary grade) calls for a usurpation of the existing French government in the name of legitimacy.

In France (by contrast with America, a federal and prudential society) things proceed from time to time by popular explosion. Bound in a sort of psychological straitjacket, the country proceeds historically by a series of national dramas where the people express themselves by upheaval: 1789, 1815, 1830, 1848, 1871, 1940, 1958, 1968.

The French Revolution, with its idea of the tabula rasa, has led France into an instability that if not endemic is at least latent—at any rate until recently. Even with the anchoring the Fifth Republic has constituted— the increased powers of the president, who names his own prime minister (Constitution of 1958), and the election of the president by universal suffrage (amendment of 1962)— one is never quite sure which political route the country is going to take.

Even today the political construction of France remains unfinished, causing the severest French critics (and French critics generally prefer that criticism of France be in French hands) to decry this "banana republic" aspect of affairs. The French method of voting (proportional or majority and/or variants) is perennially being changed, depending on the dynamics of the party in power. Alongside this perpetual inconstancy on such a fundamental matter, gerrymandering is but a venial affair.

The diverging political cultures emphasize the antinomy of these two democracies that—almost unique in the world—each considers itself the bearer of a universal message on the "equality of conditions" of mankind. These are two democracies with quite different conceptions about the organization of the state and of political life. For a Frenchman, America is the absence of politics, or rather the lack of an ideological content in political life. For an American, France is a mélange, difficult to grasp, of authoritarianism and anarchy. Most pertinently, and in the words of Stanley Hoffmann, France is a divided country.[39]

This having been said, one can discern, with the anchoring of the Fifth Republic and the age of the "global village," a coming together of the models of these two republican democracies, first in the domain of the executive, with a "president-king" established in the life of the Fifth Republic and the increase in the powers of the American president, now deemed "imperial." Second, in the judicial area, the French Constitutional Council, established in 1945, "modified itself jurisprudentially in the 1970s," Furet notes, to the point where it overruled the socialist government on the issue of the nationalizations voted by the National Assembly in the early period of Mitterrand's presidency. Third, in the administrative area, with the decentralization laws of 1983, France has taken a significant step away from the tradition of the centralized, Jacobin state. Finally, in the political area, we also see a rapprochement between the two models.

Although observers have long noted the extraordinary lack of ideological depth in the United States, where the political platforms are tepid and the political debate lacks aggressiveness, a certain polarization developed in the Reagan years. By contrast, on the French side one discerns "the end of the French exception," the subtitle of the recent book by François Furet, Jacques Julliard, and Pierre Rosenvallon.[40] The softening of political habits, the diminution of divisions within the country with the political parties being drawn toward the center, may signal the fading away of the murderous game in France known as "verbal civil war" (la guerre civile verbale).

In the constitutional realm, France may be near to reaching a national consensus—some two hundred years after the profound fissure created by the French Revolution. What emerges is a system that is more presidential than parliamentary, based on universal suffrage for the election of a president and on parliamentary representation, but in which the president holds the upper hand over the National Assembly, as was demonstrated in the cohabitation period of 1986–88. Whether, by way of backlash, the various recent calls for a strengthening of the parliament will end in significant changes remains to be seen, but it would appear doubtful.

THE PREWAR PERIOD

There are certainly fundamental differences between the two countries that go back to the dawn of history, by the extension of the history of England, mother country of the United States. Jean-Baptiste Duroselle has noted the deep differences that separated the British and the French colonists in the New World:

In the colonial era there were no worse enemies than the French and British settlers in America, and one may even say that the long conflict between France and Britain, in which, between 1689 and 1815, they confronted each other in eight successive and ruthless wars, was in large part due to the feud between their respective "Americans."[41]

In French terms, America is an Anglo-Saxon country, that is, an historical extension of Great Britain and therefore implicitly an element in the historic competition between the French and the British.

In spite of the "alliance of circumstances," the pact between Benjamin Franklin and the Court of Louis XVI in 1778, rivalry emerged rapidly after the Treaty of Paris in 1793 ended the Revolutionary War in America. The French, as well as the British, harassed the ships of the new nation trying to carry on maritime commerce. French-American engagements took place on the high seas.

Other half-manifestations of the French and British will to contain the thrust of this young country followed, especially the tentative attempt to recognize the Confederacy that was aimed, objectively, at splitting the United States in two. The comportment of American troops, or more fundamentally the mere presence of these troops on French soil in 1916–18, and the refusal of Washington to link the French war debt to the United States with German reparations to France did not have the effect of making relations more serene.

As noted above there was a certain repugnance on the part of French public opinion, rooted in a Catholic and rural past, toward American capitalism with its base of Calvinism, which made of commerce a virtue. A strong current of opinion that reviled "American materialism" appeared to gain strength in France in the period between the two world wars.

It was particularly in 1940 that real trouble began between the two countries, and a decisive turning point came in the relations between the two nations with the collapse of the French Army and the diminution of the French state. The French Army had served, in a certain sense, as a compensation for the delayed arrival of France in the Industrial Revolution. Without its army France would have appeared to be falling even farther behind.

In 1940 there erupted in France a civil war of succession, in which the Roosevelt administration came down squarely in favor of the continuity of the French state as represented by the regime of Vichy (understandable, perhaps, in 1940 but inexcusable as the war wore on), thereby demonstrating the traditional American reflex of dealing with the government that holds power—the reflex of a nation born in revolution but having become a pillar of the status quo—and the reflex of the prudential mentality which tends to focus on legalities and therefore to recognize and deal with the power in place.

The next chapter will be devoted to the trouble that began with the disaster of France in 1940, a disaster that, in the eyes of the Roosevelt administration and many in the American establishment, was unpardonable. All the history of the past was swept away by Roosevelt, who was furious at the French defeat. As of 1940, and under the policy line set by Roosevelt, American officials and public figures generally adopted an attitude of condescension toward France, largely ignoring the role it played during World War I. In the course of a seminal meeting on June 19, 1943, at Algiers, de Gaulle told General Eisenhower,

Do you recall that during the last war, France played a role analogous to that which the United States is playing today with regard to arms to several Allied countries? At that time it was France who armed the Belgians and the Serbs, procured many resources for the Russians and the Rumanians, and lastly outfitted your army with a large share of its materiel. Yes, during World War I, you Americans fired only our cannon, drove only our tanks, flew only our planes.[42]

Two days before de Gaulle uttered these words, President Roosevelt sent a personal telegram to Eisenhower that contained the following words: "It is important that you know, for your own secret information, that we could possibly break with General de Gaulle within the coming several days.''[43] It was arguably the most difficult moment in the relations between de Gaulle and Roosevelt, and this relationship will be the subject of the next chapter. The rupture between the Free French and the United States never took place because down deep, beneath the moving sands, the opinion of the French in Algeria and in France was in the process of swinging in favor of de Gaulle. Perhaps de Gaulle, who seemed to admire the formula—audacity in words and prudence in actions[44]—did not know on June 19, 1943, how close he was to the abyss.

NOTES

1. Paris, Editions Garnier Frères, 1967, which mentions (p. 36) that "it should be noted that all the manuscripts say *the French*, and all the [print] editions [say] *men*." The translation here is from *The Maxims of the Duc de la Rochefoucauld*, trans. Constantine FitzGibbon (London: Allan Wingate, 1947), 33–34.

2. Christopher Hitchens, *Blood, Class and Nostalgia: Anglo-American Ironies* (New York: Farrar, Straus & Giroux, 1990), 124. Strong's work was originally published in 1885.

3. Sarah Bradford, *Disraeli* (London: Weidenfeld and Nicolson, 1982), 350.

4. Jacques Rougerie, "The Commune of Paris," *Le Monde*, March 17–18, 1991, 2.

5. Alfred Grosser, *The Western Alliance* (New York: Continuum, 1980), xv.

6. Jacques Attali, *Lignes d'Horizon* (Paris: Fayard, 1990). Translated by John Gage, Sun Microsystems. Note: Page numbers from this work in the notes below refer to the Gage juxtaposed, page-by-page, translation.

7. Ibid., 26.

8. Ibid., 24–25.

9. Ibid., 4.

10. Ibid., 43.

11. Ibid., 56.

12. Ibid., 62.

13. Gilles Martinet, "La Politique de l'apparence," *Le Monde*, March 13, 1991, 2.

14. Jean Lacouture, *De Gaulle: The Ruler 1945–1970*, trans. Alan Sheridan (New York: Simon and Schuster, 1991), 217.

15. *New York Times*, January 10, 1991, A18.

16. Press conference of President Mitterrand, December 19, 1990. *Le Monde*, December 21, 1990, 2.

17. Jean Carpentier and François Lebrun, eds., *Histoire de France* (Paris: Seuil, 1987), 262.

18. Great Britain attained eleven million only in 1801. *Encyclopaedia Britannica, Macropaedia*, 1978, 14: 816.

19. Charles de Gaulle, *Memoirs of Hope*, trans. Terence Kilmartin (London: Weidenfeld and Nicolson), 1971, 178.

20. Charles de Gaulle, *Le Fil de l'Epée* (Geneva: Editions Edito-Service, 1972), 3.

21. William Shakespeare, *Hamlet*, the Pelican Shakespeare (London: Penguin Books, 1970), 127.

22. Charles de Gaulle, *The Complete War Memoirs of Charles de Gaulle*, vol. 1, *The*

Call to Honour, 1940–1942 trans. Jonathan Griffin (New York: Simon and Schuster, 1964), 27.

23. "At the age of sixteen I bought a bowler hat and assumed my responsibilities." Jean Monnet, *Memoirs* (Garden City, N.Y.: Doubleday, 1978), 40.

24. Ibid., 433.

25. Ibid., 221.

26. Taken from an address by Professor Vaïsse on November 23, 1990, at a colloquium in Paris on General de Gaulle.

27. Ibid.

28. De Gaulle, *War Memoirs*, 1: 94.

29. Stanley Hoffmann, "The Man Who Would Be France," *The New Republic*, December 17, 1990, 34.

30. Monnet, *Memoirs*, 228.

31. Jean Laloy, *Yalta: Yesterday, Today, Tomorrow*, trans. William R. Tyler (New York: Harper and Row, 1988), 61–62 (N.B., the quoted material in this passage is from de Gaulle's *War Memoirs*). Laloy was the French interpreter between Stalin and de Gaulle in Moscow in December 1944. Later he was in disagreement with de Gaulle, especially after the return of the general to power in 1958.

32. Marek Halter, "Abdiquer! Adresse au roi Hussein de Jordanie," *Le Monde*, January 5, 1991, 4.

33. *Le Monde*, December 11, 1990, 2.

34. Except as otherwise noted, the statements of Professor Furet cited in this chapter are from two lectures (January 24 and 31, 1989), which were part of the seminar "The Revolution of 1789 and Us," organized by the Fondation Saint-Simon in Paris, January 17–March 21, 1989. Translations are by the author.

35. Jean-Noël Jeanneney, "Jean Jaurès: Captation d'héritage," *Le Monde*, March 10–11, 1991, 2. The quotation is taken from *Jean Jaurès, anthologie*, ed. Louis Levy (Paris: Calmann-Lévy, 1983), 119.

36. *Le Monde*, June 17–18, 1990, 2.

37. Kathleen M. Sullivan, "Bush's Supreme Court Red Herring," *The New York Times*, July 29, 1990, section 4, 19.

38. Furet was speaking of the insider-trading scandals that surfaced in the press in France in 1988–89.

39. From a lecture at Harvard University in the course "French Thought about Politics and Society," Spring 1991.

40. François Furet, Jacques Julliard, and Pierre Rosenvallon, *La République du Centre: La fin de l'exception française* (Paris: Calmann-Lévy, 1988).

41. Jean-Baptiste Duroselle, *France and the United States: From the Beginnings to the Present*, trans. Derek Coltman (Chicago: University of Chicago Press, 1978), 1.

42. De Gaulle, *War Memoirs*, vol. 2, *Unity, 1942–1944*, trans. Richard Howard, 434. (N.B., the translation cites "trucks" for *chars*, but it is probable that de Gaulle meant "tanks.")

43. Franklin D. Roosevelt Presidential Library, Map Room, File on France (FOF), Box 30, France: de Gaulle, 1943, Message Freedom 511, personal from the president to General Eisenhower, June 17, 1943.

44. De Gaulle, *War Memoirs*, 2: 634.

❖ 2 ❖

The Falling Out

Paris! Paris outraged! Paris broken! Paris martyrized! But Paris liberated! Liberated by itself, liberated by its people with the help of the armies of France, with the support and the help of the whole of France, of France that is fighting, of France alone, of true France, of eternal France.

> Charles de Gaulle,
> at the time of the liberation of Paris[1]

He is very touchy about the honor of France but I think he is essentially selfish.

> Franklin D. Roosevelt
> on Charles de Gaulle[2]

There is such a thing as gratitude. De Gaulle obviously is not aware of it.

> *Shreveport Times*,
> June 12, 1944[3]

IRON WILL, HEART OF BRONZE, MULTIPLE INCOMPATIBILITIES

The first of the quotations given above was included in a review of the translation of the first volume of the biography *De Gaulle* by Jean Lacouture. The author of the review, Stephen E. Ambrose, commented as follows on this quotation: "Not one word in the last sentence was true, but through these words de Gaulle gave back to France not only her honor but her soul."[4]

Literally speaking, however, there was some truth in de Gaulle's words. At the moment of his address, August 25, 1944, there were not many Anglo-Saxon troops in Paris. The city was liberated for the most part by French forces. This had a tenuous relation to an agreement between de Gaulle and Eisenhower at the end of the previous year. According to de Gaulle, he told Eisenhower that it was necessary that French troops take possession of the capital and Eisenhower acquiesced.[5]

This conversation recounted by de Gaulle took place on December 30, 1943, just before Eisenhower was to leave Algiers to go to Washington and then to London, where, as de Gaulle was aware, he was to prepare for the invasion of France.[6] There was nothing in his account to indicate he felt his troops would be excluded again from an Allied landing (the first being the invasion of North Africa in November 1942). This time it would be in the metropole (i.e., Metropolitan France) itself, or to use a more emotive term, the mother country. Supreme offense.

There is no reason to doubt de Gaulle's words, although there could have been some exaggeration in this account of his conversation with Eisenhower. The acquiescence and understanding de Gaulle drew from Eisenhower was in contrast with the subsequent decision by Franklin Roosevelt to keep de Gaulle and the Free French away from the Allied landing in Normandy. After the invasion there followed the competition between AMGOT[7] teams and Gaullist teams to seize the machinery of administration in the liberated areas, including the dispute over what the currency in these territories should look like and who should issue it, and finally de Gaulle's decision to disregard the American command and exercise the "right" of French troops to get to Paris first.

How did the misunderstanding come to this? Essentially through Franklin Roosevelt himself, who ruled over American foreign policy, including and especially toward France, with a master hand. According to Stanley Hoffmann, the opinion of Jean Lacouture, the great French expert on de Gaulle, is that "the shabby treatment of de Gaulle by Roosevelt, which [Lacouture] analyzes in detail [in his biography], and which he attributes in large part to the influence of American and French advisors, remains mysterious."[8]

Douglas Dillon, former U.S. Ambassador to France and later Secretary of the Treasury, recounted that in the summer of 1953, several months after his arrival in Paris, he asked whether it might be useful if he met General de Gaulle.[9] The Deputy Chief of Mission, Theodore Achilles, told Dillon he did not think this would be possible, as there had earlier been a dispute with de Gaulle. It was not known what the origin was, but in any event, no one from the embassy had met de Gaulle since 1946. Dillon had an inquiry made about this in the embassy files, and he found that, in fact, relations with de Gaulle had been cut since 1946. It was due to the fact that the then ambassador, Jefferson Caffery, felt that, since de Gaulle had left the government in January 1946, it was incumbent on him to make a visit to the ambassador and not the other way around. The general refused, and a sort of blockage set in. Looking back on it, it is difficult to imagine that General de Gaulle, even in the depths of his "crossing of the desert" (traversée du désert) in 1953, would have accepted paying a visit to Cafferey inside the premises of the American Mission. Out of the question!

Several senior officials at the embassy had maintained friendly relations with some of de Gaulle's lieutenants. Discreet probes were made, and it was settled that, in the course of his next visit to Paris, General de Gaulle would be happy to receive the American ambassador.

The meeting was set for nine o'clock in the evening in a small salon next to the main dining room of the Hotel Pérouse, the favorite meeting place of the general during this period when he was out of power. The one-on-one meeting lasted about two hours. In Dillon's recollection,

De Gaulle unburdened himself. He talked about all sorts of things. He said how sorry he was to have created so many difficulties for President Roosevelt at a time when the president was carrying on his shoulders the whole burden of the world. But he had to take the side of France. He hated having to do that, but he had to do it; Roosevelt was "a wonderful fellow."

De Gaulle's words to Ambassador Dillon do not necessarily indicate that de Gaulle was not capable of deception vis-à-vis Roosevelt; far from it. But all the same, de Gaulle had a tendency to disdain personal considerations as "subaltern." Indeed, Stanley Hoffmann asserts that "de Gaulle kept his admiration for Roosevelt," but he also adds, "and his sympathy for men like Eisenhower who had understood him and respected him."[10]

General de Gaulle's words on Roosevelt call to mind a passage in the *War Memoirs* when the general spoke of the "painful affair" of his relations with General Henri Giraud and the inexorable eclipse of his rival:

Along the road that led to the nation's unity, I encountered many times such personal questions, in which the duties of my trust transcended but nevertheless afflicted my own feelings. I may say that in no case [than that of General Giraud] did it cost me more to impose the iron law of national interest (*la loi d'airain de l'intérêt national*).[11]

To note in passing, the ancient and literary meaning of the word *airain* is "bronze."

Thus, on the one hand, there is the image of an egotistical, quarrelsome, and ingrate de Gaulle, and contrastingly, a de Gaulle who carried within himself the honor of France—an honor many times trampled on since the scene of the armistice that was a surrender, signed on June 22, 1940, at Rethonde, in the same railroad car as the one of 1918.[12]

THE TWO ENCOUNTERS: THE NONCONVERSATIONS BETWEEN THE PATRICIAN AND THE PRETENDER

Act I: Anfa, 1943

The first encounter between President Roosevelt and General de Gaulle took place on January 22, 1943 at Anfa, at the time of the Casablanca Conference.

A month earlier, de Gaulle had had a conversation with Admiral Harold Stark, the official U.S. representative to the French National Committee in London. Admiral Stark's aide-de-camp, Captain Tracy B. Kittredge, wrote to Robert E. Sherwood a record of this conversation, of which the following is an extract:

[De Gaulle] was also convinced that French culture, intelligence and capacities of leadership were so widely diffused in France that when any elite or governing class failed France, through decadence or defeatism, new individuals were always projected upward out of the French masses to give a new and enlightened leadership to "eternal France"; that had been true throughout the centuries from the time of Charlemagne to that of Hitler. . . . Thus de Gaulle referred to the rise of the Capetian royal house, to Joan of Arc, to Henri IV, to the revolutionary leaders (1789–1793), to Napoleon, finally to Poincaré and Clemenceau; de Gaulle added—"perhaps this time I am one of those thrust into leadership by circumstances, and by the failure of other leaders."

The following commentary by Captain Kittredge was appended to the record of this conversation: "Admiral Stark was much impressed by this historical and philosophical analysis and suggested that de Gaulle, on meeting Roosevelt (a great student of French history and politics), should attempt to make the President understand his concepts."[13]

These are concepts that are scarcely democratic in the prudential and Anglo-Saxon sense but quite in the tradition of French political thought. The mystical notion of "eternal France" has a resonance akin to the Rousseauist theme of *la volonté générale*. The underlying anti-parliamentary theme of de Gaulle's words are not surprising, given his monarchist family tradition and his own military background. Proceeding by "rupture," as de Gaulle suggests, in getting rid of a "decadent and defeatist" ruling class, is completely foreign to what has come to be established as the prudential tradition of the American state, represented quintessentially by American elites and in this particular era by Franklin Roosevelt.

Admiral Stark was planning to be present at the meeting between Roosevelt and de Gaulle, which was to have taken place in Washington; the conversation above occurred on December 15, 1942, the eve of the admiral's departure for Washington. On December 24 the assassination of Admiral François Darlan took place in Algiers, and there were whisperings of a Gaullist hand behind it. The visit of the general was put off.

Three weeks later de Gaulle gave in to pressure from Churchill to come to Casablanca, and there he had his first meeting with the U.S. president. The circumstances could not have been worse. In the background was the invasion of North Africa in November 1942 without de Gaulle's having been consulted or officially informed. Following that, the administrative measures put into effect by the American military command had not been discussed with the general either, in particular the bringing to power of Admiral Darlan, the man from Vichy who happened to be in North Africa at the time of the invasion. Finally, the Casablanca Conference, in the Sultanate of Morocco under a French protectorate, was organized without de Gaulle's being involved.

According to American records, this first encounter between Roosevelt and de Gaulle, on January 22, 1943, lasted from 10:30 to 10:55 in the evening at the Residence in Anfa, under the bothersome though not acknowledged presence of American Secret Service agents behind the curtains. There is not a complete account of this first interview. The general arrived "cold and austere," accompanied by an aide-de-camp, according to Harry Hopkins, who did not stay for the whole meeting and did not make a formal report on it.[14] Robert Murphy, the senior American diplomat in North Africa, who had met de Gaulle just before the meeting, was not there either, because the president wanted to have a private meeting.[15]

From the American side, navy Captain John L. McCrea made some notes, but he took down only the words of the president ("the following observations were made by me from a relatively poor point of vantage—a crack in a door slightly ajar. In view of the fact that General de Gaulle talked in so low a tone of voice as to be inaudible to me, I cannot supply any comments made by him").[16] McCrea noted only that de Gaulle made a reference to the sovereignty of French Morocco, to which the president replied that

the sovereignty of the occupied territory was not under consideration, that none of the contenders for power in North Africa had the right to say that he, and only he, represented the sovereignty of France . . . [which] as in our country, rested with the people, but . . . unfortunately the people of France were not now in a position to exercise that sovereignty. . . . [T]he Allied Nations . . . were fighting for the liberation of France and . . . should hold the political situation in "trusteeship" for the French people. In other words, the President stated[,] . . . France is in the position of a little child unable to look out and fend for itself and that in such a case, a court would appoint a trustee to do the necessary.[17]

In his *War Memoirs*, de Gaulle gives few details on this first conversation with Roosevelt that, according to the general, lasted an hour, with both men sitting on the same couch. De Gaulle detected some movements behind the curtains in the corners of the room and noted, "Because of these indistinct presences, the atmosphere of our first discussion was a strange one."[18]

On the other hand, in recounting the meeting, de Gaulle made some general observations on American policy and on Roosevelt:

The United States, delighting in her resources, feeling that she no longer had within herself sufficient scope for her energies, wishing to help those who were in misery or bondage the world over, yielded in her turn to that taste for intervention in which the instinct for domination cloaked itself. It was precisely this tendency that President Roosevelt espoused.[19]

And given that Roosevelt wanted "the peace to be an American peace," and "that France in particular should recognize him as its savior and its arbiter," a French central authority bothered him, according to de Gaulle: "Politically, he felt no inclination toward me. . . . It must be added that like any star performer he was touchy as to the roles that fell to other actors. In short, beneath his patrician mask of courtesy, Roosevelt regarded me without benevolence."[20] Nevertheless, de Gaulle was careful not to offend the president. "We took care not to meet head on . . . we each had much to gain by getting along together," observed the general.[21]

Captain McCrea noted that, after some twenty minutes of conversation, de Gaulle "with some show of cordiality" took his leave. Roosevelt said to Murphy after the meeting that the conversation left something to be desired, and that de Gaulle had shown himself to be rigid and unforthcoming regarding Roosevelt's wish to pursue the war energetically.[22]

It appears that de Gaulle tried to get across to Roosevelt his theme of how decadent French elites are cast aside by new elements emerging out of the French population, an argument that had so impressed Admiral Stark,[23] but he did not get very far. According to Captain Kittredge, in a letter to Robert E. Sherwood,

De Gaulle attempted [this] at Casablanca; but later told Admiral Stark that he had hardly ever been permitted to finish a sentence. The President was determined to make de Gaulle understand and accept the attitude of the Roosevelt administration toward France; and did not seem interested in, or have any patience with, de Gaulle's views, perhaps expressed in his usual cold, standoffish and brusque manner.[24]

Sherwood also wrote, according to Kittredge, that "de Gaulle was later informed that Roosevelt had told the Joan of Arc and Clemenceau story to [President] General [Emilio] Vargas in Brazil, and de Gaulle was so deeply offended 'he never wanted to see the President again.' "[25]

Act II: Washington, 1944

One can see from the *War Memoirs* that de Gaulle maintained a subtle distinction between his distrust and disdain for the president's policy on the one hand and his esteem for Roosevelt's "grand esprit." There is a reference to this "grand esprit" in the general's commentary on his trip to the United States from July 6 to 10, 1944, the second series of encounters between the two men. De Gaulle preceded his commentary with an account of what he had said— rather overemphatically—to Roosevelt during that visit. After stating that nothing can equal the "value, the power, the shining examples" of the "ancient peoples" of Western Europe, de Gaulle said, "This is true of France above all, which of all the great nations of Europe is the only one which was, is and always will be your ally." Therefore, France should not be "excluded from the organization of the great world powers and their decisions," should not lose "her African and Asian territories," and should not emerge from the peace settlement with "the psychology of the vanquished."[26] He then added the following commentary:

The powerful mind ["grand esprit"] of Roosevelt was open to these considerations. Furthermore, he felt a genuine affection for France, or at least for the notion of it he had once been able to conceive. But it was precisely because of this inclination of his that he was at heart disappointed and irritated by yesterday's disaster among us and by the mediocre reactions the latter had aroused among so many Frenchmen, particularly those who he knew personally.... As for the future, he was anything but convinced of the rebirth and renewal of our regime.[27]

It was almost as though in Roosevelt's mind, France was responsible for the position of strategic weakness in which the United States found itself in 1940. In considering that France had been reduced to the status of a third-rate power, Roosevelt appeared incapable of taking into account the sweep of history (a failing not foreign to the cult of newness in this nation of pioneers), and in particular the historic position of France. One should add to this a leaven of lofty morality, characteristic of the East Coast aristocracy, and in Roosevelt's case a morality reinforced by an iron will developed in overcoming a terrible personal trial: polio.

If de Gaulle retained a certain esteem for Roosevelt, he was otherwise very distrustful of the American president's foreign policy. Another commentary on his conversations with Roosevelt during the July 1944 visit retains all its timeliness, although one should qualify the remarkable predictive qualities of de Gaulle—he probably wrote these words not at the time of the meetings but some twelve years later.

His [Roosevelt's] conception seemed to me an imposing one although disquieting for Europe and for France ... it was a permanent system of intervention that he intended to impose by international law. In his mind, a four-power directory—America, Soviet Russia, China and Great Britain—would settle the world's problems. A parliament of the allied nations would give a democratic appearance to the authority of the "big four." ... Roosevelt thus intended to lure the Soviets into a group that would contain their ambitions and in which American could unite its dependents.[28]

In the space of less than one year after the July 1944 encounter, the "four-power directory" acquired a fifth member: France recovered its rank and overcame the "supreme insult" of being excluded from Yalta in spite of its express request to be invited.[29]

What happened between July 1944 and the entry of France into the United Nations Security Council less than a year later were the fantastic mass plebiscite constituted by de Gaulle's parade down the Champs-Elysées on August 26, 1944 ("forty million Frenchmen can't be wrong"), and last but not least the fact that

Churchill, whose predictive qualities were akin to those of de Gaulle, exacted from the others at Yalta: (1) a French zone of occupation in Germany; (2) a French seat on the Allied Control Council in Berlin; and (3) a seat for France as a permanent member of the United Nations Security Council. Although Roosevelt confided to Stalin, according to Jean Laloy, that it was out of "the goodness of his heart" that France had been given a zone of occupation in Germany,[30] the point to consider was that it was "France which Churchill saw as the breakwater of resistance to a resurgence of aggressiveness in Germany and, above all, to Soviet expansion on the Continent, which in his mind presupposed the support and the presence of the United States."[31]

Happily for France and for the Western alliance!

In fact, de Gaulle had a great talent for masking reality, for representing more than he really possessed. Henry Kissinger wrote in 1965 that "for the greater part of his career [de Gaulle] has had to be an illusionist. In the face of all evidence to the contrary, he has striven to restore France's greatness by his passionate belief in it."[32] But the fact was that France was too big to be classed among the other "conquered" countries of the Continent—although she was seen that way through a certain perspective. George Ball recalled that

Britain, with America's help, had won the war, while the other members of the group [the Organization of European Economic Cooperation—OEEC] were, as one of my Dutch friends put it, "a club of defeated nations." The British thus thought of their country as on a different level from the nations of the continent; being a co-victor, it should deal with the United States as an equal. . . . Since the smaller European countries feared that England and France would dominate the new organization, the eloquent Belgian Paul-Henri Spaak was made chairman [of the OEEC].[33]

Thanks to de Gaulle, France was able to emerge from the war not as a conquered nation. Though not properly speaking a conquering nation in the full sense of the word, France obtained—finally—a seat at the winners' table.

In a briefing memorandum for the meetings in Washington in July 1944, Roosevelt was reminded of the difficulty in talking about the French colonies. It was the intention of the American side to remain vague and evasive on this subject:

De Gaulle may bring up rumors that the U.S. contemplates setting aside bases of operations in French Colonial possessions. This is a difficult question and the only immediately apparent reply is: the establishment of United Nations' bases for the prevention of future international wars is a matter that must be agreed to by the Allied Nations after our present enemies are forced to surrender and not before that time.[34]

In this situation it was not only a case of Roosevelt's anticolonialism; it was a question of using French bases after the war, at Dakar and elsewhere, so that the great danger of 1940—caused by the French, said some—would not happen again. An article written in June 1944 by the commentator David Lawrence, who was apparently used by government officials to get across their point of view, stated: "What America wants is some means of leasing or securing naval and air bases from France and internationalizing these so as to prevent American lives from being sacrificed again because of the criminal neglect by French politicians in Paris of national armament and overseas protection."[35]

With Roosevelt, the anticolonialist impulse was also clearly there. He seemed motivated by a desire to "decolonize" the French Empire and give to the peoples under French domination at least the possibility of free expression and later on self-determination. Roosevelt seemed to want to accomplish this noble task over a prostrate France, which was much easier to do than against the "bulldog" Churchill, who had considerable military forces in the British colonies and whose country had kept its credibility intact because of its resistance to the Germans.

It is worth emphasizing in this particular context the differing relations among the three Western leaders of World War II. Jean Laloy noted, "One only has to recall the effect of the multiple incompatibilities between de Gaulle and Roosevelt to attribute great importance to the bonds between the prime minister and the president."[36]

The lack of consideration for France and the "decadence" of its civilization did not extend only to Americans. The Soviet attitude paralleled that of Roosevelt. There was a sort of mutual consensus that the French political class and the French system were rotten, and therefore one could not accord to France strategic positions outside the country in the postwar period. Laloy described Stalin's position at the Teheran Conference at the end of 1943: "France, in Stalin's view, no longer counted. France must lose her colonies, chief among which was Indochina, and offer her allies bases at Bizerte and Dakar. At least this was what he told Roosevelt."[37]

Act III (Botched): Algiers, 1945

There never was a third series of encounters between Roosevelt and de Gaulle, the latter, in a supreme snub, refusing the invitation of the conquering Roosevelt, returning from the Yalta Conference, for a meeting at Algiers. It was not up to Roosevelt to invite him to French territory, de Gaulle reminded Roosevelt in his letter declining the invitation—supreme impertinence toward the liberator of North Africa but an understandable reply from the "uninvited" at Yalta—this conference, so-called, of powers "with not less than five million men under arms."[38]

A QUARREL OVER LEGITIMACY

De Gaulle's reference to Joan of Arc and Clemenceau before Admiral Stark in London falls under the rubric of the general's master themes. This reference is repeatedly derided by Roosevelt in correspondence during the war. "It is the proper time effectively to eliminate the Jeanne d'Arc complex and return to realism,'' wrote Roosevelt to Eisenhower and Churchill in December 1943.[39]

For de Gaulle, this reference had to do with his concept of legitimacy. In Ireland, after his departure from power in April 1969, he unburdened himself of some reflections on this subject, in the course of a conversation with his faithful aide-de-camp, Admiral François Flohic:

But there is a question that goes beyond my person. It is that of legitimacy. Since 1940, I represent it. It was not the government of the Third Republic that won the Great War, but the French people, with at its head successively Joffre, Clemenceau, Foch who were the legitimacy. Now it is I who incarnate it and that will remain so until my death.[40]

For de Gaulle, the Vichy government was the usurper. And there had been precedents for abrupt, and sometimes violent, changes of regime: the Revolution itself and its prolongations; the restoration that followed the defeat of Napoleon; the July Revolution in 1830; the Revolution of 1848; and the Third Republic which succeeded the Commune of Paris which in turn had risen following the Franco-Prussian War.

For Vichy, de Gaulle was a traitor, the man who had challenged the legal authority, in the person of Pétain. The latter had been named prime minister by the president of the republic on June 16, 1940, and then had become the sole master of France by a vote of the parliament (549 to 80) on July 10, 1940.

''Work, Family, Country'' was the new ''legitimacy'' claimed by the Pétainists, the new expression of ''the general will'' that they saw themselves as incarnating in this fundamentally divided country. Just as de Gaulle, Pétain wished to bring an end to an era of weakness of the French state and to launch a new ''national revolution'': ''that the impotence of the State cease to paralyze the Nation.''[41]

For the vast majority of Frenchmen, particularly the military, it was not a difficult choice between de Gaulle et Pétain. Edouard Frédéric Dupont, at that time a lieutenant and later a French deputy from Paris, listened to the voice of wisdom of one of his noncommissioned officers:

Lieutenant, I don't understand. Marshal Pétain is the Marshal. He says we must have an armistice. And then along comes a man called Lieutenant Colonel de Gaulle, at any rate he has the papers of a colonel. I'm supposed to tell you that we should fight alongside him? In any case it's not a lieutenant colonel who lays down the law to the Marshal.[42]

Jean Lacouture, de Gaulle's biographer, does not permit the use of the term ''traitor,'' but he does allow himself the use of the term ''rebel'' for the general.[43] By his action, de Gaulle rejected the concept of rule by parliamentary majority in favor of that of ''legitimacy.'' A very strange, indeed dangerous, notion in the United States where, to recall the words of François Furet, ''the Constitution takes on the character of a Sacred Arch.''[44]

In France the constitution is not immutable. (Indeed, "revolution" implies that the construction of society is never finished.) Thus de Gaulle was able to look to legitimacy and the Rousseauist notion of *la volonté générale* to justify the incredible leap into the unknown—and into illegality—that was the declaration of June 18, 1940, a declaration he could not have come to without considerable inner turmoil, as shown in the telegram he sent the next day to General Charles Noguès, commander of the French forces in North Africa: "I am at your disposition, either to fight under your orders or for any demarche that would be useful to you."[45] Even on June 24, de Gaulle was still seeking a superior authority, again General Noguès:

I have taken the initiative of constituting here a National Committee, which would represent the French Resistance on the outside. . . . The British Government has just declared officially that it is prepared to recognize such a committee. . . . It would be essential, General, that you accept to take this committee under your control.[46]

These demarches evoked no response from Noguès. They were followed by a summons to de Gaulle to surrender himself to French authorities at Bordeaux, to which de Gaulle replied this presented "not the slightest interest" to him,[47] and by a death sentence pronounced on him on August 2, 1940.

That de Gaulle would have dared to take this incredible step was due, at least in part, to the fact that he had been elevated to the political level on June 6, 1940, when he entered the cabinet of Paul Reynaud. By being named Under Secretary of State for National Defense, he went out of the military hierarchy in a sense, although his military rank, which he retained (and which counted considerably in this "vertical" society), was below that of a number of senior officers, including General Maxime Weygand, the new commander of the French Army, and of course Marshal Pétain.

As a member of the Reynaud government, de Gaulle was able for the first time to exercise political options. Reynaud charged him with a liaison mission to Prime Minister Churchill. Reynaud also asked him to prepare a plan for a fallback of the French government and armed forces to Brittany—the so-called *réduit breton* (Breton Reedoubt)—a highly political choice that met with the sharp disapproval of Weygand:

[On June 12] Reynaud spoke officially to the Council [of Ministers] for the first time about the "Breton Redoubt" plan which he had had General de Gaulle prepare. General Weygand protested violently against the plan itself, which he called absurd, and even more so against the fact that a plan for a strategic retreat of the armies he commanded had been established without his having been consulted.[48]

Thus a fissure opened up in French society, coincident with the defeat of 1940. As was noted previously, this was not the first time in the history of France that a national tragedy produced a change of regime as well a political split in this unitary but not unified nation. Besides being in the general pattern of a change of regime following a national collapse, there was the unique position of the army. It was a sort of "state within a state," with its contempt for the permissiveness represented by the Popular Front government of the Third Republic and with its isolation from the French parliamentary system. The army was, in a certain sense, the conservative alternate to the French parliament. All this facilitated the disengagement of the Pétainist regime, with the help of the military chiefs, from the governments of the Third Republic that had preceded it.

It was in fact the chief of the army, in the name of the army, who refused the "Holland solution": surrender by the army and the move of the government elsewhere. In the French case this would have been to North Africa, as proposed by Reynaud. Weygand's reply to him was that while Queen Wilhelmina could incarnate the continuity of the Netherlands regime, such was not the case for Reynaud, the ephemeral representative of an ephemeral republic. "I refuse . . . to cover our [battle] flags with this shame." Christine Rimbaud, who quoted these words, commented that "these arguments betrayed a state of mind scarcely 'republican.' [They] gave to understand that the Nation was not necessarily one and the same as the Republic, and that the Army was not intrinsic to the Nation and at its service but constituted in a way a body apart."

Rimbaud added:

[Weygand] could not really admit that his intransigeant stance was equally determined by his desire to make the government bear the responsibility for the defeat; and it would therefore be incumbent upon the government to ask for the armistice. The shadow of the future French state was already taking shape. Its obstinacy in discrediting the Third Republic was taking root.[49]

Weygand provided his own justification for his actions in a testimonial document from which the following is an excerpt:

The Commander in Chief asked the Government on June 12 to negotiate the conclusion of an armistice. The Government, which was in favor of continuing the struggle in the overseas territories with the help of the naval and air forces, asked of the Commander in Chief that he agree to sign the capitulation of the land forces. . . . The Government would not be involved in this action of an exclusively military nature. It would remain therefore free to stay faithful to its Ally and to continue the war at her side. . . . [The] Commander in Chief . . . indignantly refused to carry out this crushing and irremediable attack on the military honor of a nation because: the code of military justice considers that capitulation in the open field as the most serious crime that a [military] leader can commit. No written order of the Government could clear either his conscience or our [battle] flags from such a shame.[50]

The fallback solutions, first the Breton Redoubt and then the move of the government to North Africa, which de Gaulle was subsequently asked to organize, never came to pass. Reynaud, unable to face up to the army and seized with a nervous crisis[51] that was only assuaged when he turned over the reins of government to Pétain on June 16, passed from power and with him de Gaulle.

Faced with Pétain, de Gaulle had one cardinal advantage: his predictive capacity. It was de Gaulle who perceived in June 1940, and said so in his famous speech from London on the eighteenth of that month, that the war was going to transform itself into a world war. Later, with the entry of the United States into the war in December 1941, de Gaulle immediately sensed that the outcome was no longer in doubt: the Allies were going to win. Though he was not the only one to conclude this, there were many others who continued to believe that the power of the Germans was such that they would be able to come out of the war not too badly. This feeling would remain even into 1943.

De Gaulle was not a major figure in the military defeat of the Axis. That he was able to succeed, in the final analysis, in obtaining for France a seat at the winners' table after many disappointments and snubs, is a testament not only to his strength of character, determination, courage, and boldness but to this predictive capacity. Brought to Casablanca virtually under duress, de Gaulle saw himself a little more than two years later, in the spring of 1945, admitted as one of the Big Five. He neither wavered in his determination nor, apparently, in the certitude of his vision, in spite of repeated blows against him by Roosevelt.

Obviously the "current did not pass" between Roosevelt and de Gaulle. This was a major factor: a large part of the history of France and America during and in the aftermath of the war stems from this unfortunate chemistry. The patrician Roosevelt was the uncontested master of U.S. foreign policy. It was the beginning of the "imperial presidency." Elected for an unprecedented third term in 1940, it was virtually up to him, and him alone, to decide American policy toward France, toward Europe, toward the Soviet Union, in brief toward the world.

Roosevelt wanted to continue the vision of Woodrow Wilson while at the same time correct the errors of his predecessor, particularly regarding the latter's poor relations with Congress. (Indeed, it was mainly for that reason that he named former Senator Cordell Hull to be Secretary of State—which incidentally had the effect of concentrating even more authority over foreign policy in Roosevelt's hands.) There was a streak of obstinacy and blindness in the otherwise utilitarian outlook of Roosevelt. In his policy toward the Soviet Union and France, he proved himself to be much less the realist than Churchill.

In sum, since Roosevelt had already taken an anti–de Gaulle stance, there was nothing much that could be done. Well before their first nocturnal meeting at Casablanca, the American president had formed an unfavorable opinion of the general. This went back to a year earlier, to the St. Pierre-Miquelon affair, and even father back than that.

Of course, the failed chemistry had something to do with de Gaulle's own haughty and bellicose personality, his "heart of bronze." André Fontaine put his finger on this aspect of de Gaulle's persona in an editorial following de

Gaulle's defeat in the referendum of April 1969: "This too-military style, what harm it has done to Gaullist diplomacy! . . . [De Gaulle] succeeded in turning away from him a number of people who would have been quite ready to recognize in fact our country's preponderance in Europe if only he had not seemed to demand it as a right."[52]

DIVERGENCES AND SOLIDARITIES AMONG THE ANGLO-SAXONS

On June 16, 1940, at Bordeaux, Charles de Gaulle, Under Secretary of State for National Defense in the government of Paul Reynaud, decided to leave for England. On the same date the government decided to give way to one headed by Philippe Pétain. De Gaulle could oppose the capitulationist policy of the marshal all he wanted, but the fact was that, as of that moment, Pétain represented the legally constituted French government. Sumner Welles, the U.S. Under Secretary of State, stated the American position in a conversation with an official interlocutor of the Free French, Raoul Aglion: "The National Committee of General de Gaulle cannot be recognized as a government in exile. Those who are at London are legitimate governments who fled the German invasion. This is not the case with France, where the Government decided not to go into exile."[53]

The British, by contrast, adopted another position. In a statement of June 23, 1940, His Majesty's government denied the independent character of the government of Pétain. In a second declaration on the same date, the British government, as recounted by de Gaulle in his *War Memoirs*, "took note of the proposal to form a French National Committee and expressed, in advance, the intention of recognizing it and dealing with it on all matters relative to the carrying-on of the war."[54]

On June 28, 1940, General de Gaulle was publicly recognized by the British government as the "leader of the Free French," noted the general in his *War Memoirs*.[55] As it turned out, the formation of a French National Committee in London had to be put off because of the overall failure of French personalities to rally to de Gaulle. Instead of this committee, a Defense Council of the Empire was established by de Gaulle on October 27, 1940, at Brazzaville.[56] The National Committee did not come into being until September 24, 1941.

What was the basis for this difference of appreciation between the Americans and the British toward de Gaulle and the Free French movement, apart from the fact that the British considered him "their" man, discovered and sponsored by them?

First, it is worthwhile noting that the positions of Great Britain and the United States were very different. Great Britain had been an ally of France in this lightning war, and in the course of the debacle a feeling of mutual bitterness took hold between the two partners. To the British, the French had given in to panic. In the opinion of many Frenchmen, Great Britain had failed in its duty.

The land forces sent by Great Britain were much less numerous than in World War I, and the British had not even begun a draft at the time of the Battle of France in May 1940. More serious still in the mind of the French leadership, the British, at this moment of French agony, declined to provide substantial air support to the French troops.

These arguments were aired by William C. Bullitt, the American ambassador in Paris, in one of his breathless telegrams to Roosevelt in the middle of the collapse of June 1940: "I cannot express my admiration for the courage with which the French are meeting one of the most tragic situations in history. The British are still keeping at home three-fourths of their pursuit planes."[57]

Churchill himself recognized the inequality of the Allied forces during the Battle of France ("the fact that we have been unavoidably largely outside of this terrible battle weighed with us"), but at the same time he noted that "I did not hesitate in the name of the British Government to refuse to give my agreement to an armistice or separate peace."[58]

Clearly, it was necessary for Churchill to husband his fighter aircraft in view of the imminence of the Battle of Britain. He noted to Roosevelt, "I made clear to the French that we had good hopes of victory and anyhow had no doubts whatever of what our duty was."[59]

And so a torrent of recriminations against the British poured out from the French at the time of the disaster of May–June 1940. (And, as can be judged from Churchill's understatement cited above, recriminations also came from the other direction.) France had lost 120,000 men[60] in six weeks of the Battle of France, a rate more devastating than that during World War I.

Obviously there was something of a failure of duty, even of treason, in those "days of stampede" at Bordeaux, when the French government swung over to the camp of surrender: the failure of nerve of Paul Reynaud, giving up the post of prime minister; the turnabout of Admiral Darlan, who in a moment of bravado promised to take "his" fleet to England if an armistice were agreed to, then reversed himself the next day and advised the president of the National Assembly, Edouard Herriot, not to leave for North Africa[61]; the corridor maneuvers of Pierre Laval[62] and others to turn aside the proposal for an instant union between France and Great Britain.

The British were not the only ones to reproach the French. On July 24, 1940, Robert Murphy, then chargé d'affaires at Vichy, used the following words with Ambassador Charles-Roux, secretary general of the Foreign Office: "Many Americans did not understand France's failure to transfer its naval forces to its ally prior to the armistice negotiations."[63]

Murphy's statement seems to relate to a commitment the British apparently thought they had extracted from the French at the beginning of the armistice negotiations. According to Jean-Pierre Azéma, Churchill sent a telegram to Paul Reynaud agreeing to the proposal of Camille Chautemps, vice president of the council, that France approach the Germans to ask what would be the conditions of an armistice. Churchill accepted this "on the sole condition that the French

Fleet would immediately be sent to British ports before the opening of negotiations.''[64] But Reynaud "preferred to keep [to himself] this telegram [from Churchill] which in effect cancelled the Franco-British plan [for an instant union].''[65]

In fact, the new Pétain government had in the final analysis disregarded France's standing commitment with Great Britain not to make a separate peace and had gone off on its own. Pétain's rationale in a speech on June 25 at Bordeaux was that, though the army was to be disbanded and the fleet disarmed in port, no one could make use of them and therefore "honor was saved.''[66] But if the fleet were to be disarmed in port, by what force would the Germans be prevented from seizing this weapon of capital importance?

The armistice-surrender of June 1940 was soon followed by the affair of Mers-el-Kébir. On July 3, 1940, a British squadron attacked the French fleet in the port after a call to give up the ships was not heeded. The vast majority of the vessels were put out of commission, and 1,300 French naval personnel were killed or missing. The incident carried to the extreme France's anger at its former ally. Two days later Vichy broke diplomatic relations with London.

In retrospect, one can say that the Mers-el-Kébir attack was justified militarily because there was not a sufficient guarantee that Vichy would not succumb to eventual pressure by the Germans on the disposition of the French fleet, notwithstanding the repeated commitments of Pétain and Darlan not to turn it over to anyone.

The United States was in a quite different position vis-à-vis Vichy: that of a neutral country (indeed, during the Battle of France this position had drawn forth French grievances, notably at the moment when Paul Reynaud pleaded desperately that Washington send planes and American pilots).[67]

In the beginning American policy toward Vichy was characterized by a strong reserve. This was clear during the summer and fall of 1940. The culminating point was the curt letter sent by Roosevelt to Marshal Pétain on October 25, 1940, one day after the alarming meeting between Pétain and Hitler at Montoire. The United States sought to brandish the bugbear of a break between itself and France in order to bring Vichy, and in particular Pierre Laval, then vice president of the council, to more moderation toward the British and less collaboration with the Germans.

The French leaders at Vichy were wounded at the lack of respect toward the marshal that appeared in Roosevelt's letter, and Cordell Hull explained to French authorities afterward why the United States was not happy with them. In a conversation on November 4, 1940, with the ambassador of Vichy, Gaston Henry-Haye, Hull referred to the "great misfortune of the French Government in not pursuing the long-term objectives within sufficient time for its safety.''[68] In other words, the French government had failed in its duty by not preparing a fallback to North Africa.

But was it reasonable to expect that the French government could fall back into North Africa or, failing that, deliver its fleet to the British? Would the oldest country on the Continent turn over such an asset to its historic rival of nearly a thousand years? Even today, many Frenchmen would contend that it was not realistic to think that the struggle could have been carried on in North Africa under the banner of the French government.

THE RALLYING OF WASHINGTON TO THE THESES OF PÉTAIN

Little by little after the signing of the armistice, the United States was brought to acknowledge that France had to follow its provisions scrupulously. Hull, in the same conversation of November 4, 1940, cited above, told Henry-Haye that France was a "captive nation" and had to conform to the terms of the armistice.[69]

But this assessment of the facts did not mean that the United States had nothing for which to reproach the Vichy government. Hull observed to Henry-Haye, again in the same conversation, that "this Government has the usual normal relations with all other governments except those at Tokyo, Berlin, Rome, and Vichy."[70] In sum, American relations with Vichy were strained.

Gradually the American government gained confidence, if not in the Vichy government then at least in the person of Marshal Pétain. The lack of a significant rallying to the Free French movement certainly played a role. Freeman Matthews, the second in charge after Murphy at Vichy, following a conversation with Pétain on November 16, 1940, described him as

the one man who today for all his age can alone speak for France, and who alone possesses the prestige and affection of his people. Without him this Government would not last 10 minutes. A defeatist in some respects history shows him to be, but I came away with the firm impression that he will never consciously agree to any step which by his lights and standards and in his words is contrary "to the honor of France." He sold me completely on that.[71]

Whatever Pétain's "lights and standards" were, they were not sufficient to keep intact the honor of France, which was not "saved," in the marshal's phrase. Some, notably de Gaulle, knew it; others sensed it. But most probably concluded that, in the face of the German juggernaut, there was little else they could do.

If there was an initial reserve on the part of Washington toward Vichy, this did not mean that the Roosevelt administration saw in de Gaulle an alternate solution. In Washington, de Gaulle was looked upon in part as a man of the British, who had supported him from the beginning, in June 1940. The British, in a state of extreme peril, had something in hand, de Gaulle, and felt impelled to play that card. Whatever their problems with him, he represented a card they kept, perhaps jealously, throughout the war.

Furthermore, one can pose this question: if de Gaulle, as Under Secretary of

State for National Defense, had not been charged with putting together a plan for transporting to North Africa all possible elements, civil and military, and if he had not met Churchill on this matter on June 9 in London,[72] would he have thought in the days that followed to lead the pursuit of the war from England?[73]

It is possible that Roosevelt was intent on pursuing his own political course toward France and did not want to seem to be tailing after the British—always a concern for American presidents who have to take account of certain American minorities and other individual Americans who are deeply anti-British. In any event Roosevelt, far removed from events in Europe which were unfolding at a stunning speed, did not attach much importance to de Gaulle. In fact, throughout the period of American participation in the war, he constantly sought a French "third alternative" to de Gaulle or Vichy, but this proved to be a chimera.[74]

ANTERIOR PREJUDICES

Roosevelt was reinforced in his attitude of indifference, laced with hostility, toward de Gaulle by most of the people surrounding him in the White House and State Department, not the least of whom was Admiral William Leahy, who by mid-1943 had returned from Vichy and had taken up the position of chief of staff to the president. Roosevelt was also influenced by the advice of a number of Frenchmen in the United States. According to Anton de Porte, author of several works on France during World War II and the aftermath, this came down essentially to three leading personalities: Jean Monnet, Alexis Leger, and Camille Chautemps.[75] The latter, vice president of the council at the time of the German attack in May 1940, was the first to suggest, in the following month, that the French government might well find out what would be the German conditions for an armistice, after which it could best decide what course of action to pursue.[76] Though Chautemps claimed it was not his intention, the slippery slope toward surrender was from that moment engaged. Chautemps later on became for a time an unofficial emissary of Pétain to the American government.

The anti-Gaullist influence of Leger, which was quite open, and that of Monnet, which was more muffled, were much more important than that of Chautemps with respect to the policy Roosevelt came to adopt.

When de Gaulle was first in London in June 1940, a number of French personalities were also there for different reasons. One was Monnet, delegate to the Franco-British armaments mission. Another was Leger, the secretary general of the Ministry of Foreign Affairs during the 1930s, who had been brusquely replaced by the government of Paul Reynaud on May 19, 1940.[77] This was shortly before Reynaud named de Gaulle Under Secretary of State for Defense, on June 6.

Leger

The Free French movement tried by many means to attract Alexis Leger to its side. This effort did not bear fruit. "I asked M. [Jacques] Maritain and M.

Leger for their help," wrote de Gaulle. "The replies were courteous but negative."[78]

Leger, who was also known under his nom de plume, Saint-John Perse (he received the Nobel Prize for literature in 1960), was not in the least a man of Vichy. Cabinet director for Foreign Minister Aristide Briand and very involved in the Locarno Declaration (1925) and the Kellogg-Briand Pact (1928), he had been the author of a memorandum of the League of Nations concerning "the organization of a federal union in Europe."[79] After the death of Briand, Leger stayed on as secretary general of the Quai d'Orsay until May 1940. In the words of André Velter, "denounced as bellicose by all the potential collaborators, [Leger] was surreptitiously dismissed by Paul Reynaud after the decisive advance of the German Army in May 1940."[80]

Refusing the post of ambassador to Washington, Leger went on leave of absence and left for London. He arrived in Canada on July 14, 1940. Shortly afterward he learned that the Vichy government had stripped him of his French nationality and that the Gestapo had ransacked his apartment in Paris.[81]

Throughout the war, Leger was a resolute opponent of de Gaulle's policies, seeing in him an avatar of French authoritarianism, even fascism. Possibly there was also a personal side to it, Leger having been fired from the Quai d'Orsay with, at minimum, the complicity of Paul Reynaud, who shortly afterward named Charles de Gaulle to his government.

Leger maintained a particularly close relationship with Sumner Welles, the American Under Secretary of State. The two men had known each other before the war due to the analogous roles they had occupied in their respective diplomatic services. Leger, who was given a sinecure of consultant to the Library of Congress during the war, played a role (along with others) in convincing Roosevelt that de Gaulle could not pretend to represent the French state.

In particular, there was a letter addressed to Roosevelt by Sumner Welles on August 13, 1942, shortly before Operation Torch in North Africa (from which de Gaulle was excluded at the express demand of Roosevelt). The letter transmitted an account of a conversation he had had that day with Leger. Welles noted to Roosevelt that the information was particularly significant at that juncture.[82]

Leger, who emphasized to Welles that what he was going to recount should be held in the utmost secrecy, said he had encountered a close friend, a certain M. Istel,[83] a French scientist and economist. Istel, who had returned from London, having been summoned there by de Gaulle, carried a message from the general that Istel had written down. It was another urgent appeal from de Gaulle to Leger, exhorting him to join the Free French movement. In the message de Gaulle laid out his vision for France in the postwar period.

De Gaulle told Istel that he envisaged French policy as based on pure nationalism with, at its base, a far-reaching agreement between the Soviet Union and France in the military and political fields. It was the only way to prevent Anglo-American predominance. Welles's memorandum continued: "As regards Great Britain, French policy should show recognition of the role which Great

Britain had played in the liberation of France, not more. As regards the United States, French interests should be purely economic and 'at the level of French relations with the Latin-American Republics.' ''

As regards internal policy, Welles's memorandum continued, de Gaulle was expecting that a national government would be formed under his aegis at the time of an armistice ending the war. This government would remain in power for a period of six months, at the end of which there would be a national election for a Constituent Assembly which would draft a new constitution and conduct elections leading to a new government. The new government would be one of order and discipline, and through it, it would be necessary to correct the errors of the system that had prevailed during the Third Republic.

Leger made a commentary on the message Istel had conveyed to him. Leger estimated that a policy of rigid nationalism and a close relationship with the Soviet Union had been decided upon by de Gaulle in order to assure himself control over the government, which would install itself in France for a six-month period following the armistice; that is, through the influence of the Soviet Union over the French population and through Soviet manipulation of the French Communist Party.

Leger added that Istel's message had only confirmed his great doubts about de Gaulle and had also confirmed his decision not to participate in any way whatsoever in de Gaulle's committee. Obviously, observed Leger, de Gaulle's policy was totally opposed to any kind of international cooperation or world organization (subjects particularly dear to Roosevelt, partisan of a ''corrected'' Wilsonianism).

One could not imagine a letter that could do more damage to de Gaulle's image in the mind of the man who held all the strings of United States policy toward Europe, especially France. And the messenger was no ordinary messenger. As far as Roosevelt was concerned, Welles was in the orbit of ''the ties that bind.'' They had a common background, rooted in Groton and its legendary and influential headmaster, Endicott Peabody. Welles was a sort of protégé: he had been a page at the wedding of Franklin and Eleanor. He had direct access to the president, and his opinions counted. Therefore, by extension, the opinions of Welles's close contact Leger must have had an influence on the president.

According to William R. Emerson, former director of the Franklin D. Roosevelt Library, the antipathy between Leger and de Gaulle was total and uncompromising, based in part on personal considerations but more on constitutional principles:

The issue turned on the composition, ultimately, of a provisional French government after liberation. De Gaulle's intention was to impose his Algiers-based National Committee made up partly of minor (mostly) Third Republic figures, partly of representatives of the Resistance, all self chosen. Leger's and Roosevelt's conception was a broadly-based Consultative Assembly, freely elected by regional assemblies of the French *départements*, consistent with the Treveneuc Law of 1872.[84]

Curiously, this Tréveneuc Law appeared in a response made by General Henri Giraud to propositions drawn up by General de Gaulle and the National Committee (then in London) on February 23, 1943. De Gaulle had proposed the formation of a central government in order that France "have at its disposal in the war a single responsible authority and a single representation."[85]

The reply of General Giraud, received by the French National Committee in London on April 10, 1943, maintained that he himself, as commander in chief, and by virtue of the state of siege existing, should assure public order and name functionaries throughout France. De Gaulle commented on this letter in the following terms:

Thus, without a genuine central French authority, the essentials of power would be at the discretion of a military chief dependent on a foreign general. This strange apparatus was to operate as long as the war lasted. After that, far from proceeding at once to a national plebiscite, there were plans to invoke a law dating back to 1872, the so-called Tréveneuc Law, which provided that in the absence of a National Assembly it devolved upon the general councils to provide an administration and appoint a government. All in all, according to the memorandum signed by General Giraud, everything would transpire as though France no longer existed as a state, at least until the victory. Such was indeed Roosevelt's intention.[86]

This is in essence Leger's thesis: the members of a consultative assembly, elected by the general councils, in the French départements, were the only ones entitled to constitute a new government or, more exactly, a new French regime.[87]

It was also, as de Gaulle discerned, in the spirit of Roosevelt's thinking. As the president wrote to General George C. Marshall, four days before D Day: "I have a moral duty that transcends 'an easy way.' It is to see to it that the people of France have nothing foisted on them by outside powers. It must be a French choice—and that means, as far as possible, forty million people. It carries with it a very deep principle in human affairs."[88]

Monnet

In the first of a chain of "supranational" initiatives that were to mark his career, Jean Monnet, who was then in London (as was General de Gaulle), was the coauthor of the Franco-British plan for union, launched in extremis in the middle of June 1940. The plan was supported by de Gaulle, who had the vision to do so, although he recognized in it many difficulties of a practical order. The plan never saw the light of day because the government of Paul Reynaud gave way to that of Marshal Pétain, and the latter immediately sought an armistice.[89]

Looking back on it, the plan of Monnet and Lord Halifax represented a way to continue the war by recognizing that France had borne the brunt of the war until that time; the fact that France, while collapsing, was given equal rank on paper at least was a testimony to that. A reconstituted French government created in union with Britain would have been of a quite different status than, for example, that of the Netherlands (sometimes referred to by British royalty as "the bicycle kingdom," from the habit of the Dutch royal family to ride around on bicycles), whose Queen Wilhelmina installed herself in London. But just as with sending the French fleet to British ports, the union plan represented de facto too much of a surrender of sovereignty by France to its rival of nearly one thousand years which had become its tenuous ally only since 1904. However, under either option—the British-French union or the "Holland" solution—French honor would have been saved. As it was, a visionary loner, General de Gaulle—the ultimate non-*attentiste*—took it upon himself to try to put the pieces of French honor back together.

Monnet, one of the leading French personalities to have gone to London, supported General de Gaulle in the latter's effort to continue the war, which in Monnet's view should have been undertaken from the French Empire abroad. The Franco-British union proposal would have given a strong boost to this effort.

However, Monnet looked with quite a different eye on de Gaulle's effort to create a political organization behind French resistance. This divergence was a prefiguration of their subsequent ambiguous and reserved relations. "Monnet is waffling" was de Gaulle's description[90] at the time of the contretemps between Giraudists et Gaullists on the issue of forming a joint National Committee at Algiers, where Monnet had arrived as an adviser of Giraud at the end of February 1943.

Shortly after the announcement of the Free French movement in 1940, Monnet wrote to de Gaulle that, while it was right to continue the struggle, it was wrong to create an organization that appeared to be under the protection of Great Britain.[91]

De Gaulle, on the other hand, looked at the situation quite differently: without forming themselves politically, Frenchmen scattered abroad after the French defeat were liable to lose their freedom of action. In his *War Memoirs*, de Gaulle described the bulk of French exiles as

small French groups which, on the pretext of being political, were more or less astir in Great Britain and in the United States. They were willing that de Gaulle should act as a soldier and provide the Allies with the reinforcement of a contingent. But they would not admit that the leader of the Free French should take upon him governmental responsibilities. Not having rallied to me, they rejected my authority and preferred to entrust to foreigners—that is, in fact to Roosevelt, Churchill, and Stalin—the future of France.[92]

The above passage evokes what appears to be a leitmotif in de Gaulle's thinking: a concern that Frenchmen in general tend to knuckle under to foreigners and to be swayed by the arguments of foreigners.

At the end of August 1940 Monnet left London and settled in Washington. Equipped with a British passport, he became a member of the British Supply Council. Before long his influence began to be felt in the establishment of the capital, particularly among the senior civil servants and leading journalists such as Walter Lippmann and James Reston: ''Among these people there was a ceaseless exchange of information and ideas. We dined together—often at our house in Foxhall Road; we telephoned each other; we exchanged notes at all hours of the day or night. Military men joined in our talks.''[93]

Although Monnet saw the president only on rare occasions, he developed intimate relationships with Roosevelt's close friends, particularly Felix Frankfurter and Harry Hopkins, and with other very influential men such as Under Secretary for War John McCloy. The presence of Monnet in Washington seemed to be a key factor in the image of France that developed in the American foreign policy elite. Walter Isaacson and Evan Thomas, in their book about this elite, sum up Monnet in the following terms: ''As would happen to other leaders of the American Establishment, [John] McCloy became entranced by Jean Monnet, the brilliant French brandy heir, economist, and statesman who later became the eminence grise to the wise men of American foreign policy.''[94]

With his wide range of contacts in the American administration, Monnet seems to have served as a counter-model to de Gaulle. His influence was not very ostentatious because he was a man of compromise, the one who liked to ''unite men.''[95] He did not oppose de Gaulle frontally, but his actions spoke volumes: refusal to join the Gaullist movement in London in June 1940; supporter of the Tréveneuc thesis; adviser to Giraud at the beginning of 1943; and so on.

An example of the decisive influence Monnet must have wielded can be found in a memorandum he sent on December 24, 1942, to Harry Hopkins with a copy to Felix Frankfurter.[96] He cites this memorandum in his *Memoirs*. The document, said Monnet, reflected an

approach [that] seemed to me reasonable, and I was able to persuade Frankfurter and Hopkins to agree with it. On these problems, they were Roosevelt's most influential advisers: Secretary of State Cordell Hull and the State Department as a whole were kept quite outside of White House policy on France.[97]

Monnet also noted that the memorandum was later published in Hopkins's papers and that ''it both suggested and reflected Roosevelt's own ideas.''[98] Monnet's memorandum was written at a critical time in the French-American relationship. There was the formidable stir created by the installation of Admiral Darlan in power in North Africa, which Roosevelt himself felt compelled to defend—rather weakly—in public. (In fact, Monnet's memorandum is dated Christmas Eve, the date of Darlan's assassination, but obviously Monnet did not know about it at the time. Moreover, Monnet stated in his *Memoirs* that he submitted it on the 23rd.)[99] In the memorandum, Monnet's overall theme was, ''The sovereignty of the French people, the expression of which was suspended by the Occupation of France, must be completely safeguarded, and any organization outside of France should be prevented from arrogating to itself the slightest atom of a right to the leadership of the French people.''

The most important thing to do, the Monnet memorandum stated, was to form a French army in North Africa, equipped by the United States and Great Britain. This army would be

under the orders of General Giraud . . . [and] an integral part of the Allied forces under a single command . . . the statute of the French Army will result from a proclamation of the President of the United States announcing the safeguard of the sovereignty of the French people. . . . A French Army fighting with the Allies will have the effect, in time, of turning public opinion in England, in America, and certainly in France, away from the current political quarrels of Darlan, of de Gaulle, etc., and toward the military renewal of France. . . . These factions will soon realize that, to keep their public credibility, they will have to join the French military effort. At that time, one can scarcely doubt that the forces of de Gaulle will rally to the new French Army.

For Monnet, it was the duty of the United States and Great Britain to prevent the formation of a French national authority before the liberation of the country:

The sovereignty of France belongs to the French people. Only its expression was suspended with the German occupation. The indispensable element of the reestablishment of France is an assurance that conditions will exist, at the proper time, to make possible this expression. No French political authority can exist or be authorized to be created outside of France. It is the duty of the United States and Great Britain to preserve for the French people the right and the occasion to decide for themselves what government they will have. . . . The current dissensions are due to a hidden struggle for political power in the future. De Gaulle is seeking recognition by the United States and Great Britain on the basis of a suppressed but presumed support of the French people. Darlan will try to build a regime on the notion that he represents Pétain, that is the constituted regime of France. The sympathy expressed by the French for de Gaulle is a reflection not of the choice of de Gaulle as a future leader of the French Government but of the desire of the French to continue fighting Germany alongside England and the United States. However, they would certainly show resistance to a government, even a provisional one, which owed its initial authority to foreign recognition.

Finally, and again in complete opposition to the Gaullist theses, Monnet advocated, in effect, that the French place themselves in the hands of the Americans, in a passage that has a faint aura of *petit-français*[100]:

In the imagination of the French people, their army should be closely linked to the American Army. The event which without doubt has most impressed Europe and the French people is that an American Army has landed in Africa. This was the first sign of deliverance, although its first consequence was the occupation of all of France. Although the British resistance played an immense role in strengthening the French resistance in the interior, French hopes remain without doubt with the United States. Nothing can keep their hopes alive in the hard period which lies ahead like the knowledge that a French Army has been reestablished with the help of the Americans and is fighting effectively as part of the army of the deliverance of France, under the orders of a French General completely occupied by the war and not by politics.

Between December 1942, the date of the memorandum, and 1944 Monnet had changed his opinion on de Gaulle, as had many others. In November 1943 he again settled back in Washington, where he tried to extract from the United States government a recognition of the French Committee of National Liberation (formed on June 3, 1943) as the provisional governing authority for France, and he described de Gaulle at that time in the following terms: "In the eyes of those to whom he addressed his imperious claims, de Gaulle appeared less interested in the conduct of the war than concerned for his own role afterward. To me this judgment seemed unfounded."[101]

These opinions were far from those of the memorandum of December 1942. Though the less charitable, such as de Gaulle, would say "Monnet waffles,"[102] it should be borne in mind that in the meantime there had taken place a massive swing of public opinion in France in favor of de Gaulle.[103]

It was the question of recognition by the Allies of a provisional French government that dwarfed all the other issues and became the symbol of the great misunderstanding between France and the United States that grew out of World War II. Because of the symbolic and ritual nature of state power, and because of France's extraordinarily long history as a nation, this question of recognition, which was not fully accorded by the United States until October 23, 1944, was arguably the most acute of all the differences between France and the United States during the war. Monnet described in his *Memoirs* (1976) that

the recognition of the provisional government . . . in itself was merely a minor episode; but like a recurrent fever it has troubled Franco-American relations for the past thirty years. Many of the attitudes . . . would be inexplicable, were it not for the illusions born of wounded pride in a memory that never forgot.[104]

It was not through lack of effort that Monnet, returning to Washington in November 1943, was unable to convince the Roosevelt administration to recognize the French Committee of National Liberation without delay. In fact, it appears to have been largely due to his interventions with Secretary of War Henry Stimson, Under Secretary John McCloy, and General Eisenhower that Roosevelt's hand was finally forced: de Gaulle was invited to Washington in July 1944, and immediately thereafter a de facto (though not de jure) recognition was accorded.

The refusal to recognize, until virtually too late, the French provisional government was the major wound inflicted by Roosevelt on a weakened France, although Roosevelt apparently believed that his actions were not harmful to the French people—quite the contrary—but to de Gaulle. Hull and McCloy, on the other hand, both feared that the policy of nonrecognition would have adverse repercussions within the French population in the postwar period.

Roosevelt remained stubborn to the end. As late as October 18, 1944, he wrote to Hull:

From all I hear, I think it would be a mistake go to ahead at this moment with [full] recognition of the Provisional Government of France. Practically all of France today is directly under General Eisenhower, who . . . is about to set up ''an Interior Zone.'' When this is done, I think we should recognize the Provisional Government of France, because then they will have something to administer, which they have not got now.[105]

Evidently for Roosevelt, ''from all I hear,'' especially as regarded France, was selective. An Office of Strategic Services report (ironically dated October 23, 1944, the date full recognition was granted) made clear the damage nonrecognition was causing:

On one point there appears to be complete unanimity, except in the ranks of the Communists. The Provisional Government of de Gaulle should be recognized by the United States, Great Britain and Russia at the earliest possible moment. . . . Even de Gaulle's personal and political opponents, insofar as they are true Frenchmen, are united on this point. Today they consider the failure to recognize de Gaulle as a slight, not to de Gaulle, but to France, and as such they resent it. . . .

If we say that we will not recognize that government until there has been a formal approval by the French people, we may deprive the provisional Government of the prestige and authority to proceed to any such consultation. There cannot be any real doubt today that the Provisional Government is the only body which conceivably could exercise governmental authority in France, unless such authority is exercised by the Communists.[106]

LACK OF KNOWLEDGE, FAULTY APPROACH

In the final analysis, there was a gross failing on the part of de Gaulle not to have promoted successfully his cause in the United States, and more fundamentally, not to have recognized early on that U.S. influence was in the process of dwarfing that of Great Britain. De Gaulle paid the price of a failed relationship with Roosevelt by his less than forthcoming personality on the one hand, and by the faulty initial approach of the Gaullist movement in the United States on the other. Even the man chosen by de Gaulle as principal delegate of the Free French movement in the United States, Adrien Tixier, appears from time to time to have mentioned de Gaulle in unfavorable terms to American officials.[107]

De Gaulle did not attach sufficient importance to his contacts in the United States until it became too late. Moreover, at the time World War II broke out, de Gaulle had little knowledge of the United States and did not seem to attach much importance to American support. The United States, after all, was not at war. What is more, de Gaulle seems to have had a ''continental'' point of view, stemming from the epoch of his youth: it was the revanchist period, when everything focused on Germany and when many Frenchmen, including de Gaulle, studied German in school.

De Gaulle rejected outright the idea of basing his movement in the United States, although in the course of the war, and especially after the entry of the United States into the war, Roosevelt had the upper hand in deciding Allied policy toward France, and Churchill could only follow along with him. To many in Washington, the Free French movement of de Gaulle represented only a faction of exiles under British sponsorship.

According to Raoul Aglion, who was, along with Tixier and two others, one of the four delegates of the Free French movement to the United States government, two incidents in particular damaged seriously the image of de Gaulle in Washington in the early years of the war. The first was a press conference in Brazzaville in August 1941, at which de Gaulle publicly "offered" French bases overseas to the United States and seemed to turn his back on his allies of the first hour, the British.[108]

The second incident, several months later, was much more serious: the affair of St. Pierre-Miquelon in Christmas 1941. The Free French forces seized the islands in spite of what American officials considered to have been de Gaulle's oral promise not to do so without consultations. The affair, which embarrassed the United States in its delicate negotiations with Vichy in the New World, conducted through the intermediary of Admiral Robert in Martinique, left Cordell Hull practically beside himself. He did not get over this until later in the war.

In sum, apart from the fact that what the American political elites learned about the Gaullist movement, whether from French or American sources, was almost uniformly unfavorable, the fault was also in part de Gaulle's—due largely to his lack of knowledge of the United States.

REFLECTIONS

When one observes the events of May–June 1940 in a long, backward glance, there is the aura of inevitability of a Greek tragedy. There was only a relatively obscure officer, "with the papers of a colonel,"[109] who was willing to take the lead in continuing the war. It was a premature arrival on the scene for General de Gaulle—a man too new, too inexperienced in the affairs of state, and of a rank not high enough to be heeded seriously by Pétain or Weygand. On the other side there was Pétain, the "providential" man (but also the man who had emerged as a defeatist out of the slaughter at Verdun).[110]

When all is said and done, the Tréveneuc thesis[111] (very likely put on Giraud's agenda by Monnet, who was Giraud's adviser), which consisted of a new government "risen from the ashes," was not realistic, especially in the passionate climate that raged in France at the end of the German occupation. It was indeed a time of rupture, when the administration of France was wrested from the regime that had remained in place during the war. How the general councils could convene in this atmosphere, let alone proceed to elections, made the thesis moot.

It was particularly Monnet and Alexis Leger who advocated the Tréveneuc thesis (whether or not under that name), which Roosevelt took as his own, obstinately, to the end. That a democratic country, as France was supposed to be, could introduce a political change by rupture did not figure in the prudential universe of Roosevelt.

Though the American president criticized the French parliamentary system and its endemic instability, like many of his compatriots he was so focused on his own idea of democracy, and so concerned about fascism, that he could not see that an "imperial hand" was needed above that parliamentary system. The fact is that this system, as practiced during the Third (and Fourth) Republics, functioned rather badly—except during the period of extraordinary national cohesion during most of World War I.

For Roosevelt, de Gaulle was an obstacle on the road leading to victory. The president's tendency, understandable from his point of view, was to get this obstacle out of the way. A Roosevelt note to Hull in October 1944 stated: ''I am having a terrible time on the military and naval operations because the French want to join in every staff conference and are making a nuisance of themselves. There is little they can contribute at the moment in a military or naval sense.''[112]

In truth, de Gaulle represented very little, especially at the outset of the Free French movement, and he felt this keenly, as he said in a speech in London on April 1, 1942:

How ultimately could they admit that in their attitude toward Fighting France, the democracies gave in to a pathetic snobbism and let themselves be influenced by their regret at not having seen therein many of the previously known prestigious names? . . . There is in this a particularly serious ignorance of a fact that today dominates the entire French question and is called "revolution." Because it is a revolution, the greatest in its history, that France, betrayed by its governing elites and its privileged classes, has begun. And I must say in this regard that the people in this world who imagine that they are going to be able to find, after the last shot is fired, a France that is politically, socially and morally like the one they knew previously will be making a notable error.[113]

Certainly an attitude to cause concern in the governing elite in the United States, an attitude to invite criticism of de Gaulle as a fascist or even a communist. The fact that he wanted to change the French regime by reinforcing the executive, and put an end to a system that had been dominated by the parliament, plus his dominating and brutal style, was enough to convince many American leaders and officials that de Gaulle had fascist tendencies. His plan to nationalize key French industries after the war was in a tradition that dates back to Louis XIV's finance minister, Jean-Baptiste Colbert, but American officials took it as a sign of fascism or communism. In truth, de Gaulle's contempt for the shifting alliances and deals (*combinaisons*) of the parties in the parliament did not mean he was not devoted to the republic. He was. But, since the French Revolution, tradition permitted that a republic could be transformed; it could be started from *rien*.

Clearly, it was not easy at the beginning for this band of Gaullists, this "elite that began from nothing" (*cette élite partie de rien*), as de Gaulle called it, to win over the administration in France, this "vertical society," which had only a limited access by merit. Indeed one sees in the past in France how a new elite seeks to wrest power at a moment of upheaval in the society. Thus Napoleon succeeded in his attempt to create a new elite by grafting a meritocracy out of the *Grand Armée* onto the old landowning families—until his demented ambition brought the system down. As François Furet said, "If [Napoleon] did not have a foreign policy that was so adventurous, he had a chance to found the Monarchy of the Revolution. Moreover, this is so true that a second one was established which did not have the same qualities."[114]

The collapse of 1940 inflicted incalculable psychological and moral damage on France. It would have been better psychologically to have accepted the French-British union solution, or the Holland solution, with the French government displacing itself to London or North Africa. As it was, the armistice was in effect a surrender, and French honor, in spite of the affirmations of Pétain, was not saved. However, curiously, the scenario of the armistice was made less incredible for France by the fact that something similar had already taken place. For Pétain, the armistice seems to have been but another chapter in the long history of France, with its highs and lows.

For the aged Pétain, perhaps this scene represented a remake of the seventy-year-old Franco-German struggle. He was at the very impressionable age of fifteen years when the French government, on January 28, 1871, signed an armistice with the Prussians. On March 10, 1871, the government, temporarily installed at Bordeaux, decided to move north to Versailles, the city of kings.[115] And Adolphe Thiers, leader of the "Party of Order,"[116] undertook the reconquest of a Paris that had risen in rebellion after the cession of Alsace-Lorraine. Pétain must have been surprised—and delighted—that the Germans did not demand such a cession in 1940.

The choice for France in June 1940 was essentially one of two solutions, defined by Henri Rousso in the following terms: "An amistice is a suspension of hostilities between two states, signed by the public authorities; a capitulation without conditions is a military surrender signed by the general staffs."[117] The distinction is real, as pointed out by Jean-Pierre Azéma:

The stakes were not minimal: capitulation—which is strictly of a military nature—without question abandons the population to the pleasure of the conqueror, but leaves complete latitude to a government to continue the struggle in what seems to be the most adequate way (as the Norwegians and the Dutch had decided to do); on the other hand, an armistice is a political convention that ties a state to another state, and forbids any continuation of the war under whatever form, in offering a greater protection to the citizens of the conquered country since they admit that the war is ended.[118]

It was the first option that Weygand refused before Reynaud.[119] If this option had been chosen, if a sort of Holland solution had developed, this is not to say that it would have been better in strategic or practical terms. Without the armistice, Hitler likely would have proceeded directly to the occupation of North Africa. It is unlikely that the British and the remainder of the French Army in North Africa, plus the French fleet, could have prevented that. But in the final analysis, General Francisco Franco of Spain, by his refusal to enter the war on the Axis side, was a greater obstacle to Germany's arrival in the heart of the French Empire, North Africa, than was Pétain, the supposed "shield." Franco, plus the fact that the success of Rommel in Egypt and Libya rendered less necessary a German occupation of the Maghreb.

It was rather on the psychological and moral plane that the damage to France and its image as a leading power were brought on by the armistice. William L. Langer, commissioned by Hull to do a study of charges that America's pro-Vichy policy was wrong-headed, had this to say:

France came out of her defeat much more fortunate than anyone could have expected. Not only were Hitler's terms remarkably lenient, permitting the continued existence of a French nation and a French government, but through de Gaulle France was to have at least some of the advantages of an exile government loyal to Britain and her allies. When through further developments of the war, Pétain's government became played out, de Gaulle and the Fighting French could take its place. So France was able to play both ends against the middle—France had eggs in two baskets.[120]

Not having a real government-in-exile in London and continuing with a government obedient to Germany in Vichy had its consequences: in his proclamation to the "captive nations" at the time of the Normandy invasion in 1944, General Eisenhower established political control only over France. Of course it was strictly a question, at that particular moment, of the invasion of France (although, being an invasion of the Continent, the liberation of other countries could be expected to follow): for the Allies, the immediate problem was establishing control over the administrative machinery of the French state, having failed to arrive at an accord beforehand with the Free French, especially over the issuance of currency.

This having been said, one can nevertheless advance the hypothesis that objectively France was being treated in this way because its legitimate government had decided not to leave the country and continue the war from abroad. In his *War Memoirs*, de Gaulle noted:

According to this text [the proclamation at the time of the invasion], Eisenhower spoke first to the people of Norway, Holland, Belgium and Luxembourg in his capacity as a soldier in charge of a military operation having nothing to do with their political destiny. But subsequently, in quite another tone, he addressed himself to the French nation. He urged that nation to "carry out his orders." He declared that "in the administration, everyone will continue to fulfill his functions unless contrary instructions are received"; that once France was liberated, "the French themselves would choose their representatives and their government." In short, he appeared to be taking charge of our country even though he was merely an Allied general entitled to command troops but not in the least qualified to intervene in the country's government. . . . In this factum, not a word of the French authority which for years had aroused and directed the war effort of our people and which had done Eisenhower the honor of placing under his command a great part of the French Army.[121]

The end of the war in 1945 saw France less damaged materially than, for example, Poland, but more damaged on the psychological plane. As French Deputy Edouard Frédéric Dupont stated: "Among countries like Poland and Belgium, France suffered the least from the German occupation. And it was Marshal Pétain who gained us that."[122]

For not having succeeded in surmounting its moral dilemma in 1940, France was, to borrow the phrase of François Furet, "yearning for expiation" (*en mal d'expiation*). Though Weygand refused to "dishonor" the French Army and instead put the blame on the politicians of the Third Republic, it was not surprising that the army—which was at the heart of this defeat and of this division of French society, which made impossible a "solution in unity" in 1940— became the instrument of expiation in the postwar period.

NOTES

1. Charles de Gaulle, *Discours et Messages* (Geneva: Editions Edito-Service, 1970), 2: 92 (address at the Hôtel de Ville, Paris, August 25, 1944).

2. Letter from President Franklin Roosevelt to Joseph Clark Baldwin of the House of Representatives, July 19, 1944, shortly after the visit of Charles de Gaulle to Washington. Franklin D. Roosevelt Presidential Library (FDRL), Official File (OF), Box 2, France 1944–45. De Gaulle learned of this letter afterward, when an anonymous person sent him a photocopy. Charles de Gaulle, *The Complete War Memoirs of Charles de Gaulle*, vol. 2, *Unity, 1942–1944*, trans. Richard Howard (New York: Simon and Schuster, 1964), 576.

3. Excerpt of an editorial sent to President Roosevelt by New York lawyer James N. Gerard on June 15, 1944, with the note: "Enclosed is an excellent editorial from the Shreveport "Times" of June 12, '44 about that cussed de Gaulle." FDRL, President's Secretary's File (PSF), Box 31, France: de Gaulle, 1944–45.

4. *The New York Times Book Review*, November 11, 1990, 58.

5. De Gaulle, *War Memoirs*, 2: 545.

6. Ibid.

7. Allied Military Government in the Occupied Territories.

8. Stanley Hoffmann, "The Man Who Would Be France," *The New Republic*, December 17, 1990, 33.

9. Interview with the author, October 25, 1990.

10. Hoffmann, "Man Who Would Be France," 33.

11. De Gaulle, *War Memoirs*, 2: 429.

12. The car no longer exists: it was removed by the Germans to Berlin where, as fate would have it, it was destroyed in an Allied bombing.

13. Robert E. Sherwood, *Roosevelt and Hopkins: An Intimate History* (New York: Harper, 1948), 956. Also see Arthur L. Funk, *Charles de Gaulle: The Crucial Years 1943–1944* (Norman: University of Oklahoma Press, 1959), 47–48, which contains a reference to this record of conversation.

14. Ibid., 685–86 (undated Hopkins memorandum).

15. *Foreign Relations of the United States (FRUS)*, Conferences at Washington and Casablanca, 694.

16. Ibid.

17. Ibid., 695–96.

18. De Gaulle, *War Memoirs*, 2: 391.

19. Ibid., 392.

20. Ibid., 392–93.

21. Ibid., 393.

22. *FRUS*, Conferences at Washington and Casablanca, 696.

23. See p. 22.

24. Sherwood, *Roosevelt and Hopkins*, 956.

25. Ibid.

26. De Gaulle, *War Memoirs*, 2: 574.

27. Ibid., 575.

28. Ibid., 573.

29. Jean Laloy, *Yalta: Yesterday, Today, Tomorrow*, trans. William R. Tyler (New York: Harper and Row, 1988), 65.

30. Ibid., 72–73.

31. Ibid., 61.

32. Henry A. Kissinger, *The Troubled Partnership* (New York: McGraw-Hill, 1965), 44.

33. George Ball, *The Past Has Another Pattern: Memoirs* (New York: W. W. Norton, 1982), 81.

34. FDRL, PSF, Box 31, France: de Gaulle, 1944–45, Memorandum of July 4, 1944, 2.

35. Memorandum from Mr. Stephen Early, White House Press Secretary, to Mr. Hasset, June 19, 1944. The memorandum transmitted a copy of Mr. Lawrence's article. FDRL, PSF, Box 31, France: de Gaulle, 1944–45; President's Personal File (PPF), document 9085, de Gaulle; Official File (OF) 203, Box 2, France: 1944–45.

36. Laloy, *Yalta*, 15.

37. Ibid., 40.

38. The words of British historian Michael Howard at a conference on Yalta at the Center for European Studies, Harvard University, February 1991.

39. FRDL, Map Room, File on France (FOF), Box 30, North Africa: French National Committee Section 3, From War to Freedom, No. 5457, December 22, 1943.

40. François Flohic, *Souvenirs d'Outre-Gaulle* (Paris: Plon, 1979), 195.

41. "L'Histoire en Direct: le Suicide d'une République," *France Culture*, July 3, 1989. (The words of Pétain after the parliamentary vote on July 10, 1940.)

42. Ibid.

43. The first volume of Lacouture's work is entitled "Le Rebelle."

44. See p. 12.

45. Charles de Gaulle, *Mémoires de Guerre*, vol. 1, *L'appel, 1940–1942* (Paris: Plon, 1954), 330 (certain appended documents in the original French version are not included in the English translation.)

46. Charles de Gaulle, *Lettres Notes et Carnets* (Paris: Plon, 1981), June 1940–July 1941: 16.

47. From de Gaulle's reply to the French chargé d'affaires in London, July 3, 1940. *Mémoires de Guerre*, 1: 335.

48. Camille Chautemps, *Cahiers secrets de l'armistice* (Paris: Plon, 1963), 129.

49. Christiane Rimbaud, *L'Affaire du Massilia* (Paris: Seuil, 1984), 22–23.

50. Hoover Institution on War, Revolution and Peace (HI), Papers of Robert D. Murphy, Document: Général Weygand, undated, 2–4.

51. According to Hull, Reynaud nearly had a nervous breakdown just before his resignation. Cordell Hull, *The Memoirs of Cordell Hull* (New York: Macmillan, 1948), 1: 793.

52. *Le Monde*, April 29, 1969, 1.

53. Conversation on May 26, 1942, between Welles and Aglion, one of the Free French delegates in the United States. Raoul Aglion, *De Gaulle et Roosevelt* (Paris: Plon, 1984), 73.

54. De Gaulle, *War Memoirs*, 1: 94.

55. Ibid.

56. Ibid., 139.

57. *FRUS*, 1940, 1: 245. (Paris telegram No. 1120, June 10, 1940, signed Bullitt.)

58. Ibid., 250. (Message from Churchill to Roosevelt, following a meeting with French leaders at the French General Headquarters at Briare near Tours on June 13, 1940. Telegram No. 1645 from the American Embassy in London, June 14, 1940.)

59. Ibid., 247. (Message from Churchill to Roosevelt after his meeting with French leaders at Briare on June 11–12, 1940. Telegram No. 1622 from the American Embassy in London, June 12, 1940.)

60. For the entire period of World War II the figure is much higher: "France lost 600,000 men in the Second World War—an enormous loss for a country as small as France. Most of this loss came from the same generation which had suffered so much between 1914 et 1918." (The words of Prime Minister René Pleven to President Harry Truman, January 30, 1951, at the White House. Harry S. Truman Presidential Library (HSTL), President's Secretary's File (PSF), Box 186, Subject File: Foreign Affairs (Pleven-Reports), Notes on the second Truman-Pleven meeting, January 30, 1951, 26.)

61. Rimbaud, *L'Affaire du Massilia*, 25–26.

62. "Laval was the inspirer and the genius of the present French system of government," wrote Freeman Matthews, American chargé d'affaires at Vichy, in a telegram on December 18, 1940. "It was he above all who in the critical days at Bordeaux fought with great determination and success against the removal of the Government to Africa." (*FRUS*, 1940, 2: 424).

63. Ibid., 498.

64. Jean-Pierre Azéma, *1940 l'année terrible* (Paris: Seuil, 1990), 151.

65. Ibid.

66. "L'Histoire en Direct."

67. This became a point of contention later with Vichy, as a shipment of American planes had reached Martinique at the time of the armistice.

68. *FRUS*, 1940, 2: 401.

69. Ibid.

70. Ibid., 400.

71. Ibid., 413–14.

72. De Gaulle, *War Memoirs*, 1: 56–57.

73. Churchill met de Gaulle a second time on June 11–12 at the French General Headquarters at Tours, as he recounted in a letter to Roosevelt: "Reynaud . . . [in contrast to Pétain] is for fighting on and he has a young General de Gaulle who believes much can be done." *FRUS*, 1940, 1: 247.

74. For a summary of this American search prior to the North African invasion, see Marc Ferro, *Pétain* (Paris: Fayard, 1987), 421–22.

75. Interview with the author, February 3, 1991.

76. Chautemps, *Cahiers Secrets*, 155.

77. Saint-John Perse, *Oeuvres Complètes* (Paris: Gallimard, 1972), 601–603. (N.B., Perse came to be the pen name of Alexis Leger.)

78. De Gaulle, *War Memoirs*, 1: 256.

79. *Le Monde*, October 21–22, 1990, 2.

80. Ibid.

81. Ibid.

82. FDRL, PSF: State Department, Welles to FDR with attachment, August 13, 1942.

83. Not otherwise identified but almost certainly André Istel.

84. William R. Emerson, "Roosevelt and de Gaulle," *The View from Hyde Park*, Winter 1989, 8 (review of Aglion's book *De Gaulle et Roosevelt*).

85. De Gaulle, *War Memoirs*, 2: 407.

86. Ibid., 412–13.

87. Emerson's review of Aglion's book. See note 84 above.

88. Ibid.

89. See p. 31.

90. De Gaulle, *Mémoires de Guerre*, 2: 437.

91. De Gaulle, *War Memoirs*, 1: 99.

92. Ibid., 254.

93. Jean Monnet, *Memoirs* (Garden City, N.Y.: Doubleday, 1978), 155.

94. Walter Isaacson and Evan Thomas, *The Wise Men* (New York: Simon and Schuster, 1986), 122.

95. "I always followed the same line of thought. . . . My sole preoccupation was to unite men, to solve the problems that divide them, and to persuade them to see their common interest." Monnet, *Memoirs*, 221. See p. 6.

96. The complete text of this document can be found in FDRL, Harry Hopkins papers, Box 330, Book 7: Casablanca I, Monnet to Hopkins, December 24, 1942. References to the document are taken from the document itself, except for Monnet's comments on it in his *Memoirs*.

97. Monnet, *Memoirs*, 182.

98. Ibid., 181–82.

99. Ibid., 183.

100. *Petit-français* roughly refers to Frenchmen who have a humble opinion of themselves.

101. Monnet, *Memoirs*, 120.

102. See p. 40.

103. Hoffmann, "The Man Who Would Be France," 33.

104. Monnet, *Memoirs*, 220.

105. FDRL, Map Room, Files on France (FOF), Box 31, France: Civil Affairs (1), President to Hull, October 18, 1944.

106. Ibid., PSF-OSS, Box 171, OSS Reports February–April 1945: Donovan to Roosevelt, October 25, 1944 (transmitting OSS report cited).

107. Aglion, *De Gaulle et Roosevelt*, 36.

108. Interview with the author, November 22, 1990. (N.B., Ambassador John Winant referred to this press conference in a letter to Roosevelt: "Wherever he [de Gaulle] has been he has left a trail of Anglophobia behind him. An interview he gave at Brazzaville in August 1941 was only the first of many attempts to play Great Britain off against the United States and vice versa. . . . It is part of his policy to gain prestige in France by showing how rough he can be with the British and now with the Americans. He has undoubtedly Fascist and dictatorial tendencies." FDRL, Map Room, FOF, Box 30, North Africa: French National Committee, Winant to Roosevelt, June 14, 1943.)

109. See p. 28.

110. "L'Histoire en direct." (Statement by Emile Fouchard, parliamentarian in 1940.)

111. See pp. 38–39.

112. FDRL, Map Room, FOF, Box 31, France: Civil Affairs (1), President to Hull, October 18, 1944.

113. De Gaulle, *Mémoires de Guerre*, 1: 422–23. See also p. 21–22.

114. A reference to the regime of Louis-Napoleon Bonaparte (1848–70).

115. Jacques Rougerie, "La Commune de Paris," *Le Monde*, March 17–18, 1991, 2.

116. A combination of the liberals (favoring the House of Orléans) and the legitimists (partisans of the Bourbon restoration in France).

117. Henri Rousso, *Le Syndrome de Vichy* (Paris: Seuil, 1987), 238.

118. Azéma, *1940*, 149.

119. See p. 30.

120. William L. Langer, *Our Vichy Gamble* (New York: Knopf, 1947), 65.

121. De Gaulle, *War Memoirs*, 2: 559.

122. "L'Histoire en direct."

❖ **3** ❖

The Turning Point

There are a few occasions in history when a decision so purely technical
on the surface has produced such tremendous consequences.

Jean-Baptiste Duroselle
on the interim aid to France in 1947[1]

THE "MAL FRANCAIS" OF THE PERIOD

Jean Monnet, in his *Memoirs*, described penetratingly the ''mal français'' of the
period of the Fourth Republic (1946–1958):

Resignation had become the habitual response of Governments in the face of difficulties
and trials of strength. The chance of escaping burdensome responsibilities, together with
the permanent danger of being outvoted by an Assembly which ran no risk of dissolution,
had made governmental instability a political way of life. Crisis had become the most
natural and simple way of dealing with problems that demanded courage: it was a case
of solving them by default.[2]

Democracy, snatched from the French nation by the parliamentary hara-kiri
of July 10, 1940, at Vichy, was restored almost immediately following the peace.
An assembly that was also constituent was elected on October 21, 1945. This
formally ended the Third Republic, which had in reality been concluded by the
''parenthesis'' of Vichy.

There followed the resignation of General de Gaulle from the presidency of
the Provisional Government in January 1946, in the midst of the work of the
Constituent Assembly; the rejection by the electorate of the draft constitution

(June 1946); the adoption of a new draft constitution by the voters in October 1946; and the election of Vincent Auriol as the first president of the Fourth Republic (January 1947) with powers not very different from those of his predecessors of the Third.[3] Governmental instability and rule by parliament had again returned to France.

THE DIVIDE OF 1947

The International Context and the Marshall Plan

The year 1947 constituted a divide in the international relations of the postwar era. After the war the victors of the conflict, as they recovered from the ordeal, took the measure of each other's intentions, East and West. Although Churchill had publicly announced on March 6, 1946, that "an Iron Curtain has descended on the Continent" (and he had actually used the term ten months before in a telegram to Truman), it was only in the spring of 1947 that the East-West climate definitively darkened. As Professor Maurice Vaïsse stated: "Two years after the end of the war, Europe was split into two political and ideological blocs. . . . The year 1947 represented a real watershed.[4]

The rebellion in Greece, which had been in gestation since 1946, impelled President Truman to ask Congress for an exceptional grant of aid to combat the Soviet menace in that region. The Truman Doctrine was announced to Congress on March 12, 1947. Professor Vaïsse commented, "Truman thus took the step that led his people from their traditional isolationism to the leadership of the Western world."[5]

At the same time, a Conference of Ministers of Foreign Affairs[6] began in Moscow, where Foreign Minister Molotov proposed the creation of a single authority in Germany that would be a "provisional government" set up in Berlin. According to Jean Laloy, "it did not follow from this that the USSR intended to set up Communist regimes everywhere. It was merely that its long-term objective was to exert the preponderant influence over the [European] continent as a whole. Hence the importance of the German question."[7]

Stalin had plenty of time. As he said to General George C. Marshall, the Secretary of State, during the Conference of Foreign Ministers, "We have plenty of time to come to an agreement, whether the next time or the time after."[8]

During almost two months, between March and May 1947, the talks dragged on in Moscow, finally ending in failure. Secretary Marshall returned on April 26, 1947. Truman noted in his *Memoirs* that Marshall returned from the conference in a pessimistic mood and that "the Russians . . . were interested only in their own plans and were coldly determined to exploit the helpless condition of Europe to further Communism rather than cooperating with the rest of the world."[9]

Already a machinery of countermeasures was being set in motion. Dean Acheson, then Deputy Secretary of State, explained the situation in a memorandum dated March 5, 1947, one week after Truman had given his agreement in principle for aid to Greece and Turkey. Acheson noted that this was only part of a "much larger problem growing out of the change in Great Britain's strength and other circumstances" and that it was urgent to "study situations elsewhere in the world which may require analogous financial, technical and military aid on our part."[10]

It was the genesis of the Marshall Plan.

Two organizations in the government set about the task laid down by Acheson: the State, War and Navy Coordinating Committee (SWNCC), within which was formed an ad hoc committee to study the problem, and the new Policy Planning Staff of the State Department, headed by George Kennan, author of the famous "long telegram" from Moscow in November 1946, which presented the rationale for the policy that came to be known as containment. A public version of the telegram appeared later in *Foreign Affairs* of July 1947 under the pseudonym "X." The Policy Planning Staff took on as its first task a study of the critical situation in Western Europe, where economic recovery since the war had clearly fallen short of expectations.

As regards the aid already programmed for Greece and Turkey, Kennan noted with regret that in the public mind there had been the predominant theme of a struggle against communism. For Western Europe, said Kennan, it was necessary that the accent be put on the positive side: the recovery and economic development of Europe.[11]

Pending the report of the ad hoc committee of the SWNCC, an officer in economic affairs in the State Department, C. Tyler Wood, emphasized the particularly critical situation in France in a memorandum dated April 17, 1947. Existing financial institutions, said Wood, would be able to take care of France's financial needs through fiscal 1948, provided the International Bank (for Reconstruction and Development, IBRD) granted France a requested loan of $500 million, adequate coal supplies would be available, and inflation in France could be contained.[12]

In the report of the ad hoc committee dated April 21, 1947, France was the only country for which aid was deemed necessary "for political and not economic reasons."[13] Although the committee seemed to underestimate the extent of economic misery in France, it was quite aware of the political stakes involved in this spring of 1947.

Under the guidance of Will Clayton, the respected Under Secretary of State for Economic Affairs, a rescue plan for Europe was put together. The plan was announced by General Marshall, the most unassailable figure in the Truman administration, including the president himself. In his speech at Harvard University on June 5, 1947, announcing what came to be known as the Marshall Plan, General Marshall emphasized the importance of a European effort: it was up to the Europeans themselves to come up with a program of assistance.

At the same time, Washington had decided that the United States should not be seen as responsible for the division of Europe. Therefore, the Soviets and

East Europeans should be invited to join in this endeavor. However, the Soviet Union, because of the extreme suspicion of its leaders, particularly Stalin, rejected the Marshall Plan offer and took upon itself the responsibility for the division of Europe. Thus Marshall's speech had the effect of setting in motion the great East-West divide.

Moreover, because of the American insistence on a unified approach on the part of the Europeans, a formidable impulsion was created in Europe in favor of supranational initiatives. The Schuman Plan (May 5, 1950) followed within three years and gave birth to the first supranational organization in Europe, the Coal and Steel Community (CSC).

Jean Monnet, the author of the stillborn plan for a British-French union in the somber hours of June 1940, had turned his attention toward the Continent in the postwar period: "by now the question of Germany was uppermost in my mind."[14]

In 1950 Monnet confided his line of thought to a close American friend: Great Britain was not going to distance itself from the United States sufficiently to become really European. The Americans could not be admitted into a European entity because they would then become "the boss." As for the Germans and the French, they needed something bigger than themselves, but not so big for them not to believe in it. A French-German relationship was the key for Europe. The other continentals were essentially on the periphery.[15]

Several months after the announcement of the Schuman plan for a European Coal and Steel Community, Monnet came up with yet another plan, this time for a European army: a plan that was premature, by the admission of Monnet himself,[16] but deemed necessary for the defense of Europe in the wake of the invasion of South Korea in June 1950. This Pleven Plan, announced by French Prime Minister René Pleven on October 24, 1950, which was turned into the European Defense Community at the Treaty of Paris (May 27, 1952) and then rejected by the French Parliament a little more than two years later, is the subject of the next chapter.

The Franco-Soviet Relationship

The divide in international relations that took place in the spring and summer of 1947 affected not only Anglo-American relations with the USSR but also the bilateral Franco-Soviet relationship. After the signing by de Gaulle of a friendship treaty with Moscow on December 10, 1944, the French government had seen itself as playing the role of intermediary between East and West. In spite of the brusque resignation of de Gaulle in the beginning of 1946, there was a certain continuity in French foreign policy, in part from the fact that Georges Bidault had remained Foreign Minister since November 1944.[17]

The Treaty of Moscow, which was more constricting for France than it should have been, was not an Anglo-Saxon constriction. What de Gaulle was seeking was the support of the Soviet Union to lessen the crushing weight of Anglo-

American influence in Europe. In the negotiations, de Gaulle agreed to two major concessions: at the eleventh hour he agreed to send an unofficial French representative to the pro-Soviet government in Warsaw; and in the pact itself, there was a provision that mutual assistance was required not only in the case of German aggression against one or the other of the signatories, but also if one of the parties became involved in hostilities with Germany for having taken ''all necessary measures to eliminate any new threat originating in Germany.'' The same clause was contained in the treaties signed by the Soviet Union with Czechoslovakia, Yugoslavia, and Poland in the period 1943–45.[18]

In judging de Gaulle's opening toward Moscow in December 1944, it should be borne in mind that the general had political objectives involving the Soviets that were related to the French internal scene. He had every interest at the end of 1944 that ''the party'' (such as the French Communist Party was called in the postwar period because of its pre-eminence), which had borne the brunt of the resistance inside France, not make trouble for him. And the party, which was part of the government from 1944 to 1947, generally did not.

The Moscow Conference of March to May 1947 put an end to this initiative toward a Franco-Soviet rapprochement. Foreign Minister Vyacheslav Molotov refused to sanction the detachment of the Saar from the French Occupation Zone and its linking to France under a sort of protectorate—an action that had been undertaken unilaterally by the French government in December 1946. The consequence of the refusal of the Soviet foreign minister was that Georges Bidault abandoned his self-imposed role as mediator between the Anglo-Americans and the Soviets.[19]

THE POLITICAL CONTEXT

The ''Third Force''

Even after the resignation in January 1946 of General de Gaulle, who was the architect of the Franco-Soviet rapprochement as a means of counterbalancing Anglo-Saxon influence, the détente with the Soviet Union continued, as did the détente with the French Communist Party. When the Socialist Vincent Auriol became the first president of the Fourth Republic on January 16, 1947, and Paul Ramadier, also a Socialist, was named president of the Council (prime minister), a Communist, Maurice Thorez, became one of two vice presidents of the Council. And for the first time, there was a Communist as Minister of Defense.

This cooperation with the Communist Party did not last, however. The antagonism was deep between the Socialists (the SFIO—Section Française de l'Internationale Ouvrière) and the Communist Party, former political brothers until the split of 1920 at the Conference of Tours. In May 1947, in the wake of the failed Conference of Foreign Ministers at Moscow, the two French parties of the left fell out openly.

The interim aid to France, so called because it was to tide the country over until the Marshall Plan came into effect on April 1, 1948, coincided with the coming into being of the "Third Force"[20] governments in France which followed the period of tripartite governments (Communists, Christian Democrats [*Mouvement Républicain Populaire*—MRP], and SFIO). The existence of this Third Force (neither Communist nor Gaullist) was to facilitate the granting of this aid to France and the application of the Marshall Plan.

Two key events in the spring of 1947 contributed to the advent of Third Force governments. First, the Communist ministers were dismissed from the government on May 5, 1947, after they protested the prime minister's conservative wage policy. This was to lead to all-out opposition of the Communists to the government in the fall of 1947, following the formation of the Kominform. Second, General de Gaulle on April 7, 1947, announced the formation of a movement, the Rally for the French People (*Rassemblement du peuple français*, RPF), with the objective of revising French institutions, in particular the creation of a strong executive.

The arrival on scene of the Third Force was manna for Washington, for which the earlier era of tripartite governments had been a sort of political miasma. This earlier period was described by U.S. Ambassador to France Jefferson Cafferey in a telegram of October 29, 1946, shortly before the second referendum on a new constitution, as one of profound "malaise" in France, in which democracy was perceived as not producing results. Politically aware Frenchmen saw the only alternatives as a dictatorship by the Communist Party or an authoritarian regime under de Gaulle. Though a majority preferred the latter, because the former would have put France behind the Iron Curtain, "many would do so with the greatest misgivings and with the feeling that France was being launched on an unknown adventure which might lead anywhere."[21]

The Third Force stretched from the SFIO to the center right. The principal element from the latter was the Mouvement Républicain Populaire (MRP), a post–World War II creation of Christian Democrats. This was the first time such a movement had been organized in France, with its still recent anticlerical past. Added to the Third Force cluster was the remainder of the Radical Party, a republican and bourgeois party that had been the pivot of the governments of the Third Republic, and the Independents grouped principally around Antoine Pinay.

Essentially two pillars, the SFIO and MRP, formed the base of this Third Force coalition and remained, with difficulty, until 1952, when the Socialists went over to the opposition. (Later, in 1953, the Gaullists, who had been released from a commitment to de Gaulle, saw some of their leaders enter the government). As Jean-Baptiste Duroselle put it, the Marshall Plan "could not have arrived at a better time to consolidate the new 'third force' governments taking power in France."[22]

The United States government put its full weight in favor of the new Third Force coalition, led by the Socialist Paul Ramadier. Five days after the expulsion of the Communists from the government on May 5, 1947, Ambassador Cafferey wrote from Paris apropos this new situation that it was "the best that could be hoped for." A Communist victory would greatly facilitate Soviet penetration in the region and make the Allied position in Germany virtually untenable, and if de Gaulle won, "France would be headed into a new and unknown adventure which by the nature of the forces generated in such a struggle would make the practice in France of democracy as we understand it difficult if not impossible for some time to come."[23]

Unfortunately the United States was not in a position to make a strong government of this coalition of the center right and the non-Communist left. In October 1947 Paul Ramadier's coalition received a severe shock in the municipal elections. The Gaullists crushed the center, in particular the MRP, winning 40 percent of the votes, while the Communists held their position with 30 percent. This meant, in short, that seven out of ten Frenchmen were not in tune with the philosophy of a Third Force government.

Shortly after the municipal elections, an associate of General de Gaulle's, Gaston Palewski, said to an American Embassy officer that if de Gaulle were asked to return, he would request full powers to bring about the necessary institutional reforms to set the country right. In reply the State Department expressed "dismay" and noted that the American press had "expressed extreme concern lest dictatorial methods imputed to de Gaulle will mean the substitution of dictatorship of the Right for parliamentary methods."[24]

By the autumn of 1947, as the polarization between left and right increased concerns in Washington about a possible communist dictatorship or a fascist-style Gaullist one, a certain discouragement set in on the part of the moderate parties. Obviously there was a need to close ranks, to save the Third Force idea, and in November 1947, a new prime minister was designated, the socialist Léon Blum, who symbolized the rejection of the Communists on the one hand and the Gaullists on the other. However, in an overly blunt speech before the National Assembly, Blum ended by offending the Gaullist RPF rank and file plus other members of the right. He asked that all "republicans rally round him: all those who refuse to be under the impersonal dictatorship not of the proletariat but of a political party; all those who refuse to seek a recourse against this peril in the personal power of one man."[25]

According to *Le Monde* of the period, "the President of the Council succumbed to too much frankness."[26] The upshot was that Blum's parliamentary margin of maneuver withered away: not only had he offended the right but he also lost the support of other parties of the non-Communist left, the Rassemblement des gauches (Radicals and the USDR, Union socialiste et démocratique de la résistance). The recourse became a member of the MRP as president of the council: Robert Schuman. *Le Monde* reported that "the new government is in the image of the previous one, with the center of gravity having been displaced from the SFIO to the MRP."[27] The newspaper's editorialist, Jacques Fauvet, commented that "the now more coherent bloc of the socialists and the Popular Republicans" had put together "a sort of moral contract, for better or for worse . . . between those whose ambition, as Léon Blum put it, was not to separate the cause of social justice from the cause of political democracy."[28]

The MRP-SFIO tandem had become indispensable for the continuation of Fourth Republic governments. A strengthened ruling team had emerged in November 1947, with the Alsatian Robert Schuman as MRP prime minister and the Socialist Jules Moch as interior minister. Although the left-right polarization in France (which was mirrored on the international scene) had thrown the moderate parties on the defensive, it had also intensified the split between the Communists and the Socialists; this was to be reflected rapidly on the trade union front.

Social Unrest and Upheaval

What came to pass in the fall of 1947 was a sort of repetition of the rebellion in Greece, displaced to Western Europe and transformed into a labor union struggle centered in Italy and France, particularly the latter. The break between the communist world and the socialists of Western Europe became definite as a result of a secret meeting in Warsaw at the end of September which shortly thereafter surfaced in the press. The meeting was attended by representatives of all the Communist parties in power plus those of Italy and France. The rupture with the socialists was symbolized in these words from the subsequent declaration announcing the birth of the Kominform as a result of this meeting: "above all the French Socialists and the British Laborites—Ramadier, Blum, Attlee and Bevan—facilitate by their subservience the work of American Capital, incite it to acts of violence, and lead their own countries toward a state of dependent vassalage toward the United States."[29]

In the fall of 1947 there was fear of a severe winter like the previous one, which had been followed by a drought over the summer, resulting in a disastrous harvest. The food situation was rapidly becoming critical. The French Communist Party decided, following the creation of the Kominform, to launch a spectacular challenge to the government by the method of general strikes.

Social unrest combined with Communist agitation reached its apogee in November 1947. The atmosphere was prerevolutionary, if not revolutionary itself. The new government of Robert Schuman took office on November 24, following Paul Ramadier's resignation five days earlier. The Council of Ministers received parliamentary approval for a declaration assuring the freedom to work and the defense of the republic, and the government ordered a draft call-up as a means of coping with the social unrest. The new Minister of the Interior, Jules Moch, held firm, and the Communist threat subsided.

It was evident from the beginning of this wave of labor union violence that many workers were hesitant about participating in an agitation that was also highly political. After the union pressure subsided, an open split took place on December 20, 1947, within the principal labor union organization, the Communist-dominated Confédération générale du travail (CGT). A number of Socialists formed themselves into a separate organization, the Force ouvrière (FO). According to Jean-Pierre Rioux, from November 29 to December 10, until the Communists of the CGT gave the signal for a general retreat, the split among the strikers was obvious.[30] In this atmosphere of a struggle with East-West overtones, U.S. policy came to be enunciated as follows: "the most effective way of weakening the CGT is to strengthen the non-Communist unions."[31] As Thomas Braden, who had headed the International Organizations Division in the CIA's Directorate of Plans, put it in a television interview, "they [the Communists] set up a successful communist labor union in France right after the war. We countered it with *Force ouvrière*."[32] In a separate article in the *Saturday Evening Post*, Braden was more explicit:

In 1947 the Communist *Confédération générale du travail* led a strike in Paris which came very near to paralyzing the French economy. A takeover of the government was feared. Into this crisis stepped [Jay] Lovestone and his assistant Irving Brown. With funds from [David] Dubinsky's [International Ladies Garment Workers] union, they organized *Force ouvrière*, a non-Communist union. When they ran out of funds, they appealed to the CIA. Thus began the secret subsidy of free trade unions which soon spread to Italy. Without that subsidy, postwar history might have gone very differently.[33]

In this context, it is worth noting the words of Annie Lacroix-Riz:

The assent to the Marshall Plan took shape more progressively. *Force ouvrière* blew hot and cold from week to week, before casting off its initial ambiguities and coming down with a definitive choice in October 1947—the moment of a very discreet trip by [its president], L[éon] Jouhaux (which the publication of FO failed to mention).[34]

The destination of this "discreet trip," not specified, is thus all the more emphasized.

THE ECONOMIC CONTEXT

Economic relations between the United States and the French Provisional Government went back to the Lend-Lease Agreement concluded with the French National Committee in London in September 1942 and with its successor entity, the French Committee of National Liberation (Comité français de libération nationale, CFLN), a year later in Algiers. Jean Monnet obtained an extension of the Lend-Lease arrangements on February 28, 1945.[35]

However, the end of the war in August 1945 brought an abrupt end to Lend-Lease. Goods ordered but not delivered were to be incorporated into loans at a very low interest rate. The Provisional Government had henceforth to deal with the new Export-Import Bank, and Monnet, after getting the negotiations started, returned to Paris in November 1945.[36] In the following month an agreement was signed between the Provisional Government and the new Export-Import

Bank opening up a credit of $550 million for France. The loan was repayable over thirty years[37] at an interest rate of slightly more than 3 percent.[38]

On January 3, 1946, Monnet was named Commissioner of Planning by General de Gaulle, who himself resigned on January 20. At the end of January, Léon Blum, his prestige at a high because of his principled comportment during the war, was designated an ambassador charged with negotiating economic agreement with the Allies. Once named, Blum planned to engage immediately in talks with the United States government aimed at obtaining substantial economic aid for France. Because of his uncertain health, however, his departure had to be put off.

At the end of the previous year, on December 6, 1945, Congress had accorded a very substantial loan to Great Britain, in the amount of $3.75 billion on very favorable terms it decided would not be repeated for other countries. "So we had come at the worst possible time," commented Monnet, who accompanied Blum to Washington in March 1946.[39]

Before the arrival of the French visitors, the negotiating field was circumscribed. "An approach to Congress for a credit to France along lines of Brit[ish] loan is not practicable," Secretary of State James M. Byrnes stated in a telegram to Ambassador Cafferey on February 4, 1946.[40] As an alternative, William Clayton, the State Department's Under Secretary of State for Economic Affairs, suggested several days later to French Ambassador Henri Bonnet that France could ask for additional credit from the Export-Import Bank, over and above the $550 million accorded in December 1945. However, the bank had to deal with many requests from borrower countries. The disappointed Bonnet, who had earlier asked for a loan of $2 billion, only to be told that Washington had already loaned $1 billion to France to finance purchases under the Lend-Lease Agreement, was further informed by Clayton that as far as loans for reconstruction were concerned, the International Bank (for Reconstruction and Development) was being organized for that purpose and was to be ready for operation at the end of 1946 or the early part of 1947.[41]

In truth, France's position was ambiguous, not to say unique. Great Britain considered herself in a class apart. The countries of the Continent, on the other hand, were a "club of defeated nations," as one of George Ball's Dutch friends had put it.[42] However, France was too big to be considered in the same category as the Benelux countries or Norway. What is more, France, though beaten in 1940, had come back and contributed to the Allied victory. In brief, France was special: not an enemy country, obviously; not a conquered country, at any rate not anymore; but not one of the three great victors of the war. Quite apart from Anglo-Saxon affinities, there was no question in Washington of France being put on the same footing with Great Britain, but at the same time, France was too important to be ignored—once again, victim and beneficiary of its own geography and size. Politically, France was the key to Western Europe, and hence an economic rescue plan for France was eminently political.

If the United States's favored treatment of Great Britain was an understandable, though bitter, reality for the French, the case of Germany was completely different. France had emerged from the war traumatized by four years of occupation, only to be faced anew with the prospect, more or less continually present, of a new world war. In this new situation of East-West confrontation, the average Frenchman tended to view with jealousy the U.S. effort to rebuild the German economy as a means of defense against the Soviet threat. West Germany, according to an observer of the left (and there were many in France in the period following the war), was "pampered by Washington and promised priority in reconstruction."[43]

One can follow the thread of this postwar French anxiety toward Germany through accounts of official conversations between French and American leaders, beginning with the talks that took place between President Truman and General de Gaulle in August 1945 in Washington. De Gaulle was so insistent on a defense of France at the line of the Rhine and the detachment of the Ruhr from Germany that Truman finally stated that the Russians also wanted an internationalization of the Ruhr and had asked to send troops there. This seemed to cut short further conversation on the subject.[44]

After more than two months of negotiations, an agreement between Léon Blum and Secretary of State Byrnes was signed on May 28, 1946. According to one of the provisions in this agreement,[45] the wartime debts of France to the United States plus the sales of surplus American goods were set at $720 million. For repayment of this amount, the French obtained an interest rate of 2 percent, the same as the British had for their loan, but over thirty-five years instead of the fifty accorded to the British. Also, there was a provision in the British loan agreement for waiver of interest payments.[46] Although the French side was anxious that the agreement not appear different in the eyes of French public opinion, the National Advisory Council (NAC) in Washington, the highest-level organ for economic policy, was against such a waiver.[47] The final text of the agreement stated only that in extraordinary conditions an installment payment could be postponed by mutual agreement.[48]

As it turned out, the French tried to avoid meeting the first payment under the terms of this agreement but were dissuaded by American officials, who cautioned that this would create a bad impression from the very beginning.[49]

According to a second provision in the Blum-Byrnes Agreement, an additional credit of $650 million was opened for France by the Export-Import Bank, over and above the $550 million allocated in December 1945.[50] A third provision concerned discussions that were to be undertaken for another credit that would enable the French to acquire American cargo ships of a tonnage up to 750,000 tons. And in a fourth provision France committed itself to the policy of freedom of commerce enunciated in the Bretton Woods Agreements of 1944.

Finally, there was a special provision, which became extremely controversial in France, by which the United States obtained the right of entry into France of American films without an import quota, as had been the case in the 1930s. French films were allowed a very limited right to exclusive showings in movie houses in France, a so-called screen quota. "Starting from July 1, 1946, the screen quota reserved for French films will not exceed four weeks every four months," stated the agreement.[51] In case of a dispute in this regard, the two parties could reexamine the agreement, but if they did not come to new arrangements, the original one would remain in force. The ultimate objective was that, once France had recovered economically, these special quotas would be abolished entirely.

According to Jean Monnet, over and above the Blum-Byrnes accord there was an agreement by the United States at the time that the new World Bank (IBRD) would approve a loan of between $500 and 600 million to France in the future.[52] The American version is slightly less categoric. According to documents prepared for discussions between the Secretary of the Treasury, John W. Snyder, and the Minister of Finance, Robert Schuman, in September 1946— four months after the signing of the Blum-Byrnes Agreement—the matter was still pending. France had asked for a credit of $500 million from the IBRD, but the complete documentation was still awaited from the French side.[53] Following the visit of Schuman on October 8, 1946, the formal French request was received.[54] (On May 7, 1947, in response to this French request, the first IBRD loan was announced: $250 million with the overall objective of helping to finance economic recovery in France.)[55]

The Blum-Byrnes Agreement was unanimously ratified on August 1, 1946, by the new National Assembly.[56] In reply to a question from Communist Deputy Jacques Duclos, Léon Blum said that the specific agreement on the entry of American films would not be submitted to the National Assembly for ratification.[57]

THE QUESTION OF INTERIM AID

It rapidly became apparent that the Blum-Byrnes Agreement was not going to be sufficient. Between July and December 1946, according to Monnet, prices went up 50 percent in France.[58] This quickly made the benefits of the Blum-Byrnes Agreement inadequate. Obviously it was necessary to put into effect a wage and price stabilization program, as the money supply was constantly swelling because of salary increases decided by the government in periods of high social tension, and which required government borrowings from the Bank of France.

Inflation not only undermined social stability but also caused a decrease in French exports. Thus, largely deprived of the possibility of accumulating dollars through substantial exports, France found itself virtually unable to import the capital goods and raw materials necessary to get the economy going. This was the famous "dollar gap" problem summed up by Jean-Baptiste Duroselle: "The difficulty . . . was 'priming the pump' . . . the food and machinery France lacked could be purchased from the United States—but how, since France had no dollars and was scarcely in a state to export anything whatever to so wealthy a country?''[59]

It was Jean Monnet's estimate, as planning commissioner, that equilibrium in France's balance of payments would not be achieved until 1950. Even if France used up all its gold and hard currency reserves, it would still need an additional several billion dollars in the 1946–50 period.[60]

There was a strategic dimension as well: As Duroselle observed, the dollar gap

resolved itself quite simply in France's case into a choice of regimes: either the preservation of a liberal Western type of democracy, with American aid, or the setting up of a ''people's democracy,'' in other words a party dictatorship. One may justifiably claim that up to the spring of 1948 the fate of France hung in the balance.[61]

On May 7, 1947, the first IBRD loan to France of $250 million[62] was announced, followed a month later by the unveiling of the Marshall Plan, an ambitious and unprecedented undertaking aimed at providing systematic and continuing aid to Western Europe over a four-year period (1948–52). Though these developments were heartening, it soon became apparent that an additional loan would be necessary to cover the interim before the start of the plan on April 1, 1948.

As of the end of the summer of 1947, the French government had only $240 million in reserves to cover a trade deficit estimated at $450 million. This meant that either imports would have to be curtailed drastically at a moment of increasing social unrest, or the United States would have to be asked for further assistance.[63] As Ambassador Cafferey noted, in a telegram dated September 30, 1947, ''the present Government has been progressively orienting its policy toward the US and has continued to oppose heavy Communist pressure to re-enter the government counting largely on the Marshall Plan and interim aid until Marshall Plan can go into effect next Spring.''[64]

One effort begun in Washington was to study the issue of French reserves. As of early October 1947 several sources of additional hard currency were deemed to be available, and if and when they could be recuperated, would be in excess of $250 million.[65] Even presuming these sources could be tapped, there would still be a drastic shortfall: the minimum need over the six months ending March 31, 1948, was estimated at $615 million.[66]

Parallel to the examination of French reserves, Secretary of State Marshall brought to the attention of the Cabinet on August 8, 1947, the recommendation of the State Department that a new look be made at all the possibilities of interim aid for Europe, where the situation had become desperate. Obviously, efforts within the executive branch would not suffice. On September 29, 1947, President Truman publicly recognized this fact:

If this recovery program [for Western Europe] is to have a chance of success, means must be found for aiding France and Italy to survive this critical winter as free and independent nations. . . . Assistance this winter, in sums much larger than the Executive Branch can provide with funds now at its disposal, is essential. That assistance can only come from Congress.[67]

The statement came five days after a report by the Acting Secretary of State, Robert Lovett, to the Cabinet describing France and Italy in a "terrible state" and subject to famine and sickness over the coming winter.[68]

On October 17, 1947, Georges Bidault, the French foreign minister, put out a financial S.O.S. to the United States: in a meeting with several American senators who had come to Paris, Bidault stated "that it is essential that we not be allowed to be asphyxiated." He added that he had the "moral certitude" that the United States would find the means to aid France until the Marshall Plan took effect.[69] France, said Bidault, needed dollars to buy goods in the United States. These dollars, he assured, "would not stick to the hands of the French."[70]

Congress dragged its feet in the face of these urgent appeals. The matter was repeatedly discussed in Cabinet meetings during the fall. At a meeting on November 14, 1947, President Truman, apparently to underline the sense of urgency, disclosed that he would announce to Congress that he was putting into effect in the United States a program of price controls on food, fuel, clothing, and rents.[71] At the same meeting Lovett intervened, saying that he found it incredible that, for want of several million dollars—that is to say, $150 to 300 million—Western Europe was in the process of being lost to the Soviets.[72]

In the meantime, on November 10, the Department of State had informed the American Embassy in Paris[73] that the total amount of interim aid to France had been determined at $328 million, but this would depend on whether Congress voted favorably.

On November 17 the American Embassy in Paris transmitted to Washington a note from the Ministry of Foreign Affairs stating the necessity of having $140 to 150 million over and above the anticipated interim aid in order to cover the projected deficit.[74]

On December 2 the Department of State came to a final decision. The sum of $328 million would be sufficient for the minimum needs of France for the interim, or emergency, period. Although the French authorities still thought that a supplementary amount of $143 million would be necessary, the American government estimated that certain expenses could be avoided during the period. By this reckoning France's supplemental needs could be reduced to $70 to 75 million.[75]

On the same date Secretary Marshall sent a message from London, where he had met the same day with his British counterpart, Ernest Bevin. The message made known Marshall's "grave preoccupations" concerning the "critical situation in France" where there was taking place "a veritable struggle for power." Maurice Thorez, said Marshall, had returned from Moscow, probably with a promise of wheat to be used at the right moment to swing the balance against the United States. Marshall added:

If we are not to run the serious risk of losing France, we should act promptly. Therefore, if the House [of Representatives] is favorable to interim aid to France, it should approve it at once. Time is of the essence. . . . The situation has moved dangerously far during the last two weeks. Prompt action by the Congress would so encourage and strengthen the favorable forces in France that, in our opinion, they will be able successfully to prevent what is a flagrant attempt to seize power. You know the far-reaching significance to Germany, Italy, the Mediterranean, North Africa, and to other areas, were France to fall.[76]

On December 17, the House of Representatives approved the Foreign Aid Act of 1947. Aid totaling $522 million was made in the form of grants to France, Italy, and Austria. It was a reduction from the $597 million requested by Marshall on November 10, of which $328 million was earmarked for France, $227 million for Italy, and $42 million for Austria. However, the total was increased to $577 million in March 1948.[77] The total French share was $312 million.

The modalities of this aid were not without problems on the French side, and the American administration succeeded in removing several clauses in the draft law that were wounding to French sensibilities, two salient ones on the insistence of Secretary Marshall. He had objected to two provisions, one of which gave the United States the right to use the "franc equivalent"[78] as of June 1948, and the other the right to supervise French production of items on the list of the interim aid. The first, noted Marshall, would give the United States the power to direct and/or destroy French monetary policy, whereas the second would be an outright blow to French national dignity. The two provisions, added Marshall, would lend credence to Soviet charges that the United States was trying to reduce France to the status of an American colony. He recommended that the legislators who were meeting to reconcile the two versions of the draft law go with the Senate version, which did not contain this embarrassing language.[79]

The French side also raised a procedural problem, as the American Embassy in Paris noted on December 24, 1947, one week after the interim aid bill became law. French officials feared that if their government signed an agreement for the aid without a sort of preliminary statement emanating from their government, this could give the impression that France had weakly submitted to conditions imposed by a foreign power, to the detriment of "French national sovereignty."[80]

In parallel discussions in Washington, the French Embassy insisted on a distinction in the commitments between (1) those that were a part of the agreement between the United States and France, and (2) those taken on by the French government in the context of the French economy. The former would be a part of the agreement between the United States and France; the latter would be included in an exchange of letters between the two countries.

The American government found this arrangement unacceptable because such a method would create a distinction among the provisions of an agreement that had been decided in its totality by Congress. The State Department informed Ambassador Henri Bonnet that it did not object to the French government's making a sort of preliminary declaration such as had been suggested by the American Embassy in Paris several days earlier. Washington, in a message to its embassy in Paris on December 26, added: "Until this question is resolved, we cannot proceed farther with aid provisions respecting France. Moreover, it is likely that the agreement with Italy and Austria can be signed without delay. You are requested to urge upon [Foreign Minister] Bidault the urgency of reaching a settlement of this problem."[81]

The next day Ambassador Cafferey informed Bidault of the State Department's position. Bidault yielded: "I shall almost certainly sign it but that may be the last official act of my career. I am not at all concerned as to what the Communists will do and say, but I am very concerned about possible attacks from the friends of de Gaulle and other very nationalist elements."[82]

The agreement was signed by France on January 3, 1948, under the formula recommended by the Department of State to Ambassador Bonnet in Washington. At the same time Finance Minister René Mayer introduced measures to combat inflation: a law for an exceptional salary deduction accompanied by an 80 percent devaluation. This was Jean Monnet's comment:

The inflationary gap must be closed. To increase the country's resources was difficult: to cut back demand was possible. All it required was courage . . . the preparation of these measures was in no way commensurate with the achievement of persuading Parliament to vote for them, which was a very great ordeal for René Mayer.[83]

Though social tensions were to resume in France in 1948, the worst moment of the "disguised insurrection," and Moscow's assistance to it, passed with the end of the dark and dangerous days of late 1947. The fate of a prostrate France hung in the balance, and a sort of "wise men's"[84] consensus within the American government, symbolized by the S.O.S. telegram sent by Secretary Marshall on December 2, 1947, with which John Foster Dulles associated himself in a bipartisan gesture,[85] prevailed over a hesitant Congress. The United States finally made the necessary effort to keep France as well as Italy in the Western camp, as had been done with Greece and Turkey. To say, however, that the United States wished to reduce France to the state of a "white colony," according to an expression of the postwar period, is clearly exaggerated. Even so, one should recognize the element of truth in the words of one of the French delegates in the interim aid negotiations:

If the aid and the Marshall Plan were essentially inspired by political necessity, it was nevertheless the case that the United States tried to get out of it all possible advantages for its industry in particular and its economy in general. The attitude of American officials was thus intransigent and inquisitorial. To the objections . . . of the French . . . the American Administration replied . . . in sum by all the dilatory means aimed at bringing us to heel.[86]

To balance out the perspective, it should be recognized that the macroeconomic philosophy of the two democracies was very different. France was accustomed to a rather large umbrella of social protection from public funds. For example, until the 1980s France had not experienced the non-indexing of wages with prices. As Erik Izraelewicz commented, "With the end of the widespread indexing of incomes, the governments of M. Mitterrand were to revolutionize France."[87]

The American model of a free economy, with a more restricted public sector role, went generally against this philosophy. This difference was particularly evident in the manner of looking at "counterpart funds": those funds that accumulated as the result of sales by the French government to French buyers of American products received through the interim aid or later through the Marshall Plan. From the French side, the impulse was for free access to these counterpart funds. However, the American negotiators, such as the young and gifted "Tommy" Tomlinson (who died shortly thereafter at the age of thirty-five), wanted to see a large proportion of these funds frozen. The spigot would be opened only to prevent a recourse on the part of the government to the Bank of France. It was necessary to avoid such a recourse because the French reserves were dangerously low. At heart, Jean Monnet was not against this approach. He wanted the counterpart funds to be used for purchases of equipment in the framework of his modernization plan and not for the current expenses of the government.

The American philosophy behind this aid program was clearly anti-inflationary, as put forth in a document prepared for the occasion of a visit by President Vincent Auriol in 1951: "We believe that only by means of an increase in essential imports into France can US financial aid serve to provide increased local currency resources for the French Government. Such imports, by absorbing purchasing power, will serve as a most effective device to combat rising prices."[88]

At the same time the American position was that economic aid should not be offered to a country where it would have the effect of increasing that country's monetary reserves—unless the refusal of aid would damage the country's defense effort.[89]

The document prepared for the Auriol visit, with its emphasis on defense, was written three years after the affair of interim aid to France. In the meantime the French defense capability had grown considerably, due to the revolt in Indochina and the Soviet threat that brought about the North Atlantic Treaty in 1949 and the integrated NATO defense system in 1950. France's increasing role in defense, specifically in the defense of Europe in the 1950s, is the subject of the next chapter.

NOTES

1. Jean-Baptiste Duroselle, *France and the United States: From the Beginnings to the Present*, trans. Derek Coltman (Chicago: University of Chicago Press, 1978), 181.

2. Jean Monnet, *Memoirs* (Garden City, N.Y.: Doubleday, 1978), 429.

3. This chronology is taken from Jean Carpentier and François Lebrun, *Histoire de France* (Paris: Seuil, 1987), 345–47.

4. Maurice Vaïsse, *Les relations internationales depuis 1945* (Paris: Armand Colin, 1990), 18.

5. Ibid., 19.

6. "To draw up the peace treaties, the Big Three decided to create an organism called the Council of Foreign Ministers, made up of representatives of the five great powers having veto powers at the United Nations." Ibid., 14.

7. Jean Laloy, "Le lancement du plan Marshall," *Le Monde*, June 7–8, 1987, 2.

8. Ibid.

9. Harry S. Truman, *Memoirs* (Garden City, N.Y.: Doubleday, 1956), 2: 112.

10. *Foreign Relations of the United States (FRUS)*, 1947, 3: 197.

11. Ibid., 224–25.

12. Ibid., 203.

13. Ibid., 206.

14. Monnet, *Memoirs*, 222.

15. Summary of a conversation in London between Monnet and his friend Professor Milton Katz, the number two in the Marshall Plan Mission in Europe, whose headquarters was in Paris. (Interview of Professor Katz with the author, March 6, 1991.)

16. Words spoken by Monnet to Robert Bowie. (Interview of Mr. Bowie with the author, December 17, 1990.)

17. Alfred Grosser, *The Western Alliance* (New York: Continuum, 1980), 60.

18. Jean Laloy, *Yalta: Yesterday, Today, Tomorrow*, trans. William R. Tyler (New York: Harper and Row, 1988), 58.

19. Grosser, *Western Alliance*, 61.

20. The term "Third Force" had another, less frequent, meaning—that of an independent and powerful Europe, distinct from the two superpowers.

21. *FRUS*, 1946, 5: 469–70.

22. Duroselle, *France and the United States*, 180.

23. *FRUS*, 1947, 3: 709–12.

24. Ibid., 790–91.

25. *Le Monde*, November 22, 1947, 1.

26. *Le Monde*, November 23–24, 1947, 1.

27. *Le Monde*, November 26, 1947, 1.

28. Ibid.

29. *Le Monde*, October 7, 1947, 3.

30. *Le Monde*, November 8–9, 1987, 2.

31. Harry S. Truman Presidential Library (HSTL), Psychological Strategy Board File, Box 5, 091 France File 1: PSB D/14, November 1, 1951, Annex A, 4.

32. John Ranelagh, *The Agency: The Rise and Decline of the CIA* (New York: Simon and Schuster, 1987), 246.

33. *Saturday Evening Post*, May 20, 1967, 4.

34. Annie Lacroix-Riz, *Le Choix de Marianne: les relations franco-américaines, 1944–1948* (Paris: Messidor/Editions sociales, 1985), 195.

35. Grosser, *Western Alliance*, 36. (Monnet himself dated the agreement March 13, 1945, and described it as reciprocal aid because there were important inputs from the French side in terms of labor and services. (*Memoirs*, 225.)

36. Monnet, *Memoirs*, 228.
37. Grosser, *Western Alliance*, 36.
38. Monnet, *Memoirs*, 228.
39. Ibid., 250.
40. *FRUS*, 1946, 5: 410.
41. Ibid., 416.
42. See p. 26.
43. Lacroix-Riz, *Choix de Marianne*, 200.
44. HSTL President's Secretary's File (PSF), Foreign Affairs, Box 178, France-Germany: France, Memorandum of conversation between Truman and de Gaulle, August 22, 1945, 6–9.
45. Published in *FRUS*, 1946, 5: 463–64.
46. Ibid., 457.
47. Ibid.
48. HSTL, PSF Foreign Affairs, Box 178, France-Germany: France, annex 4, Memorandum from the Secretary of the Treasury to President Truman, dated June 3, 1946, concerning the Blum-Byrnes Agreement and the memoranda relative to the negotiations with the French delegation, 2.
49. Ibid., Papers of John W. Snyder, Secretary of the Treasury, Box 18, Foreign Funds Control (General) Gold: France—September 1946, discussion between Mr. Snyder and French Finance Minister Robert Schuman, questions that could be raised by Mr. Schuman, 2.
50. Ibid., annex 1, 1. See also pp. 63–64.
51. Ibid., annex 14, 1.
52. Monnet, *Memoirs*, 254. See also p. 57.
53. HSTL, Snyder Papers, Box 18, Foreign Funds Control (General) Gold: France—September 1946, discussions between Mr. Snyder and French Finance Minister Schuman, questions that could be raised by Mr. Schuman, 1.
54. *FRUS*, 1947, 3: 708.
55. Ibid.
56. Monnet, *Memoirs*, 251.
57. HSTL, Snyder Papers, Box 18, Foreign Funds Control (General) Gold: France—General 1946–1951, Telegram 3666 from Paris, July 26, 1946.
58. Monnet, *Memoirs*, 260.
59. Duroselle, *France and the United States*, 179.
60. Monnet, *Memoirs*, 249.
61. Duroselle, *France and the United States*, 179.
62. See p. 66.
63. Duroselle, *France and the United States*, 180–81.
64. *FRUS*, 1947, 3: 761.
65. HSTL, Snyder Papers, Box 18, Foreign Funds Control (General) Gold: France—General 1946–1951, Memorandum of Frank A. Southard, Jr., to Secretary Snyder on October 6, 1947 entitled, ''Possible Sources of Funds for France for the Next Six Months,'' 2–3.
66. Ibid., Memorandum to the President on December 29, 1947, entitled, ''The Situation Regarding an Emergency Aid to France and Italy,'' 1.
67. Ibid., Official File (OF), Box 769, OF 203 (1945–1949): Statement of the President, September 29, 1947.

68. Ibid., Papers of Matthew J. Connelly, Press Secretary, Set II, Box 2, Notes on the meetings of the Cabinet, January 3–September 19, 1947.

69. *FRUS*, 1947, 3: 787.

70. Ibid., 790.

71. HSTL, Connelly Papers, Set II, Box 2, Notes on the meetings of the Cabinet, January 3–September 19, 1947.

72. Ibid.

73. *FRUS*, 1947, 3: 801.

74. Ibid.

75. Ibid., 808–809. In spite of this reckoning, the administration's request to Congress for the interim period remained at $328 million.

76. Ibid., 807–808.

77. Peter Calvocoressi, *Survey of International Affairs, 1947–1948* (London: Oxford University Press, 1952), 46, 47, 81.

78. These were the "counterpart funds." See p. 71.

79. *FRUS*, 1947, 3: 814–15.

80. Ibid., 820–21.

81. Ibid., 822–23.

82. Ibid., 823.

83. Monnet, *Memoirs*, 310–11.

84. The term is from the title of the book *The Wise Men*. See p. 41 and the accompanying note 94.

85. See pp. 68–69. Dulles was present in London along with Marshall as a delegate to the meeting of the Council of Foreign Ministers.

86. Lacroix-Riz, *Choix de Marianne*, 188. N.B., the name of the French delegate was not mentioned.

87. "M. Mitterrand, modernisateur du capitalism," *Le Monde*, May 8, 1991, 8.

88. HSTL, PSF, Foreign Affairs, Box 178, France-Germany: France—President Vincent Auriol, March 1951, Memorandum on the Visit of President Auriol, "Financial Aid to France," 2.

89. Ibid.

❖ 4 ❖

La Grande Nation, la Grande Armée[1]

Of course, France, among all the great nations which today have an army, is the only one to lose hers.

Charles de Gaulle, following the signature at Paris in May 1952 of the treaty instituting a European Defense Community.[2]

This chapter examines the debate concerning the European Defense Community (EDC), an event described at the time by *Le Monde* in the following vein: "The rejection of the EDC by the National Assembly marks one of the most important stages in French political life and in the external situation since 1946–1947."[3]

The paradox of the EDC can be summarized in this formulation: the EDC, conceived by *some* (though not *all*) Frenchmen to get around American insistence on German rearmament in the wake of the invasion of South Korea, was finally rejected by the French themselves—who almost immediately thereafter turned around and accepted essentially what the Americans had preferred at the beginning: a German Army as part of a sovereign German state within NATO. As Raymond Aron noted apropros of the EDC, in his "Historical Sketch of a Great Ideological Quarrel," "Thus, the end of the story ironically contradicted the beginning; the National Assembly ended up by preferring the solution that the American Government had proposed in 1950 to the solution proposed by the French Government."[4]

This is the key paradox among others in this drama, which lasted from the autumn of 1950 until the end of 1954. And it was in its protractedness that the EDC was destined to fail and at the same time to become transformed into something else. In the final analysis, and at the end of these four years, the

French preferred to keep their independence at the risk of seeing a remilitarized Germany.

THE INTERNATIONAL SCENE

During the long, tortuous affair of the EDC, France felt itself the most threatened by a possible German rearmament. It was potentially the country most in danger from Germany, and on the largest scale. In 1871, 1914, and 1940, it had been *the* country for the Germans to defeat. Everything excuses itself, everything explains itself in terms of this perception. France had to play the politics of its geography.

The overlapping dilemmas the EDC sought to overcome were summed up in the formula of Geneviève Rouche: "How, in the final analysis, could the Federal Republic be rearmed—without losing control of it, without frightening France, and without risking the outbreak of a new war?"[5]

The three problems contained in this formula can be developed as follows, as they apply to the countries involved and to the attitudes of the United States in dealing with these problems:

- The continuing uncertainty regarding Germany, following the horrors of the war and the occupation. This was not only related to the potential economic and military might of West Germany; the anchoring of West Germany to the West did not appear completely solid. There was implicitly the fear of a new Rapallo Pact with the USSR which, from the distance of the present, appears to have been exaggerated.

- The concern that France's fixation on its rank and security could lead it to turn instead to its traditional ally, Russia. This concern too appears to have been exaggerated.

- The unpredictability of the Soviet reaction which, again with the benefit of a long look back, appears to have been an exaggerated preoccupation with American planners. The outrageous Soviet rhetoric was probably taken too seriously, although Soviet intentions to unleash hostilities remained the great imponderable, especially in this early period of the Cold War.

Since the United States, as a superpower, carried so much weight, the temptation, indeed the perceived imperative, was to put its weight into the balance in order to accomplish objectives deemed desirable for the good of the West. The United States had broad shoulders and therefore was the country to pick up the challenge of the Soviets. The European countries, and in this case France, were closer to the Soviet Union by geography, and in a power position infinitely inferior to the Soviets at that point in time. Naturally, they were less inclined to face up to Moscow.

The Suspicion of a Renewal of the Franco-Russian Alliance

During this period of the early 1950s, there was a continuum of concern in Washington that France might break the solid Western front and turn toward the Soviet Union. There was a fear that it might wreck the plans of the Atlantic Alliance for the defense of Europe, a fear made more acute by the feeling that, without France, NATO was unworkable, basically because of France's geography. Washington appears to have underestimated the desire of a majority of the French population in that period to remain in NATO, a desire that may have been obscured by the fact that many in the French political class were in the thrall of thinkers hostile to America, particularly Jean-Paul Sartre.

The "Russian temptation" reappears continually in the history of France in the modern era. After the post–World War I rupture represented by the war between the Reds on the one hand and the Whites (supported by the Western powers) on the other, there was the "desperate flirtation" of Britain and France with Moscow in 1939, which ended in a total failure, and World War II began. The original alliance of 1893 between France and tsarist Russia was in effect revived by Charles de Gaulle in December 1944, as the war approached its end. The awareness of this relationship has never, even to this day, been entirely absent from American calculations. Through the period of the Cold War, and especially in the beginning, American policymakers seemed not to forget the pact signed by de Gaulle with the Soviets. Indeed de Gaulle renewed this trend following his return to power: after being assured of the strength of U.S. determination as a result of the Cuban missile crisis, de Gaulle, his mind free of a Soviet threat which seemed to be subsiding, proceeded to reanimate the Franco-Soviet relationship. It was a flirtation that ended with the application of the Brezhnev Doctrine and the crushing of the "Prague Spring" in August 1968.

Particularly in tense moments, such as in the hand-wringing over the deliberations on the EDC, there was suspicion in Washington over the presumed tendency of the French to "play the Russian card." Before, during, and after the vote of the National Assembly that killed the EDC in August 1954, there was an American distrust, especially on the part of John Foster Dulles, toward the policy of Pierre Mendès-France which was judged as leaning too much in Moscow's direction. The entourage of Mendès-France was considered to contain suspect elements. Mendès-France was thought to be prepared to seek an agreement with Moscow as a means of avoiding German rearmament. However, from his point of view, he needed to appear before the French public, especially the French left, as the man who had tried to find a solution with the Soviets but who had not received an adequate response. This scenario would make it easier for him then to cause German rearmament to be accepted by the French public.

The British Exemption

Throughout the affair of the EDC there is an astonishing absence of Great Britain, a fact keenly resented in France at the high point of the debate in the summer of 1954, as seen in these words attributed to Gaullist Républicains Sociaux in the French Parliament: "The defense of the West . . . can be assured only by a system in which France and Great Britain find themselves on an equal footing and are linked by the same commitments.[6]

This absence was soon corrected after the failure of the EDC by the creation of the Western European Union (WEU) as a defensive organization that included the British as full-fledged members. This change was perceived as necessary immediately after the vote that killed the EDC, at which time Pierre Mendès-France hastened to "define the principles of his foreign policy, among which figured faithfulness to the Atlantic Alliance and the 'presence' of England in any pact linking France and Germany."[7]

Throughout the EDC episode, the British, who were less interested in the project than the Americans or Konrad Adenauer, and therefore less inclined to make it a crusade, showed themselves to be more sagacious, more "historical," and through the intervention of Foreign Minister Anthony Eden, they were able to save the situation at the end, with the transformation of the EDC into the WEU. The relationship between Eden and Mendès-France, solidified in Geneva during the Conference on Indochina (June–July 1954), proved itself to be of value in the period after the sudden death of the EDC in the French Assembly.

In its exhaustive attempts to bring the EDC into existence and thereby launch the process of German rearmament, the United States asked the French for more sacrifices than it asked of the British. To read today the documents on the EDC and the proposed amendments, the language appears clearly weighted in favor of Great Britain. This is understandable in a certain sense from the fact that the British came out of the war with their glory intact. However, the imbalance can be clearly discerned.

It should be noted in this context that, at the beginning of the talk about a European Army, the French had the idea that the British would be a part of it. A U.S. government document of the time stated:

The French Government intends to invite Great Britain and the free nations of continental Europe which would accept to participate with it in creating a European Army and in perfecting the principles just expounded. This study would begin in Paris as soon as the treaty for the coal and steel plan is signed.[8]

Even Churchill, when he first proposed a European Army in a speech in Strasbourg in August 1950,[9] did not consider that the British would be exempted. But he did not consider either that the European Army would be integrated into one force. On July 14, 1954, before the House of Commons, Churchill recalled his initial position: "my idea did not include any supranational institution, and I saw no problem that would prevent Great Britain from playing its full role in such a system."[10]

Once the European Army idea was transformed into a supranational context, with the British outside of it, the French found themselves placed de facto among the "Continentals," or, to recall the phrase of George Ball's Dutch friend, among the "club of defeated nations" of the Continent.[11]

What made this state of affairs all too widely accepted was the weakened position of France at the time. It had been occupied during the war. It had been openly divided as a nation, more than at any time since the Revolution, and the horrors of the occupation and the vengeful period that followed testified to this. Moreover, France, still institutionally unsettled, had returned to its chronic condition of being the political sick man of Western Europe, a condition that had been interrupted during the twentieth century only during the supreme effort of World War I that had brought about the "sacred union" under the leadership of Raymond Poincaré. But to look too fixedly on this circumstantial degradation of France was to neglect history; it was to forget the traditional status of *la Grande Nation, la Grande Armée*.

In sharp contrast to its attitude toward the French, the American side was notably sympathetic toward British sensitivities about supranationality and the EDC: "We fully understand the reasons why the U.K. objects to full participation in the EDC and we do not believe that direct participation by you is necessary for the successful conclusion of a satisfactory treaty on the EDC." This statement of position was among the points to be raised by Truman with Churchill in the latter's visit to Washington in early 1952.[12] In the discussions that followed, Churchill, who never was a fervent supporter of the EDC, said that nevertheless he would do all that he could to help the project succeed— without British participation of course. Churchill, recorded the American note-taker, "placed great importance on the 'national impulse' in fighting forces."[13]

What was irreducible for the British turned out, in the final analysis, also to be for the French—both being ancient countries (and ancient enemies). This fact seems to have been surprisingly ignored by the Americans whose attention, however, it is nevertheless fair to say, was led astray at the beginning by the fact that the European Army had been proposed by France—in this case by the preferred interlocutors of Washington, Jean Monnet, René Pleven, and Robert Schuman.

The "German Predilection" of the United States

Behind this affair of the EDC, described by Pierre Maillard as "a sort of new Dreyfus Affair"[14] (and in a similar vein by Raymond Aron before him),[15] a number of factors continued to persist, during virtually the entire Cold War, in creating a disturbance in French-American relations. The British exemption— which had as its basis the special relationship between the United States and the United Kingdom—has already been mentioned: it is the most important element in sorting out the puzzle of the EDC. Also noted was the suspicion in Washington concerning the long-term tie between France and Russia—a suspicion intensified by France's revolutionary past and by the espousal of the communist point of view by great numbers of Frenchmen. There should also be pointed out the perception in France—a perception fundamentally not misplaced—of American favoritism toward the former enemy of World War II: Germany.

The United States had had only a limited history of a conflictive relationship with Germany. Germany was not for the United States a troublesome neighbor, as it had been for France for nearly a century. The United States traditionally has a culture that at the core is Anglo-Saxon and German, and not particularly French, except for some pockets of anachronistic interest. Even after the two world wars, the prejudice of the average American toward Germany is surprisingly absent. During the EDC debate, the perception of most Frenchmen was that the United States seemed to be favoring Germany: on the basic question of whether it was necessary to rearm Germany; on whether Germany should be integrated into NATO; and on how the Saar question should be settled. On all these questions the Americans seemed, in French eyes, to be making a case for the Germans.

THE FRENCH INTERNAL SCENE

The European Army idea was launched at the height of the period of the "Third Force," a governmental combination in France that, as has been noted, excluded the Communists and the Gaullists, leaving a broad coalition of the center right and the left—from the moderates to the Christian Democrats (MRP), to the Radicals, to the Socialists (SFIO)—holding the reins of power.

The EDC affair spelled the end of these pro-American governments of the Third Force type, about which George Ball (who had been Jean Monnet's lawyer in the United States) evinced some nostalgia: "In spite of its untidiness, I had always liked the Fourth Republic; its very weakness was its most attractive virtue, because it was incapable of resisting the accommodations in favor of a greater Europe which I believed necessary."[16]

This Third Force system could not last because fundamentally too many Frenchmen were not represented in it. Although the country had slid systematically toward the right since 1945,[17] this shift was not in favor of the coalition of "pro-Europeans" in power. In the legislative elections of June 17, 1951, the MRP continued its slow loss of support and the SFIO lost seats also. But the Rally of the French People (RPF) of Charles de Gaulle gained ground. Jacques Fauvet of Le Monde had the following observation: "Begun under a legislature that was favorable to it, the policy of European integration had to be carried on under a legislature that was less favorable, if not hostile, to it."[18]

In the case of France, the United States was not dealing with an ally acting in a fully integrated manner. While the French prime ministers—at least until Pierre Mendès-France—were "Europeans" favorable to the EDC, the contrasting situation in the Assembly was such that "the opponents of the treaty determined the existence of the governments, or rather their death, hence that of the [EDC] plan itself."[19]

During this entire period (and beyond), France was subjected to chronic parliamentary (and therefore governmental) instability. Whereas in the other countries of Europe there was notable leadership—Adenauer in Germany, Churchill in Great Britain, even de Gasperi in Italy (until his death in the middle of August 1954 at the height of the EDC debate)—France's interlocutors were without a political base and without charisma: Robert Schuman, Antoine Pinay, René Mayer, Joseph Laniel. All were well-intentioned men but without international weight, except, to a degree, Schuman and Pinay. France, still in the grip of its "legicentrism" inherited from the Revolution, had not found a way to escape from this condition of "sick man of Europe," to the point where Churchill, in the aftermath of the EDC debate, referred to the "tyrannical weakness" of the French Parliament, a formula Eisenhower found right on the mark.[20]

THE ORIGINS OF THE EDC

The EDC was born out of the Pleven Plan, announced by French Prime Minister René Pleven before the National Assembly on October 24, 1950. Five months earlier the first of the great supranational initiatives in Europe, the Coal and Steel Community (CSC), known then as the Schuman Plan, saw the light of day, on May 9, 1950. The idea was that first coal and steel would be denationalized or, more properly, supranationalized, and then defense would be. Each would involve the Europe of the Six: France, the Federal Republic of Germany, Italy, and the Benelux countries.

The Pleven Plan, like its precursor, the Schuman Plan, was a surprise. Conceived in secret, without consultation with the leading figures in the French political class, these plans were more elitist than representative; both sprang from the mind of Jean Monnet, although the idea of a European Army had previously been evoked publicly by Winston Churchill in August 1950, as has been noted. Because Monnet formed part of a "transatlantic political class"[21] that was in the process of being formed, this facilitated the acceptance of these plans in the United States and Europe. This "Monnet factor" was especially important in gaining support for the EDC, which originally met with little enthusiasm in Great Britain and the United States. (Indeed, the paradox of Monnet was that, while Americans found him the ultimately accommodating Frenchman, his long-term agenda of a Europe independent of the United States would not have been entirely to their liking).

The two plans, Schuman's and Pleven's, were founded on the principle of supranationality, or what General de Gaulle termed, in a famous press conference on November 12, 1953, in the midst of the controversy over the EDC, as "fusion." Monnet, without being cited by name, was "the instigator," ("l'inspirateur"), who on two previous occasions had proposed to de Gaulle "the panacea which is called fusion":

In June 1940 . . . the instigator brought to me a proposition for a fusion of France and England which I got accepted by Churchill and his Government. But Churchill and I saw in it only an ultimate show of Franco-British solidarity and a supreme reason offered to the French ministers to move to Algiers. The instigator himself thought it was possible to integrate King George VI with President Lebrun, the House of Lords with our Senate, the Home Guards with the Republican Guards [la Garde Républicaine]. . . . Three years later, as the United States had, after a fashion, set up an organization at Algiers that was in competition with Free France and not going well, the instigator came to their help in proposing to lump together General Giraud and General de Gaulle in one and the same government. Once again, I accepted the mélange, knowing well what would happen.

Then came the EDC: "after these two failures, what a magnificent occasion was offered for his panacea: the difficulty of bringing France and Germany together for the rearmament of the Reich!"[22]

Though it was originally an idea of the French government, the EDC was not in the strict sense of the word a "French" idea. It was a European idea. This conception of Monnet, and others in his orbit, could not, and would not, receive the approval of a majority of the French political elites—far from it.

The EDC was conceived by Monnet as a necessary but not wholly desirable follow-on to the Coal and Steel Community. According to Robert Bowie, a personal friend of Monnet and one of the principal American supporters of the EDC, Monnet regretted having to present the Pleven Plan—the forerunner of the EDC—ahead of its time: that is, precipitously in the wake of the invasion of South Korea, on June 24, 1950. Monnet told Bowie he came up with this plan because any other alternative would have been worse. A national German Army would have aroused fierce opposition in France at that point: it was only five years since the end of the war.[23]

Thus on two occasions, in May and October 1950, Monnet, solicited by the prime minister—first Robert Schuman and then René Pleven (for whom he had worked in 1939)—drew a plan from his pocket.[24] Between these two dates the Korean War had begun, and there had been "*la grande peur*"[25]—the fear that this type of civil war, apparently sponsored by Moscow, could be repeated elsewhere—this time in the heart of Europe, in Germany. Washington considered that a new surprise attack could come at any time. It was urgently necessary to mobilize the resource represented by West German manpower.

In September 1950, at a meeting of the North Atlantic Council in New York, the American government officially proposed the rearmament of West Germany. France demurred. A month later Monnet, through Pleven, proposed creating a European Army with the Germans in it.

The question of giving weapons to Germans was not something to be taken lightly in 1950. European sensibilities, particularly in France, were still acute. However, the perception of an urgent threat swept Monnet's idea along. In this moment of great weakness in Europe, there was a feeling that not much could be done at the level of individual states. It was necessary to form a combination of them. But Great Britain, with the Commonwealth behind her, soon seemed not to be an apt member of such a combination. France too had an empire but was a continental power in the heart of Europe and therefore indispensable to the combination.

To make the pill easier to swallow, the formula was devised of a "contribution of Germany to the defense of Europe."[26] Pleven summed it up in his speech of October 4, 1950: "Germany, which is not part of the Atlantic Pact, is nevertheless going to benefit from the security system that results from it. It is therefore right that she should furnish her contribution."[27]

Not everyone accepted this rationalization. In a statement on June 6, 1952, in which he used the term "stateless mixture" (*mélange apatride*) to describe the EDC, General de Gaulle summed up the contradiction: "so that Germany would be reputed not to have an Army while at the same time reconstituting a military force."[28]

WASHINGTON AND THE EDC: FROM RESERVE TO ADVOCACY

Washington was initially reserved about the EDC because it seemed that the process of German rearmament—which was the top priority—might be delayed, perhaps indefinitely, by this complicated scheme. Some saw in the Pleven Plan a French desire to hamstring the Germans. Once convinced of the goodwill of French officials and of the seeming good sense of the plan, the United States changed its mind. At first lukewarm, the American government became the most determined supporter of the EDC. Thanks to the arguments of Jean Monnet and other "Europeans" and to the passion of Konrad Adenauer for the EDC, the Americans came to the conclusion that no other solution existed. One of the more difficult to convince, however, was General Dwight D. Eisenhower.

In February 1951 General Eisenhower took command of the forces of NATO, whose headquarters was set up at Rocquencourt, outside Paris, under the name SHAPE (Supreme Headquarters Allied Powers Europe). On October 28, 1950, when Eisenhower was still president of Columbia University, he had been invited to Washington by Truman to discuss the possibility of taking command of the Allied forces. In his journal of that date, Eisenhower noted that the French had come up with "a complicated form of partial German rearmament and a hodge-podge organization that they feel might be approved by popular French opinion."[29]

Eisenhower gradually warmed to the EDC, and the "Monnet network" seems to have played a major role in this. Monnet's close friend John J. McCloy, then American high commissioner in West Germany, appears to have persuaded Eisenhower to spend a day in Monnet's company in order to receive a briefing on the Pleven Plan. Eisenhower accepted, and the briefing took place in the summer of 1951.[30]

After this briefing, Eisenhower wrote to General George C. Marshall on August 3, 1951, noting that his initial impression was that "inherent in this plan [for a European Army] were all the kinds of obstacles, difficulties and fantastic notions that misguided humans could have put together in a single package."[31] Now, however, he felt that "the plan represents the only hope in the immediate future for developing German power—which is of vital importance to us—in conditions acceptable to the other European countries . . . there will not be real progress towards European unification except through specific projects of this type."[32]

The support of General Eisenhower for a European Army could not have been more important. His prestige, and later his accession to the presidency, were capital.

DEATH OF THE EDC; BIRTH OF A SUBSTITUTE

The speech of the French prime minister in October 1950 (the Pleven Plan) was only a statement of principle. There remained a long road to travel before the EDC could be achieved. After months of negotiations on the Pleven Plan among the six continental partners plus the Americans and the British, the Treaty of Paris of May 27, 1952, gave birth to the EDC. One day earlier France, the United States, and Great Britain signed at Bonn the so-called "contractuals" involving the cessation of the occupation regime and the establishment of the sovereignty of the Federal Republic of Germany.

But there remained the problem of ratifying these twin accords. Several months earlier, in February 1952, the French National Assembly had registered a vote of confidence tied to the EDC but had accompanied the vote with pre-conditions that had not been resolved at the time of the signing of the Treaty of Paris. These had to be submitted to and approved by the various national parliaments, which in time was done.[33]

During the same month of February 1952 the NATO Council meeting in Lisbon adopted the report of Robert Schuman (then French Minister of Foreign Affairs) on "force goals" of NATO, which bore on the breakdown of forces within the EDC. The levels were set at fourteen French divisions, twelve German divisions, twelve Italian divisions, five divisions from Belgium and the Netherlands combined, and four British divisions with their own air support—the British being in association with the EDC but not members subject to its supranational provisions.[34]

Because the Paris treaty on the EDC did not have the general approval of the French political class but only that of the "Europeans," and not all of the latter, the tendency was to wait. French governments came into power and then went away. At the moment they came into office, the new prime ministers pleaded for time; time was always necessary.

During this long period, the entry of West Germany directly into NATO and the reestablishment of the German Army, particularly with its own general staff, remained a taboo, especially for the French. This was also true initially for the Germans (who, however, eventually wound up accepting a German Army as a gauge of their return to the concert of the great Western powers). This taboo was generally accepted in Washington. "I am not clear in my mind as to any alternative [to the EDC]," wrote John Foster Dulles to Winston Churchill as late as mid-August 1954.[35]

By 1954 the Treaty of Paris on the EDC was in the process of ratification by the parliaments of the six participating countries. Attention came to be focused on France, which was the keystone, at least psychologically and politically, of the whole edifice. Only the French and Italian parliaments were still dragging their feet, but the heart of the problem was in Paris.

Finally, in the summer of 1954, there arrived in power a man out of the ordinary: a man who had decided to act. Coming out of the small Radical Party, Pierre Mendès-France registered one stunning success after another, right after taking over power: Indochina, then Tunisia. Although still at the mercy of the parliament, he presented the image of someone who could overcome obstacles and raise hopes—especially after the success of the Geneva Conference on Indochina (June–July 1954). The American Embassy spoke of "a new situation which recalls the first days of the Government of de Gaulle . . . [although] Mendès does not have a solid coalition behind him."[36]

But Mendès-France was not completely to the liking of John Foster Dulles, who had succeeded Dean Acheson at the head of American diplomacy. For Dulles, Mendès-France was "a strange character."[37]

By the summer of 1954, after nearly four years of debate on the EDC, the international context had changed considerably. The initial high sense of alert over the invasion of South Korea subsided. The situation in the peninsula stalemated near the 38th parallel after the winter of 1950–51 and the painful American withdrawal from the Chosin Reservoir. Stalin died in March 1953. An armistice in Korea was achieved in July of the same year. A third world war seemed less of a possibility.

From the French point of view the most important event was the armistice concluded in July 1954 in Geneva, thus ending France's war in Indochina; the most intense period in this first phase of the Cold War had ended. Since the beginning of the decade France had become more and more involved in Indochina, in a vain effort to save this part of the empire. As involvement became greater than expected, the European part of the French Army diminished.

More profoundly, the cost of the war to France, the loss in men, the crushing defeat at Dien Bien Phu in May 1954, the anger of the French Army and its sense of having been left in the lurch: all this frustration arrived at its zenith in the summer of 1954 when the debate over the EDC reached its denouement. France's back was to the wall. It was being asked to submerge its military traditions at a moment when the French Army, hardened by the war in Indochina, was taking form again as a major military force. From the earliest history of France, military might had been the symbol of the nation, as General de Gaulle noted in his *War Memoirs*: "For fourteen centuries, military power had been second nature to France . . . eminently capable of the greatest military actions."[38]

By the summer of 1954 France was like a man flayed alive. The instrument of expiation of the shame of 1940 seemed about to disappear in its traditional form, at least in the European area. For what purpose? It appeared now, four years after the Pleven Plan was announced to the French National Assembly, that the United States, in order to obtain German rearmament, was ready to sacrifice the ancient traditions of the French state.

At the moment of his accession to power, on June 18, 1954, Pierre Mendès-France, who also took over the portfolio of foreign affairs, gave indications that he was prepared to force the issue on the EDC. He insisted that the French Parliament come to a decision on this issue before the end of its summer session. Although it was the first time since the launching of the Pleven Plan four years earlier that a declared "European" was not prime minister, the Americans were relieved at the determination of Mendès-France. On July 13, 1954, during their first meeting after Mendès-France had come to power, Dulles, who did not fail to mention the "billions of dollars" the United States had given to France for Indochina and elsewhere, laid out the U.S. position in his typical fashion, just short of hectoring:

[T]he U.S. had confidence in Mendès-France and welcomed his fresh approach to some of France's most pressing problems in which the U.S. also had a common interest. Speaking with complete frankness, the Secretary said that French indecision and inability to make difficult decisions had in the past created a real problem with respect to France's relations not only with the U.S. but also with other allied countries. . . . Traditionally there is a great sentimental attachment for France in the U.S., but there is a growing concern in the U.S. over apparent French vacillation and backing out on commitments. M. Mendès-France's forthright statements that he would press for decisions on urgent problems was therefore greatly welcomed.[39]

Alternating the carrot and the stick, Dulles, who had in December 1953 spoken of an "agonizing reappraisal" of American policy in case the EDC was not ratified,[40] then said to Mendès-France, probably largely for effect, that

if this does not soon occur [France's agreement to a German role in the defense of Europe], it would be better to write off what we have tried to do to build up the defensive strength of Western Europe as a noble but unproductive experiment. There would be the strongest pressures for the U.S. to engage in a peripheral form of defense involving the U.K., Spain, Greece, Turkey and other peripheral countries.[41]

But this warning shot by Dulles, who soon thereafter wrote to Churchill that "French soil is essential to an effective continental defense system,"[42] was not something to be taken too seriously.

The truth was that, in spite of manifold pressures on the part of Washington to hasten the ratification of the EDC, a majority in the French National Assembly in favor of it was simply not there. Jean Lacouture recounted that during the same meeting of July 13, 1954, in Paris, Mendès-France informed Secretary

Dulles that the text of the EDC treaty would not be approved by the parliament, "which shocked his interlocutor, whose numerous informers in Paris seem not to have been up to the mark."[43]

In view of this divisive situation in the assembly, Mendès-France sought to bring together the various French points of view on the EDC and named a committee of two ministers to study the subject. The effort at consensus failed; on August 13, 1954, in a gesture of protest against this effort to pass the EDC by means of a more acceptable packaging (these were in effect new protocols that would be added to the treaty), three of the six Gaullist-oriented ministers quit the cabinet—even though the Mendès-France government had still not taken a position for or against the EDC.[44]

Even these new protocols, Mendès-France now decided, would not suffice alone. One would have to play for higher stakes. On August 12, 1954, Ambassador Dillon in Paris reported that

[Mendès-France] felt that the changes which he would suggest in the EDC treaty would not of themselves be sufficient to guarantee passage at this time [by the Assembly]. He said he felt that he must take account of the Russian proposals for a further meeting on Germany and the effect these propositions had had on French public opinion and in parliament.[45]

What Mendès-France proposed to Dillon was to pass the treaty in the first reading in the assembly, then open new negotiations with the Soviets. Following this, at the end of the parliamentary vacation period, the procedure would recommence: submission of the treaty to the Council of the Republic (the name for the senate under the Fourth Republic), a second reading by the assembly, and then ratification in the first half of December, which would fit with the timetable for the ratification in Italy.[46]

In reply, Dulles stated he was "deeply shocked and disheartened" by the new plan. Mendès-France protested that he was not trying to inject a new delay. He was not proposing a new meeting with the Soviets but rather a response to them which would oblige them to clarify their position. If the Soviets did not make any concessions, there would be no new meeting. Ambassador Dillon, in reporting a meeting with him on August 13, stated that Mendès-France "said he is proceeding as he had planned and will put EDC to the French Assembly as a question of confidence in his government. In other words, he will stake the existence of his government on passing the EDC, and therefore he wants to have some chance of a successful result."[47]

The United States and Dulles in particular were caught up in a rigid mindset: the EDC was the best thing for France and for the defense of the West. There was no other way possible for the French. Were they so blind that they could not see that? On August 18, Dulles wrote to Winston Churchill, "I agree with you that it is time to bring this chapter to an end. I hope that it will be an EDC ending. I am not clear in my mind as to any alternative which will be both practical and not subject to another succession of parliamentary wrangles.''[48]

The same day Dulles told a French visitor to Washington, who reported that Mendès-France felt Dulles had lost confidence in him, that time was running out, particularly in Germany, and ''we were threatened with stark disaster.'' If Adenauer were voted out of office by the German Parliament as a result of the failure of the EDC, said Dulles, it would be ''the end of the last German with whom France could negotiate an organic unity which would prevent a repetition of the past.''[49]

Mendès-France then tried his last chance. He met in Brussels with the other chiefs of government (August 19–22) and presented them with his new protocols. He found himself chastized by Paul-Henri Spaak and by the Dutch for having tried to reduce the supranational extent of a treaty that had already been ratified by a majority of the countries involved. Adenauer, until almost the end of the talks, declined to meet with Mendès-France one on one. It was an impasse. The conference failed, although a papered-over communiqué was issued.

Mendès-France next made a quick trip to Chartwell, England, for a meeting with Winston Churchill but found no satisfaction for his point of view. Ambassador Dillon met Mendès-France again on August 24, after the latter's visit to Brussels and Chartwell, and found the prime minister rather depressed. Mendès-France had sensed a distrust toward France on the part of the other countries represented at Brussels, and he considered it a personal insult that Adenauer had refused to see him until the very end of the conference.[50] He told Dillon that his government was different from previous French governments: it kept its word. Therefore he was going to put the EDC to a vote, as planned, on August 30, after a debate that would last three days. He expected that the assembly would vote against it. There was no possibility of posing the question of confidence because that required prior agreement of the cabinet, which was impossible in the circumstances.[51] Another problem was how the members of his government would vote. It would be embarrassing if some voted for and some against.[52]

If the EDC proposal were voted down, Mendès-France said, he would favor an alternative that would be the creation of a loose seven-power military agreement including the six countries and the United Kingdom and which would have no supranational features. Because of the tie-up with Britain, he said, this would be a way of getting the French Parliament and people to accept German entry into NATO.[53]

(What Mendès-France proposed to Dillon as the EDC was about to fail appears today eminently reasonable. This could be said of all his proposals on the subject of the EDC—albeit sometimes presented in a rather evasive manner— except one: the idea of going again to the Soviets before concluding the debate on the treaty. This calls to mind the recent formulation of Paul Fabra: ''the concern not to upset the Soviets has not disappeared from French preoccupations.''[54])

On August 24, 1954, the same day of the Dillon–Mendès-France conversation cited above, Eisenhower telephoned Dulles and asked for an update on the EDC situation. Dulles told him he had just received a telegram from Churchill which was not encouraging. It appeared, said Dulles, "as though Mendès-France was pretty much letting up on this one in a perfunctory way and will not ask for a vote of confidence in the French Parliament." There was a strong feeling, said Dulles, "that if he did, he would get it through."[55] The reply of the president was the following: "Eisenhower said what puzzled him was that he did not know where the French had to go—what can they do without this? Are they deliberately saying they are going to tie up with Russia?"[56]

Finally, on August 30, 1954, the EDC was defeated by a vote of 319 to 264 on a motion of procedure (called a *motion préalable*) which amounted to a rejection of the treaty. An originally French plan was renounced by the French themselves, almost furtively.

After this defeat, Dulles, in the course of a mid-September trip to Europe which took him to London and Bonn, rather obviously omitted a Paris stop. The American Embassy in Paris reported that "Mendès [*sic*] in preparation for difficulties he will face on return of Parliament has launched press campaign to effect that U.S. Government in general and Secretary Dulles in particular are engaged in attempt to overthrow his government."[57]

But the Allies took things rapidly in hand. Through the intermediary of Anthony Eden, after he had consulted with Mendès-France, a conference began in London on September 27 with nine countries represented: the six of the aborted EDC plus Great Britain, the United States, and Canada.

By the accords of London (October 3, 1954), transmuted into the accords of Paris (October 23, 1954), the Western European Union (WEU) was instituted as a sort of substitute for the EDC. The WEU was the reincarnation of the Western Union created by the Brussels Pact in 1948, modified by the London accords to include West Germany and Italy.

Great Britain, which was a member of the 1948 Brussels Pact, had thus made what Anthony Eden termed, as reported by *Le Monde*, "a tremendous step forward:"[58] not only did she join the new WEU, but she agreed to maintain her four divisions plus accompanying tactical air support on the Continent and under the command of the SACEUR (Supreme Allied Commander Europe) for the duration of the Brussels Pact (fifty years). These divisions could not be withdrawn except by a vote of the majority of the countries of the WEU (in consultation with the SACEUR, of course). But—and a great but—"it is understood that in case of extreme urgency in the overseas territories, the British Government could be compelled to disregard this procedure."[59]

Thanks to the London accords, France avoided the political supranationality that would have been exercised through the EDC but had to accept what *Le Monde* described as "the reinforcement of the structure of NATO and the authority of the Supreme Atlantic [*sic*] Commander in Europe."[60] This reinforcement in command did not, however, involve an integration of grades and

military schools, as envisaged in the EDC. But a new element was introduced—
a system of arms control that would leave to a majority vote of the council of
the Brussels Pact a decision as to how many atomic, biological, or chemical
weapons could be retained by the continental members of the pact;[61] and for
certain other sophisticated weapons, the continental members of the pact would
not exceed the limits of their needs as defined by the annual military plan of
NATO.[62]

In other words, Britain, as an ''off-Continent'' member, escaped the WEU
arms control mechanism which, however, was to become a dead letter. Ironically, France had insisted on this arms control mechanism as a means of pre-
venting German military preponderance in the EDC. But the French had larger
goals in mind, which, however, did not come to pass: in the French view, the
WEU arms control agency would control not only the stocks of arms on the
Continent but the production and even the distribution of American arms—
including atomic weapons—destined for the Continent.[63]

True to its vacillating image, the National Assembly, after first voting for the
London/Paris accords in a confidence motion, then backtracked: on December
23, 1954, it voted *against* German rearmament (Article 1 of the Paris accords,
which adopted the London accords and *for* the entry of Germany into NATO
(Article 2). Finally, on December 30, 1954, by a vote of 280 to 259 with 76
abstentions, the assembly voted for the draft law as a whole based on the Paris
accords.

The struggle was over. To save the Atlantic alliance, a majority voted for
German rearmament, generally with regret. To save the Mendès-France government and in so doing leave the way open for negotiations with the Anglo-
Americans on the one hand (for the follow-ons to the Paris accords) and with
the Soviets on the other, a relatively large number of deputies supported Mendès-France, including most Socialists and a number of ex-Gaullists (the Rally
of the French People, RPF having disappeared as a party in May 1953). As for
the MRP, it conducted a calibrated game of not supporting the Paris accords
openly but not allowing them to fail.

For Mendès-France, it was a Pyrrhic victory. On the one hand he was recognized as the best person to conduct successfully the upcoming negotiations
with the Allies and the Soviets. But on the other hand, as Jean Lacouture observed, he had lost too much credit with his friends: ''He had caused Western
solidarity to triumph over French nationalism.''[64] And the ''Europeans'' did not
forgive him for ''the crime of August 30.'' His days were numbered. He was
overthrown two months later.

As for Washington, a certain distrust toward Mendès-France remained, even
after the decisive step of ratification by the French National Assembly on December 30, 1954. For Washington, he was still exhibiting signs of what could
be called ''the Russian temptation.'' On January 15, 1955, President Eisenhower
admonished him:

Your letter of January 5 and its accompanying memorandum, informally setting forth your views concerning your problem of assuring prompt ratification of the Paris accords by the Council of the Republic, have received my careful attention. . . . I fully share his [Dulles's] view that it would be a very serious matter indeed if we were to make at this juncture a three power approach to the Soviets, or if France were to do so alone.[65]

The Paris accords were approved by the Council of the Republic, and France's formal ratification was registered on May 5, 1955.

RETROSPECTIVE

The heart of the EDC problem was that the European Army, as it came to be conceived under the EDC formula, would have been a supranational grouping of military units from France, West Germany, the Benelux countries, and Italy—but without Great Britain. Moreover, the assemblage would have been under the command of an American general, the SACEUR.

In fact, French national identity was flouted on two counts: politically, in the supranational political structure of the EDC (from which Britain was exempted), and militarily, in the integrated command of NATO which in effect meant that those French forces dedicated to the EDC lost, in the ultimate sense, their national command. This dual derogation was fatal to the project, and sooner or later the combination of the two had to be split apart, which indeed was done by the French National Assembly in its rejection of the EDC. The ultimate solution became the integrated military command, West Germany included, without the political structure of the EDC.

Ultimately, though France was indispensable to the success of the EDC concept, the United States was not willing to grant it special considerations. Quite the contrary. Witness this excerpt from a statement by President Eisenhower in April 1954 concerning "guarantees" to members of the prospective European Defense Community: "The European Defense Community will form an integral part of the Atlantic Community. . . . The United States will encourage the closest possible integration between the European Defense Community forces on the one hand, and United States and other North Atlantic Treaty forces on the other."[66] In other words, looking at it from a French point of view, the Anglo-Saxons were separate and distinct from the EDC, while at the same time the "closest possible integration" between these various elements of NATO was to be encouraged—that is to say, the EDC would be under the military orders of NATO.

There are those who, in a sort of counter-factual nostalgia, note that France, which caused the EDC to fail, could instead have created then and there a European defense organization without Anglo-American participation. But the margin against the EDC, in the vote on August 30, was considerable: 319 to 254. It seems doubtful, even if Mendès-France had backed the treaty in its existing form and had tied it to a vote of confidence, that the treaty would have passed. The concept of a pan-European defense force was simply premature: Jean Monnet's vision was too farsighted to be politically sound. As George Ball said of his friend Monnet, the latter was a man who, whenever he encountered an obstacle, thought of nothing else but removing it or getting around it.[67] But this time the obstacle was monumental: the tradition of the French Army, and an army seeking expiation at that.[68]

Monnet's idea, at an opposite pole from de Gaulle's, was to denationalize defense just as coal and steel had been denationalized. Thereby, German rearmament—inevitable though regrettable—would be locked in with the march toward European integration. In turn, the key to the construction of Europe would be a Franco-German rapprochement. (Here Monnet's goal was very similar to de Gaulle's, except that Monnet preferred the rapprochement, and the building of Europe, to take place in a supranational rather than a national framework.) Monnet had begun the process with the Coal and Steel Community, and he was insistent that the CSC be ratified before finalizing the second link in the chain, the EDC.[69]

With the advent of the CSC, supranational institutions had been put in place: an assembly, a commissariat, and a council of ministers—all three sharing the management of the CSC—plus a court of justice. The same type of structures were envisaged for the EDC. In fact, the assembly and the court were to be the same for two communities that were obviously very different. The common assembly would be made up of delegates from national parliaments.

Monnet's more long-range project, that of a European Political Community, did not get very far. Adopted in principle on March 10, 1953, the plan had to be abandoned in 1954 after the failure of the EDC. (It is a mark of how far Monnet was ahead of his time that almost forty years later, the construction of a political union was agreed to in principle at the Maastricht Summit of December 1991.)

Curiously, the "Europeans," Monnet included, seemed to have attached little importance to the fact that a proposed European Army was being created prior to the establishment of a European political authority. In insisting on the military integration of Europe without the umbrella of an authentic European political authority, the "Europeans" wound up with something quite different. The lack of such an authority could only result in NATO's being in charge of the EDC. As Maurice Delarue noted,[70] citing de Gaulle,

this army called "European" which is intended to be built by the treaty, is placed by the latter organically, automatically and solely in the hands of the Atlantic commander in chief, that is, if one does not want to play with words, the American commander in chief in Europe—who is one of the instruments of American strategy.[71]

Though stubborn resistance remained to the supranational vision of Jean Monnet and the "Europeans" throughout the EDC debate, the same could not be said for the linked question of German rearmament. Here a change did indeed occur over the four-year period from 1950 to 1954. Though the threat of a Soviet invasion of Europe subsided, the rehabilitation of Adenauer's Federal Republic proceeded on, inexorably. The proof came when German rearmament was quickly approved in the fall of 1954 after the failure of the EDC. Most observers had thought French rejection of German rearmament was an immutable given. These included Maurice Duverger, who made a vain appeal in the aftermath of the failure of the Conference of the Six at Brussels: "the French Parliament should vote on the EDC in its present form and Paris should establish solemnly the impossibility for the Atlantic Allies to reconstitute a German armed force against French opposition."[72]

The fact was that many in the French political class had become less hostile to German rearmament in the course of these four years, and they included de Gaulle himself. However, the aim of the general was that this rearmament be accomplished essentially as a French-German event, separate from the Anglo-Saxons, and with a heavily circumscribed position for the Germans: (1) non-extension of German national territory by military means; (2) no recourse to force without consulting the other West European allies; and (3) no more German divisions in time of peace than French ones—excluding those France needed for its overseas territories.[73]

It is interesting to note the similarity between these requirements of de Gaulle, enunciated in a press interview in November 1952,[74] with what resulted from the Paris accords of October 23, 1954, ratified by the National Assembly on December 30.

On the eve of the decisive vote in the National Assembly, *Le Monde* commented that the postwar declarations and accords had put France "on exactly the same footing as Great Britain or the United States as regards decisions to be made on Germany." And yet, the newspaper noted, the Anglo-Saxons had gone ahead with the decision to rearm Germany against the advice of France.[75]

Still, a majority of Frenchmen did not want to push things to the point of their isolation from the Atlantic alliance, which would have been the equivalent, as Mendès-France put it on January 1, 1955, two days after the assembly vote, of "adventurism." In the final analysis, the French public, through its elected representatives, preferred to run the risk of German rearmament than to diminish the political sovereignty of "*la Grande Nation, la Grande Armée.*"

While "*la Grande Armée*" had to submit directly to the increasing power of the SACEUR rather than indirectly through the commissariat of the EDC, it is nevertheless worth emphasizing the difference: supranationality was highly political—and permanent. The reinforcement of the NATO military structure was not political, at least not openly, and it was not necessarily permanent. Fundamentally, the deep misgivings over the EDC had more to do with supranationality than with German rearmament.

Looking backward, it is difficult to imagine how a military mélange such as the EDC, in which units that were supposed to fight against a Soviet attack were deprived, at least in part, of national command and identity, could have been accepted by the French people. The concept could more readily have been accepted by the Germans and Italians, both seeking rehabilitation as former Axis powers, and by the Benelux nations, whose weight was not sufficient to play in the balance when the overall security of Europe was concerned.

With Britain out and France in, the EDC represented a "club of defeated nations." It therefore constituted a denial of France's national ambitions. Though France's weight could not be compared with Great Britain's at the time the European Army was proposed, it was not long before France overtook Britain economically. As France grew stronger, and as it came under the direction of a much more intransigent leadership—that of Charles de Gaulle—this discrimination against France was challenged with increasing aggressiveness. The dilemma, which in its broadest expression was that represented by the integrated military command of NATO, was never really resolved. The perspective of the American imperium differed from that of the oldest nation in continental Europe: for the imperium, someone had to be in command in the age of nuclear war. The French solved this dilemma partially by leaving the command structure but at the same time staying in touch through the alliance. Britain lay outside this problem because it could get out from under NATO command in an emergency; France could not.

In the internal French, or "Franco-French," context, the great debate of forty years ago between the pro-EDC and anti-EDC groups goes on, episodically and in remakes. The national spirit of France is in conflict with the aspirations of the French people to realize the potential Europe represents: to become, as Jean Monnet said in the immediate postwar era, greater than France—or Germany—could expect to become as individual nations.[76] This conflict is related to, but not entirely congruent with, the figures of Charles de Gaulle and Jean Monnet, those poles of attraction symbolizing the two Europes of nationality and supranationality. Their differing visions of Europe, and of France in Europe, have been the thread of a dispute lasting from the aftermath of World War II to the present.

The so-called quarrel of the EDC ended up on the one hand with a half-victory for France under the banner of independence—that is, the rejection of a discriminatory supranationality from which Great Britain was exempt—and on the other hand with a last-minute triumph of the United States, snatching victory from the jaws of defeat in forcing German rearmament without the EDC. Whether the United States would have forced German rearmament and German entry into NATO earlier is open to question. The United States may have been overly concerned about Soviet and Allied (especially French) reaction; however, it should be remembered that, at the origin of the European Army proposal, the threat of a remilitarized Germany seemed much greater than it did later on.

The vote of August 30, 1954, represented the first time since World War II that American foreign policy was set back—although only temporarily—by France. This was largely the work of General de Gaulle, then out of power and in the middle of his period in the political wilderness. Without an objective alliance between the Gaullists and the Communists, there could not have been formed at that time a solid bloc of anti-EDC forces against the will of the United States. For the general, it was his first victory on the world stage in the postwar period, after his self-eviction from power at the beginning of 1946.

In the "Franco-French" context, de Gaulle was the essential victor in the vote of August 30, 1954, which rejected an overpowering supranationality for France. But in the military vein France had to swallow at the end of the year the pill of reinforcement of the military structure of NATO accompanied, in theory at least, by an arms-control regime from which the British were exempted.

Throughout the EDC affair France was regarded in Washington as the key but at the same time not having the right to a favored treatment, unlike Great Britain. The same discrimination appeared in the 1960s in the affair of the Multilateral Force (MLF), a sort of EDC elevated to the nuclear level.

Once having arrived in power, de Gaulle tried to put an end to this British exemption,[77] without success. He then proceeded to undo the existing structures of military integration and at the same time to resist American efforts to strengthen them. Before the end of his tenure he arrived at his goal, taking France out of the integrated military command of NATO while at the same time remaining in the Atlantic alliance as a sort of odd man out. In so doing, de Gaulle finally achieved the theoretical parity (albeit a negative one) that had been lost by the defeat of 1940 but had existed before—particularly during World War I, when France, until near the end of the war, was the superior partner in the Allied camp. And the repeated references of de Gaulle to French grandeur, held up to ridicule, whether through ignorance or not, by Roosevelt and others who followed him, stemmed exactly from this earlier reality of World War I.

It was not very far, at the end of the debate on the EDC, from the collapse of the Fourth Republic. The weakness of the French system, of its "legicentrism," had been exposed time and again. An editorial in *Le Monde* at the time drew a philosophical lesson of the EDC affair: "As long as France has not been able to provide itself the means of adopting an individual policy [*une politique personnelle*] on those matters that are for her of vital interest, she should not blame anyone but herself."[78]

And the day was awaited when someone could impose "*une politique personnelle*" for "*notre dame la France.*"[79]

NOTES

1. *La Grande Nation*: term applied to France during the Revolution. *La Grande Armée*: Napoleon's army.

2. Statement of June 6, 1952, Charles de Gaulle, *Discours et Messages* (Geneva: Editions Edito-Service, 1970), 4:202.

3. *Le Monde*, September 1, 1954, 1.

4. Raymond Aron and Daniel Lerner, eds., *La querelle de la C.E.D.* (Paris: Armand Colin, 1956), 19.

5. "Le Quai d'Orsay face au problème de la souveraineté allemande," *Revue d' Histoire Diplomatique*, no. 104 (1990): 38.

6. *Le Monde*, July 1, 1954, 1.

7. *Le Monde*, September 2, 1954, 1.

8. Harry S. Truman Presidential Library (HSTL), President's Secretary's File (PSF), Foreign Affairs, Box 178, France-Germany: France, Proposals of the French Government for a European Army, 3. The reference to a joint study that was to take place in Paris after the signing of the treaty on the Coal and Steel Community (CSC) appears to have been to a meeting held in February 1951 in Paris.

9. See p. 81.

10. *Le Monde*, August 28, 1954, 3.

11. See p. 26.

12. HSTL, PSF, Box 116, General File Churchill-Truman meetings: Steering Group negotiating paper EDC, 3.

13. Ibid., memos and minutes, minutes of the fourth session, 3.

14. Pierre Maillard, *De Gaulle et l'Allemagne* (Paris: Plan, 1990), 138.

15. *Le Monde*, August 20–21, 1989, 2.

16. George W. Ball, *The Past Has Another Pattern: Memoirs* (New York: W. W. Norton, 1982), 156–57.

17. *Le Monde* noted this already at the end of 1947: "since October 1945, [the country] has continually voted less for the Left. The center of gravity in Parliament and in the leadership of government has in turn moved to the Right." *Le Monde*, November 23–24, 1947, 1.

18. Jacques Fauvet, "Birth and Death of a Treaty," in Aron and Lerner, eds., *La querelle de la C.E.D.*, 23.

19. Ibid., 33.

20. Dwight D. Eisenhower Presidential Library (DDEL), Ann Whitman File, DDE Diaries Series, Box 8, DDE diary December 1954: letter from Churchill to Eisenhower of December 7, 1954 and from Eisenhower to Churchill on December 14, 1954.

21. The expression is that of Stanley Hoffmann, who spoke of the role of Monnet in a course at Harvard University in the fall of 1990 entitled "Europe, 1945–1990: From Division to Unity."

22. De Gaulle, *Discours et Messages*, 4:268–69.

23. Interview with Robert Bowie, December 17, 1990.

24. Lecture of Stanley Hoffmann. See also note 21.

25. An expression from the early days of the French Revolution, when attacks by revolutionary mobs were feared in the French countryside.

26. *Le Monde*, August 20–21, 1989, 2.

27. Ibid.

28. De Gaulle, *Discours et Messages*, 4:202.

29. *The Papers of Dwight D. Eisenhower*, ed. Alfred D. Chandler, Jr. (Baltimore: Johns Hopkins University Press, 1984): 11:1390.

30. Robert McGeehan, *The German Rearmament Question* (Urbana: University of Illinois Press, 1971), 129.

31. *Papers of Dwight D. Eisenhower*, 12:458.

32. Ibid., 459.

33. *Foreign Relations of the United States* (*FRUS*), 1952–54, Vol. V, Part 1, p. 1050 (message from John Foster Dulles to the American Embassy in Paris, August 19, 1954).

34. In April 1954, when British guarantees to the EDC were drawn up parallel to those of the United States laid out by Eisenhower (see p. 91), Great Britain agreed to be associated with the EDC without having to submit to its supranational provisions.

35. DDEL, Dulles-Herter Series, Box 3, Dulles July 1954 (2): message from Dulles to Churchill, August 18, 1954.

36. *FRUS*, 1952–54, vol. 6, pt. 2, 1439.

37. DDEL, Ann Whitman File, DDE Diaries Series, Box 7, telephone calls, June–December 1954: conversation between Eisenhower and Dulles on October 7, 1954.

38. Charles de Gaulle, *The Complete War Memoirs of Charles de Gaulle*, vol. 2, *Unity, 1942–1944*, trans. Richard Howard (New York: Simon and Schuster, 1964), 2: 580.

39. DDEL, Dulles-Herter series, Box 3, Dulles July 1954 (1): account of the Dulles–Mendès-France meeting, July 13, 1954, 2.

40. *Le Monde*, October 26, 1954, 2.

41. DDEL, Dulles-Herter series, Box 3, Dulles January 1954 (1): account of the Dulles–Mendès-France meeting, July 13, 1954, 5.

42. *FRUS*, 1952–54, vol. 5, pt. 1, 1051 (message from Dulles to Churchill, August 20, 1954).

43. Jean Lacouture, *Pierre Mendès-France* (Paris: Seuil, 1981), 306. (According to the account of this meeting in the Dulles papers, "Mendès-France replied that he did not think there was a majority at present." DDEL, Dulles-Herter series, Box 3, Dulles July 1954 (1): account of the conversation between Dulles and Mendès-France, July 13, 1954, 8.)

44. The Rally of the French People (RPF), after its early success, disappeared as a party in May 1953.

45. *FRUS*, 1952–54, vol. 5, pt. 1, 1027.

46. Ibid., 1027–28.

47. Ibid., 1031–32.

48. Ibid., 1049. See also pp. 102–3.

49. Ibid., 1050.

50. Ibid., 1071–72.

51. Either Mendès-France had overspoken himself to Dillon in their meeting on August 13, at which time, according to the latter, he had said he would tie the EDC issue to a vote of confidence, or else he had become disillusioned by the way he was treated at the Brussels conference.

52. As it turned out, the government did not take a position for or against the EDC, and the ministers did not participate in the vote.

53. *FRUS*, 1952–54, vol. 5, pt. 1, 1074 (meeting between Ambassador Dillon and Pierre Mendès-France, August 24, 1954).

54. Paul Fabra, "Mitterrand-Metternich," *Le Monde*, July 3, 1991, 4.

55. DDEL, Ann Whitman File, DDE diaries series, Box 7, telephone calls, June–December 1954: DDE-JFD conversation of August 24, 1954 on the EDC.

56. Ibid.

57. *FRUS*, 1952–54, vol. 6, pt. 2, 1451.

58. *Le Monde*, October 1, 1954, 2 (statement of Anthony Eden at the London Conference).

59. Ibid.

60. "From the European Defense Community to the Agreements Signed at London by the 'Nine'," *Le Monde*, October 7, 1954, 2. N.B., SACEUR (Supreme Allied Commander Europe), is the person whereas SHAPE (Supreme Headquarters Allied Powers Europe) is the place. *Le Monde* used the term "Atlantic," but the proper term is "Allied."

61. *Le Monde*, October 5, 1954, 3.

62. *Le Monde*, October 26, 1954, 5.

63. *Le Monde*, December 24, 1954, 2.

64. Lacouture, *Pierre Mendès-France*, 369.

65. DDEL, White House Central Files (1953–1961), Confidential File, Subject series, Box 70, Department of State (January–February 1955): letter of Eisenhower to Mendès-France, January 15, 1955. N.B., the Council of the Republic in effect functioned as a senate during the Fourth Republic.

66. DDEL, Ann Whitman File, International Series, Box 9, European Defense Community: U.S. Assurances to EDC, State Department telegram CA-5728, April 9, 1954, 2.

67. Interview with the author, May 3, 1991.

68. The expression (*"en mal d'expiation"*) is that of François Furet. See p. 49.

69. The CSC went into effect on July 25, 1952.

70. *Le Monde*, March 6, 1990, 2.

71. De Gaulle, *Discours et Messages*, 4:243–44.

72. Maurice Duverger, "L'heure de saint Thomas," *Le Monde*, August 27, 1954, 1.

73. Maillard, *De Gaulle et l'Allemagne*, 137.

74. Ibid.

75. *Le Monde*, December 28, 1954, 1.

76. See p. 58.

77. Notably in his "Memorandum on the Directory" of September 1958, addressed to President Eisenhower and to Prime Minister MacMillan. See p. 4.

78. *Le Monde*, December 28, 1954, 1.

79. The expression in this case is from a BBC radio address by Charles de Gaulle to the children of France, December 24, 1941: "among the ladies of nations, none has ever been more beautiful, better, or braver than our lady France [*notre dame la France*]. Pierre Galante, *Le Général* (Paris: Presses de la Cité, 1968), tape 2, side 2.

❖ 5 ❖

The Reversal

The horror began on July 5 [1962], the last day of *l'Algérie française*, when several hundred Europeans were kidnapped. Months of efforts by [Jean-Pierre] Chevènement, at the time a consular official, and several démarches to Ben Bella, the new Chief of State, were in vain; only some 20 of the kidnapees were returned alive by the Algerians. From this episode, he drew a lesson: in a confrontation between two peoples, military superiority is not always the determining factor.

From a political profile on Jean-Pierre Chevènement[1]

This chapter is situated neither in 1962 nor in the present but forms a piece with the events evoked above—events that have to do with the interrelationship between the First (or Western) World and the Third World, events that reflect France's (and the West's) relationship with Islam.

In the 1990s, it has become clear that social integration, and particularly integration between the secular society of France and the culture of Islam, is not working well. But this is a problem that only tangentially affects French foreign policy, as the many Muslim immigrants in France are there of their own will, and the international image of France is scarcely affected. It was a whole other case some thirty years ago, when the relations between France and the Arab world were white hot with difficulties.

France, having now relinquished nearly all of its empire (albeit with less grace than the British), and most importantly those Islamic countries on the other side of the Mediterranean, has become again the French nation. As such it is a better carrier of its universalist message, with its emphasis on political liberties, human rights, and social justice, which is the basis of its aspiration for leadership in the world. It is not an altogether different situation from that which took place a century before in the United States—the other Western country that is the carrier of a universalist message—when the problem of slavery was removed in the course of a national crisis.

The insoluble problem of the incorporation of an overseas culture—that is, Algeria—into France no longer exists. This colonial impasse, compounded by an institutional impasse—where "French government" came to be a synonym for weakness and flight from responsibility—began to go away with the coming to power of Charles de Gaulle in 1958. This chapter will examine an episode in the annals of French-American history that is related to this reversal of French fortunes.

SUMMARY

At the beginning of 1958 the French Fourth Republic was sick, some would say dying. The French Army, still working through its expiation, had changed terrain. Pushed out of Indochina, it was holding firm in Algeria. The revolt of the native population, latent since the explosion of mobs in Sétif (1945), became an open war on All Saints' Day, November 1, 1954.

France, trapped into its parliamentary sovereignty, had struggled along from government to government. The leaders in the governing coalition, Radicals and Socialists (SFIO), strove more and more desperately not to go off the cliff. All that was needed, as Jean Lacouture put it, was a "detonator,"[2] and in fact, one came along: the raid by the French Air Force on the Tunisian village of Sakhiet-Sidi-Youssef on February 8, 1958. The outcome of this blunder caused by the exercise of the right of pursuit was seventy-five dead and eighty-three wounded—men, women and children.[3] The French Ambassador in Washington, Hervé Alphand, recounted the incident in his memoirs:

I was abruptly invited to meet M. Dulles, who had come out of the hospital, at his home at nine o'clock in the evening [of February 8]. He was beside himself: during the day, a small Tunisian village named Sakhiet-Sidi-Youssef, had been bombarded by French aircraft. There had been casualties. M. Dulles asked me to explain this action about which I obviously could not yet have been informed. For him, it was a very serious matter which threatened French-American relations. This incident, in terms of international law, did not warrant the interference of the United States. But instead of having recourse to juridical arguments, I limited myself to saying to M. Dulles that he only knew the Tunisian version of the event, and the next day I would bring him the French version. The next day the fever had subsided and the threatening communiqué had been pocketed by its author.[4]

But if the fever quickly abated, the affair nevertheless was seized upon by the world at large. The editorial of *Le Monde* of February 11, entitled, "A Step Toward Internationalization," ended with the following words: "Those who decided on the raid on Sakhiet-Sidi-Youssef are certainly not in favor of the internationalization of the Algerian conflict. It is difficult for them to ignore the fact that, whatever one's viewpoint, their initiative leads straight to it."[5]

Decomposition came quickly: two months later, the government of Felix Gaillard was overthrown by a vote of confidence on the question of an Anglo-American Good Offices mission arising out of the incident. The mission was led on the United States side by none other than the man who had brought General Henri Giraud to North Africa as the American alternative to Charles de Gaulle: Robert Murphy. Three months after the raid a Committee of Public Safety, set up at Algiers under the leadership of General Jacques Massu, issued an appeal to General de Gaulle to take power. On June 1, 1958, the National Assembly voted 329 to 224 in favor of a government headed by de Gaulle. The second coming to power of the general had taken place, and a profound transformation of the French constitutional system and the French Empire resulted.

The historians Pierre Mélandri and Frédéric Bozo, noting the causal chain from the Sakhiet-Sidi-Youssef incident to the good offices mission to the return of de Gaulle, observed that the birth of the Fifth French Republic was closely tied up with French-American relations.[6] The incident itself "only strengthened in the mind of the Americans a negative image of the foreign activities of France going back at least to the Suez crisis and confirmed by its deplorable internal situation."[7]

Indeed, the "prudential" government of the United States regarded with distaste and perplexity the spectacle of parliamentary anarchy in France—produced by a system in which the popular will was expressed virtually totally by moveable majorities in the French National Assembly. (Curiously, it seems little to have occurred to Americans in the postwar period that the trend in Europe was to refashion governments closer to the American model.[8] Rather than welcoming de Gaulle's calls for more executive leadership in the American pattern, the United States was negatively fixated on the general as an authoritarian, "neo-Fascist" figure, whose personality had been written off by the American establishment since the wartime period as "arrogant and belligerent."[9])

The French National Assembly was subjected to ever new combinations that changed and rechanged the political, and therefore the governmental, landscape: it was a system denounced by de Gaulle and by the traditional right. The situation had not fundamentally changed since the 1920s and 1930s. A new republic, the Fourth, had been formed, but only after an unsuccessful struggle by de Gaulle to reform the constitution. The traditional parties had won out. However, the successive crises of Indochina, the European Defense Community, and Algeria, compounded by the fiasco of Suez—a little more than a year before the incident at Sakhiet—were so damaging to France's prestige that the system of the Fourth Republic could not exist much longer.

One can imagine, in the mind of the French in the postwar period, that there existed two institutions that could lead France back to the position it had had before 1940: the army and the empire, which became in 1946 the French Union (l'Union Française). The former proved to be true; the latter turned out to be a snare.

In the mounting crescendo of the war in Algeria, in which the raid on Sakhiet was only a small incident, the army and the empire, which had not been central concerns for the average Frenchman, came together in a curious combination— a sort of counterpower to the authority of the French state. It became necessary to break this ensemble, to separate the army from its mission to preserve the overseas empire. Once this infinitely complicated task had been accomplished, Charles de Gaulle could make of this war-hardened army, accompanied over time with an atomic strike force, the symbol and the reality of the restored world power of France.

THE BACKGROUND

The French Empire, renamed the French Union by the Constitution of 1946, was "varied and fragmented," according to a study published in 1959 by Jean Chatelain entitled, *The New Constitution and the Political Regime of France.* The status of this "heterogeneous community"[10] was founded on a juridical and sociological duality. The latter aspect was manifest in the preamble of the Constitution of 1946: "The French Union is composed of nations and peoples who place in common or coordinate their resources and their efforts, in order to develop their respective civilizations, increase their well-being, and assure their security."[11]

On the contrary, as Chatelain pointed out, Article 60 of the same constitution emphasized the juridical aspect: "The French Union is formed on the one hand by the French Republic which comprises Metropolitan France and the overseas *départements* and territories; and on the other hand by territories and associated states."[12]

Thus, in the context we are examining, the status of the "associated states" was differentiated from the *départements*, whether in France or overseas, *in the conception of the French*. Moreover the *départements* of Algeria were considered an integral part of France. These were not faraway, overseas *départements*. They were virtually alongside France, and together with a population of 9 million Algerians was also a population of a million Europeans. This made the French-Algerian tandem indissoluble to most Frenchmen, even to a man as liberal (in the American sense) as Pierre Mendès-France. Prime minister at the time of the revolt that marked the start of the Algerian revolution, he declared to the National Assembly eleven days later, on November 12, 1954:

One does not compromise when it comes to defending the internal peace of a nation, [or] the unity and integrity of the Republic. The *départements* of Algeria form a part of the Republic. They have been French for a long time; their population . . . enjoys French citizenship and is represented in Parliament. Between her [Algeria] and the Republic, secession is not conceivable. . . . Never will France . . . give in on this fundamental principle.[13]

Le Monde, in reporting these words, noted that "the orator considered as erroneous and dangerous the parallels drawn by certain speakers to our policy in Tunisia." Mendès-France concluded in this context that "Algeria is France and not a foreign country that we are protecting."[14]

By contrast, the two "associated states" of North Africa, Tunisia and Morocco, had from the beginning refused to take part in the assembly of the French Union created by the Constitution of 1946:

In fact, the Assembly of the French Union throughout its existence was composed essentially of representatives of the Republic, some elected by the Metropole and others by the overseas *départements* and territories—the representation of the associated states being reduced in number and political importance, due particularly to the refusal of the most important among these states, Morocco and Tunisia, to send delegates to it.[15]

And yet it was a question of all the same people in North Africa, colonized and homogenized by the Arab conquest. This conquest and common experience are symbolized in Maghrebian folklore by the larger-than-life figure of Abu Bakr, the Arab conqueror who declared at the northern side of the strait separating Europe and Africa, "The enemy is in front of us. The sea is behind us. We have no choice but to advance."

There is a kindred population across North Africa: an Arabophone majority, a Berberophone minority. The proportion varies from one country to the next, but the population of the three countries (Morocco, Algeria, Tunisia) is very similar. The religion of Islam and the Arab-Berber cultural amalgam operate as a sort of leaven. But there are differences between Algeria and Tunisia and Morocco: there was not a long-standing tradition of a reigning family in Algeria; the French penetration came rather early in Algeria, in 1830, and the invasion was direct, in contrast to the indirect penetration of the two flanking countries, Tunisia and Morocco; the city of Algiers was the closest to the great city of the south of France, Marseille; and as regards Morocco and Algeria particularly, the Turkish advance did not go beyond the town of Tlemcen, in western Algeria. But these were largely differences arising from recent historical and national experiences caused by the French occupation and the French codification of the borders.

Last but not least, the enormous French and European colonization in Algeria made for a significant difference vis-à-vis Morocco and Tunisia. But even this factor changed nothing as regards the similarity of the native populations in the three countries.

The words of Mendès-France on these "flank states" during his speech of investiture on June 17, 1954, leave the reader of today just as perplexed as his above-quoted statement that followed the outbreak of the Algerian revolution five months later: "Morocco and Tunisia, to whom France has opened the way toward economic, social, and political progress, must not become, on the flanks of our Algerian *départements*, centers of insecurity and agitation; this I will never accept."[16]

Mendès-France seemed to intend these words as premonitory. In the month following his investiture he undertook two spectacular initiatives, one on Indochina and one on Tunisia. On July 31 he paid a sudden visit to Bey Sidi Lamine in Carthage, with the aim of calming the tense situation and of offering a new arrangement for Tunisia, what he called "the opening of an era of negotiations as a substitute for the period of repression."[17]

The French retreat from Indochina by mid-1954 and the start of a dialogue with the native population in Tunisia at the same time left all the more glaring the blocked situation in Algeria. The revolt that broke out there on November 1, 1954, was certainly related to these two events.

A little more than a year later, in March 1956, independence was accorded in turn to Morocco and Tunisia. The contrast between them and "our Algerian *départements*" had by then become insupportable. The events of the summer of 1954, far from easing the situation, had goaded the Algerian revolt, and the liberal spirit of Mendès-France was no longer there to attempt a new squaring of the circle. Exhausted morally and politically by the long and thankless affair of the European Defense Community, he had been voted out of power in February 1955. A year later his replacement, the Radical Edgar Faure, was no longer there either. He had been replaced in turn by the Socialist Guy Mollet, who undertook in January 1956 what was to be the longest tenure of any government of the Fourth Republic.

Given these circumstances, to expect Tunisia to observe strict neutrality in the war in Algeria was part of a dream world. It was more or less the same for Morocco, although Morocco lagged somewhat behind Tunisia in support of the Algerian nationalists. This situation was due to the faraway geography of Morocco and the particularly close psychological proximity between the Algerians and the much less numerous Tunisians. (Again, it should be recalled that the Turkish penetration, proceeding westward, stopped at Tlemcen in western Algeria.)

It should have been clear from the moment Mendès-France arrived at Tunis on July 31, 1954, and a dialogue took hold aimed at the internal autonomy of the protectorate in a more or less near term, that it was utopian to think that Algeria, or at least the original population in Algeria, would not be affected. And it was just three months after the visit that the Algerian revolution started. In a later period, at the beginning of 1960, when the countries of black Africa began to follow the example of Mali in proclaiming their independence, it was again an ostrich-like policy not to accept that the status of Algeria had to change.

It was exactly this unreal quality of French foreign policy at the time that opened the way to the Anglo-American good offices mission. The Anglo-Saxons decided to intervene at that point in order to counter the advances of the Arab extremists, assumed to be supported by the Soviets—advances that were made all the more possible by what was widely perceived as the blind and stubborn policy of France. It was necessary to intervene, with the objective of bringing the French to reason and, in so doing, ward off the "mounting danger to the West which looms in North Africa."[18]

However, the French had a flash-point sensitivity regarding North Africa. Apart from French and other European implantation in the Maghreb, there was the proximity of this region to France. The French expansion into North Africa and Africa as a whole was at its apogee during the latter half of the nineteenth century, in particular in the aftermath of the Franco-Prussian War. This extension of the "backyard" of France was supposed to be a compensation, though not wholly satisfactory, for the loss of Alsace-Lorraine—impossible to recover before sometime in the future. This was the means par excellence, advocated in particular by Prime Minister Jules Ferry, to hold high the banner of France, gravely besmirched by the defeat of 1870.

At the end of World War II, Africa, and particularly the Maghreb, remained as the jewel of the French Empire, somewhat akin to what India had been for the British. For the French, it was a prize not to be given up easily; it was thought of as an exclusive preserve of France. This was made sharper by a xenophobia never completely absent from the French state of mind and by the humiliation that had followed the defeat of 1940 and the reduction of France to a second-class power in the 1940s and 1950s. Holding on to this jewel seemed to be the proper means of struggling against decline.

Moreover, France had had long experience as a colonizing country, and only Great Britain could claim a comparable experience. (At the time, Russia was somehow not thought of generally as a colonizing power.) In this context, the United States was considered an interloper, scarcely experienced in carrying out the mission of civilizing a foreign country.

Within the French Army could be observed a sentiment of revenge, present since 1940; an ardent desire for a comeback, sharpened by the terrible ordeal in Indochina; and the frustration brought on by the Suez adventure that was supposed to have brought an end to the Algerian war. These sentiments invaded the psyche of the French military in North Africa with ferocious intensity. Some declared themselves determined "not to allow in Algeria the 'coup of Indochina'."[19]

Alastair Horne, author of a work on the Algerian war, observed, "If Indo-China had transformed its French pupils into superb warriors, it had also made them highly political animals—a fact that was to have as potent an impact on the French Republic as it did on the Algeria War."[20] The symbol, indeed the spearhead, of this sentiment was the elite of this volunteer army pushed out of Indochina—the "paras," who had become the centurions of this French Empire in North Africa.

At the beginning of 1958 the war in Algeria had begun to hurt France seriously. The firepower of the Algerian nationalists had increased visibly. The losses on the French side were "markedly higher than those suffered by our troops a year ago" noted *Le Monde* at the time.[21] Although the losses had hurt, the fact was that the French had inflicted, in the course of the year 1957, a terrible defeat on the Algerian National Liberation Front (FLN) in Algiers itself.

At the moment of the raid on Sakhiet-Sidi-Youssef, the epicenter of the war had already shifted to the Algerian-Tunisian frontier because of the Battle of Algiers. The FLN, short of arms as a result of this battle and having committed a grave tactical error by engaging in it, began to concentrate its attention on the resupply of its guerrillas from Tunisian territory. The French, in turn, sought to block off the Tunisian front by constructing an elaborate barrier along the frontier known as the Morice Line (named after then Minister of Defense André Morice), completed in September 1957. Immediately the Algerian rebels sought to breach this line from the Tunisian side, with only modest results and considerable losses in men. In the six months preceding the attack on Sakhiet-Sidi-Youssef, more than eighty firefights took place along the Algerian-Tunisian frontier.[22] The most serious was an ambush of a French patrol on January 11, 1958, by a band of guerrillas coming from the Sakhiet area. Fifteen French soldiers were killed. Three days later, in the course of the French reaction, a French aircraft was shot down over Sakhiet, where there seemed to be located an important rebel base.[23]

At a meeting of the French Council of Ministers on January 29, the possibility of raids against rebel bases in Tunisia within ten kilometers of the frontier was discussed.[24] It is not possible to determine through available documentation whether an actual decision was taken at the political level to exercise the right of pursuit across the frontier in Tunisia. In any case, it is unlikely that a decision was made to hit a specific target such as Sakhiet or a similar one during this meeting of the council. The most plausible hypothesis is that the raid on Sakhiet was conceived and executed by the commander of the military sector, as a reprisal against rebel antiaircraft fire. On the morning of February 8 a French plane overflying the area had received machine-gun fire. Three hours later three B-26 bombers of American manufacture[25] conducted an all-out attack against the village of Sakhiet. According to what Jean Lacouture has written, the Minister of Defense at the time of the raid, Jacques Chaban-Delmas, was not aware of it and had not given the order. "It was the maximal 'mistake,' the error par excellence—while at Paris, the Minister of National Defense had not even been consulted before the action by Algiers. This gave a measure of the abasement of the central authority in the face of the military."[26]

This having been said, it is the tradition in France, related to the principle of *raison d'état*, that the political authority will cover the military in such circumstances. This is quite different from the American practice, where transparency, more and more the rule, demands that the guilty be exposed; and this difference almost certainly added to the incomprehension between the two capitals at the time. There was no such transparency on the French side in the affair of Sakhiet-Sidi-Youssef.

There was a disturbing confluence in the French scene at the time: on the one hand a political authority in Paris, uncertain and weakened; on the other hand an army of 350,000 in North Africa, essentially in Algeria, supposed to be the spearhead of the execution of this uncertain policy. It was a formula for independent actions, indeed for insubordination. And it should be remembered that it was the recluse of Colombey-les-Deux-Eglises, the one who had saved as much as he could of the honor of France, who had given the supreme example of insubordination when he defied a marshal of France in June 1940. The political authority in Paris had become weakened to the point where, several weeks after the turning-point raid on Sakhiet-Sidi-Youssef, the ephemeral prime minister, René Pleven, asked the military to support the North African policy of the government that he was trying to form, by way of a public announcement to that effect: "It was at his request that Generals Salan and Jouhaud submitted to him on April 26 a memorandum demanding of the government that it commit itself solemnly never to tolerate that Algeria 'cease to be an integral part of France.' "[27]

Jean Lacouture, whose account this was, had the following comment: "thus the military arm, this instrument, was invited by the political authority to impose on the latter its views."[28]

The intention of the United States at the end of World War II was to conduct a global foreign policy, that is to say at a global echelon. This implied carrying on state-to-state relations with all countries of the world, however small, however far away. It was an ineluctable imperative of this country, sensing itself for the second time as savior of the world. After this second time the United States definitively emerged from its isolationism to become an imperium.

At first glance it was not to be expected that problems would develop between France and the United States over North Africa, especially under Eisenhower. Ike was well aware of the overall situation in North Africa because of his experience in the region during the war. Of all the leading American figures of the wartime period, he was among the most sensitive to the unique problems of France, and especially to the imperatives of the Free French movement. In particular, he had been able to manage a cordial relationship with Charles de Gaulle, in spite of the many obstacles they found in their path.

But an Eisenhower presidency brought with it a dyarchy in foreign policy, harmonious and efficient but a dyarchy nevertheless. Secretary of State John Foster Dulles was permitted to carry on direct relations with the great leaders of the world. He even had a direct correspondence with Winston Churchill. Below Dulles in the State Department were officials who were not particularly tender toward France, in particular Livingston Merchant and Robert Murphy.[29]

Although the United States had affirmed that it had no intention of replacing the French in North Africa, this did not mean that Washington intended to be a complete nullity in this region. The imperium intended to manifest itself everywhere. In his journal of November 21, 1956, President Eisenhower noted that he had just met with Habib Bourguiba: "I was struck by his sincerity, his intelligence, and his friendliness. . . . I assured him of America's friendliness, and particularly of its desire to deal directly with each one of the Moslem countries, in the effort to promote our common interests."[30]

Behind these benign words were the characteristic American anticolonialist mind-set and the intention not to let the Soviets penetrate at will in the Arab world. Unfortunately, this was not completely to the liking of the French at that period. They were very sensitive to the rank the French Empire accorded them in the world, and they were imbued with the tradition of a French preserve in Africa, especially in the Maghreb. North Africa was (and still remains) the counterpart of Central America to the United States. However, Washington would not have accepted that Paris exercise a sort of Monroe Doctrine over North Africa.

In the course of the 1950s a growing number of misunderstandings dotted the landscape of French-American relations. Already mentioned was the quarrel over the EDC, which was considered by many Frenchmen as an assault on their national sovereignty. It also should be noted, if only in passing, two other great misunderstandings, Indochina and Suez. As to the former, it represented in French eyes non-assistance to an expeditionary corps in danger and then, after the armistice, the replacement of the former colonial power by the American imperium in the southern half of the country. As for Suez, again from the French point of view, it represented the superpower leaving its smaller allies in the lurch, at a moment when the Soviets were threatening to drop atomic bombs on London and Paris.

For the French, the Suez expedition was first and foremost an exercise in preemption, a golden opportunity to choke off the rebellion in Algeria. As Alastair Horne observed, the idea that the original impetus for the Algerian war had come from Cairo "was a notion that would die hard and exert a fundamental, and disastrous, influence over the Suez operation of 1956."[31]

After the failure of Suez, in which the British had given in more rapidly than the French to American pressures, the cordial relations between the two Anglo-Saxon countries were restored relatively quickly. It was less the case for the French, who felt themselves in the forefront of the threat posed by the Algerian war. Therefore, their bitterness over Suez remained alive.

French-American misunderstandings persisted in the year that followed the Suez operation. Vice President Richard Nixon, following a visit to Bourguiba in March 1957 to celebrate the first anniversary of Tunisian independence, recommended to President Eisenhower that a referendum be held in Algeria on the question of whether to accept the framework law (*loi-cadre*) proposed by the governor general, Robert Lacoste, or else total independence.[32] Then, in July 1957, Senator John F. Kennedy advocated in a public speech that the United States support "a solution which will recognize the independent personality of Algeria and establish the basis for a settlement interdependent with France and the neighboring nations."[33]

Against the background of these periodic but passing irritations, there arose in November 1957 a new and more troublesome disagreement between the French and Americans on North Africa: the affair of American arms for Tunisia at a time when the latter had become a resupply base for the Algerian nationalists following the Battle of Algiers. One could not imagine a more unfortunate timing; however, Eisenhower's journal of the period has a different perspective: "For the past three days we have been in a terrible difficulty with France and Tunisia, based partially upon misunderstanding but mostly on what we believe to be French stupidity and refusal to face international facts as they exist."[34]

Eisenhower went on to recount that Bourguiba had asked for arms from the West, and that the Americans and British had suggested to the French that they do it. But the French had laid down unacceptable conditions for the Tunisians, notably that the sole source of arms for Tunisia be France. In the early autumn of 1957 the Americans and the British had informed Bourguiba that if the French did not deliver arms to Tunisia for the maintenance of order and minimal defense needs, they would.

A delivery date was established, November 1, but because of the fall of the government of Maurice Bourgès-Maunoury, the French asked that the delivery be put off until November 12. Then, suddenly, the new government of Félix Gaillard protested. The French stated that they did not think that a date was going to be fixed and they they considered even a minimal delivery to be an unfriendly gesture. Eisenhower noted that the French "reaction was violent, so much so that they even held that they might have to withdraw from NATO. . . . This put us in a dilemma . . . we could not afford either to see Bourguiba begin to purchase arms from the Soviets nor could we be in the position of breaking our pledged word to Tunisia."[35]

Following this, in the first half of November 1957, a new complication arose: Nasser decided to send some arms to Tunisia as a gift. Eisenhower wrote that Bourguiba, who could not afford to turn down the offer, "attached the most extraordinary importance to the delivery of some Western arms in Tunisia before the Egyptian shipment could reach there."[36] Accordingly, Eisenhower, not having been able "to persuade the French to deliver some arms themselves to the Tunisians which would not be under conditions 'incompatible with genuine independence,' "[37] informed Prime Minister Gaillard, in a letter of November 13, that he was obliged to make the American delivery the following day.[38] Eisenhower noted in his diary that "we felt we simply could not be blackmailed by the French weakness."[39] Almost as an afterthought, Eisenhower observed that "incidentally, the French objection was based on the argument that Bourguiba was trying to arm his country for far more than defensive purposes."[40]

Clearly, there existed a wide gulf of incomprehension: On the one side the French, prisoners of their "special preserve" mentality regarding North Africa; on the other side the Americans, with their anticolonialist messianism and their fixation on Bourguiba as "our most independent and enthusiastic friend in the Arab World,"[41] whose requests seemed reasonable, and all the more so since he had asked for arms for cash, and not as aid.[42] In the meantime, on the ground,

French troops and Algerian nationalists were killing each other thanks to the refuge accorded the nationalists by Tunisia.

The anticolonialist reflex was firmly anchored in American thought patterns at the time. Eisenhower himself noted to General Valluy, the French representative to the "Standing Group" of NATO, "It would be difficult for the United States to openly express support for France against the Arabs in view of the anticolonial tradition in the United States. To attempt to do this would only arouse a controversy in the United States that would not be useful to France."[43]

The French "blindness" on this subject of colonial empires was very difficult to understand from the American side. On March 3, 1958, in the midst of the good offices affair, Eisenhower wrote a personal note to Dulles: "The sentiments expressed by [Defense Minister Bahi] Ladgham, which are reported by Murphy in his cable of February 27th, coincide almost item by item with my own views. The trick is—how do we get the French to see a little sense?"[44]

Incomprehension in the political domain was one thing; in the military context it was lethal. In this case it was no longer, as in Vietnam, "non-assistance to an expeditionary corps in danger"; from the French point of view, it was worse still: it was a case of arms destined at least in part to be used in killing soldiers of the French garrisons in Algeria. What is more, the naïveté of Eisenhower in competing with Nasser to get arms to Tunisia, of which a certain amount would unquestionably end up in the hands of the Algerian nationalists, leaves the reader nonplussed. It was hardly a surprise, then, that the following words, as reported by Alastair Horne, escaped from the mouth of Prime Minister Gaillard: "If the Atlantic Pact should fall to dust one day, we will know the artisans of its failure."[45]

Horne also noted that Harold MacMillan in his memoirs expressed regret over this affair of Anglo-American arms for Tunisia: "I think we made a serious error, at a critical moment when France was already nervous and uncertain. . . . At the time I did not fully realize the true situation in France."[46]

Whatever else may be said, this matter of the sale of arms to Tunisia was not a good augur for the outcome of another affair that was to shake the relations between France and the Anglo-Saxons even more deeply: the sudden attack on the village of Sakhiet-Sidi-Youssef on February 8, 1958.

THE GOOD OFFICES MISSION

From the beginning of the affair of Sakhiet the American reaction was to intervene, apparently for two reasons: not to complicate further the Western position in the Mediterranean and North Africa; and not to remain indifferent to human suffering. On March 13, 1958, Eisenhower wrote in a letter to King Idris of Libya, in reply to a message the latter had sent concerning the incident, that "the United States cannot of course be indifferent to any situation which entails the destruction of lives and property or causes human suffering of the type which you describe."[47]

By a curious coincidence, certainly not intended expressly by the Americans, the man who symbolized American interference in North Africa during the war, and who moreover was not known for his sympathies toward the Free French movement, was named by the U.S. Government for the Good Offices Mission: Robert Murphy. *Le Monde* noted: "The past role of M. Murphy, his hostility toward General de Gaulle, his multiple interferences in French politics in Algiers at the time [of the Second World War], have not made him . . . friends here."[48] Given this background, it is not surprising that Charles de Gaulle let it be known that he did not want to see Murphy when the visiting American diplomat came to Paris during the Good Offices Mission.[49]

The personal ambience between French and American officials, still not completely free of the trauma of the Suez experience a little more than a year earlier, was not helped by the unfortunate choice of Murphy as mediator. One of Murphy's principal interlocutors, as Minister of Foreign Affairs, was Christian Pineau, who was not a friend.[50]

A career diplomat, a conservative, a Catholic, Murphy, as can be seen through his memoirs, exhibited an impatient attitude toward those Frenchmen he considered recalcitrant. There sometimes shows through a peremptoriness regarding the French in general, such as in this phrase: "It is notorious that most press leaks emanate from French delegations."[51] In a reference concerning his contacts with Tunisian Defense Minister Bahi Ladgham at the time of the Good Offices Mission, Murphy referred to the "physical conditions in French military and civilian prisons . . . [as] shockingly medieval."[52]

From the American point of view, however, Murphy was a perfectly logical choice for the mission. He was the number three official in the State Department. He had had long experience in French affairs, dating from the prewar period, when he was posted to Paris before arriving at Vichy after the French defeat of 1940 to become the chargé d'affaires.

It is not clear on the basis of available documents what was the origin of the Good Offices Mission. According to Murphy, the idea of a recourse to the Anglo-Americans came from Ambassador Alphand, after France had been censured in the United Nations.[53] In his own memoirs, Alphand does not deal with the Sakhiet affair except to recount his disagreeable conversation with Dulles,[54] and he does not mention the mission.

Apparently at the beginning the idea was not to join the Anglo-American effort but to conduct two separate missions. The American effort began in late February. Murphy went to London on the 23rd, to Paris on the 24th, and on the 25th he arrived in Tunis, where he had an initial conversation with Habib Bourguiba. When Murphy observed that the French thought Tunisia had become a belligerent in the war between France and the FLN, Bourguiba made a half-tortuous, half-astute reply:

[W]hile Tunisia could not be neutral, it was a "non-belligerent" . . . though it had not granted any belligerent rights to the FLN in Tunisia, it gave refuge to Algerian soldiers and accepted their wounded. These Algerians were also free to depart with their rifles. . . . However . . . Tunisia was not giving military aid to Algeria. . . . [Its] government was determined not to allow Tunisia to continue as a base for French action against Algeria.[55]

Fifteen days later Murphy, accompanied this time by his British counterpart, Horace Beeley, returned to Tunis where they presented the French proposals to Bourguiba. These were: the withdrawal of French troops stationed in Tunisia other than at the base of Bizerte; a neutral supervision of Tunisian airports; and a commission for the Algerian-Tunisian border.[56]

On February 25 Bourguiba had already given his approval to the stationing of neutral observers in the four airports concerned,[57] but this was not the heart of the problem. Rather, it was the Algerian-Tunisian frontier, and Bourguiba had already made known his position, as of February 25: "International control of the [Algerian-Tunisian] frontier was not practical, [Bourguiba] said, and in any case the Tunisians could not cooperate with the French to exterminate their Algerian brothers."[58]

During a meeting with Murphy and Beeley on March 11, Bourguiba observed that the difficulties Tunisia had with the French stemmed from the fact that "while Tunisia thought it had achieved full independence and sovereignty, the French considered that Tunisia had been given independence minus—independence less Bizerte, less the airports, et cetera."[59]

During this meeting Bourguiba showed to his Anglo-American interlocutors a note of March 10 from the French Embassy in Tunis stating that the Franco-Tunisian conventions on defense and foreign policy, which preceded the granting of independence, were still in force. These conventions, dated June 3, 1955, had placed under French control for an indefinite period (1) the Bizerte base and (2) certain zones along the coast. Beyond this the French maintained that the general provisions of these conventions gave them responsibilities in the defense area over and above these two categories, and that in any event the consent of both parties was required in order for the defense responsibilities laid out in the conventions to be changed. However, the legal counsellor of the State Department reasoned otherwise:

In the French-Tunisian [Independence] Agreement of March 20, 1956, it was provided [that] "France solemnly recognizes the independence of Tunisia," [and that] those provisions of the Conventions of 1955 which might be contradictory to the new statute of Tunisia " . . . will be modified or abrogated" . . . [also] . . . a national Tunisian army would be constituted.

The conclusion of the legal adviser was that Tunisia would win if the matter were referred to the International Court of Justice.[60]

THE REVERSAL

The mission of Murphy and Beeley lasted eight weeks. In the course of his visits to Tunis, Murphy scrupulously avoided in-depth discussions on the Algerian problem. At one point he told Gaillard that he had not pushed Bourguiba on the subject of a Tunisian-Algerian border commission out of concern that the Algerian question might come up.[61] However, it was the question of such a commission that was at the heart of French preoccupations.

Basically, Murphy did not want the Good Offices Mission to get involved in the Algerian question. His reasoning was that the French government was incapable of a bold solution to the North African situation, and if his mission tried for a settlement of the Algerian question, this would, for reasons of "intense chauvinism," lead to the toppling of any French government that appeared to be sympathetic to it. Murphy feared that the successor government "could be an extremely nationalist government of the right which would strongly oppose any change in Algerian policy, or perhaps one of the right formed outside Parliament which might change policy in North Africa but at the expense of Europe and of the Atlantic community."[62]

Murphy had sketched out rather presciently the contours of what was to come. After the fall of the Gaillard government in mid-April 1958, the emergence of the candidacy of Pierre Pflimlin, who was reputed to harbor liberal intentions toward Algeria, provoked the May 13 upheaval in Algiers and the formation of a Committee of Public Safety there under the leadership of General Jacques Massu.[63] To prevent a *coup de force* by the French Army in Algeria, the return of de Gaulle became ineluctable. What happened was not exactly a government "formed outside Parliament" (which indeed voted the investiture of de Gaulle on June 1 by 329 votes against 224). Nevertheless, this second takeover of power by de Gaulle, described as a "seventeenth Brumaire" by Jean Lacouture,[64] brought a profound change in the French Parliament and in French policy toward Algeria—not to mention what happened eventually within the Atlantic alliance.

At the end of the eight-week mission of Murphy and Beeley, the French press judged it to be a failure. On the weekend of April 13–14, 1958, *Le Monde* reported, "The Council of Ministers . . . is trying to find a way out of the Franco-Tunisian crisis and the failure of the 'good offices'."[65] In truth, the government of Félix Gaillard (himself a former *chef de cabinet* of Jean Monnet) found itself in a very delicate situation. None of its objectives had been achieved by the Good Offices Mission. Even its desire for a declaration of non-intervention by Tunisia had been turned aside by Murphy and Beeley, who persuaded Gaillard that the French would do better to raise this question after the French resumed direct talks with the Tunisians.[66]

In fact, all the recommendations of the mission went in the direction of appeasement of Bourguiba. French troops would be evacuated from Tunisian airports and replaced by "neutral" observers who supposedly were to make sure the arms did not wind up in the hands of the FLN. French troops would be evacuated from all areas except the Bizerte base, over which Tunisian sovereignty was recognized and whose status would be the subject of negotiations between the two governments.[67] The only concessions to the French were of an administrative or humanitarian order: the opening of French consulates closed by Bourguiba following the raid on Sakhiet and the return of some six hundred French citizens who had had to leave Tunisia following the raid.[68] The most important thing from the French point of view, and announced as such by Gaillard, was to achieve the non-permeability of the Algerian-Tunisian frontier, but this did not figure in the recommendations of Murphy and Beeley.

To judge by the recommendations of this mission and by American documents of the period, there was a clear desire on the part of Murphy, and also of President Eisenhower, to nurture Bourguiba, considered by Washington as the great leader of the region and "our most independent and enthusiastic friend in the Arab World."[69] To be sure, this was the 1950s, when the drive toward decolonization seemed irresistible and the image of Bourguiba and other Third World leaders had yet to be tainted by the cult of personality, dictatorial methods, and corruption; thus the undiscriminating acceptance of these leaders, which seems naive today, was more understandable in the light of the times. To Eisenhower, the problem was caused not at all by Bourguiba but by the French: on February 26, 1958, the president wrote to his friend "Swede" Hazlett apropos of Sakhiet and its aftermath: "I agree with you completely with regard to Bourguiba and I deplore the situation the French have gotten themselves, and indirectly us, into."[70]

Charles de Gaulle, though out of power, had ostentatiously injected himself into the Sakhiet dispute by meeting with Tunisian Ambassador Mohammed Masmoudi immediately afterward; it was just as Masmoudi was preparing to leave Paris because of the break in diplomatic relations. In so doing de Gaulle distanced himself from the French government's action and appeared suddenly sympathetic to the plight of Tunisia.

What made Prime Minister Gaillard's position particularly difficult was that the failure of the Murphy-Beeley mission would have put things straight back into the arena of the United Nations, where there likely would have ensued further embarrassment for the French government. On February 14 France had lodged a complaint with the UN asking for a condemnation of the aid provided to the Algerian rebels by Tunisia.[71] If France, eight weeks later, initiated a debate in the UN Security Council, the outcome could not be predicted, and in any case the result would be another step in the internationalization of the Algerian conflict. Going back to the UN would effectively end the Good Offices Mission, which had been a way of bypassing the UN where the Soviets were in a position to cause trouble in the Security Council. Another recourse to avoid going back to the UN could have been NATO, but here again, other countries, including the smaller NATO nations, would thereby become involved in the Algerian dispute—certainly not to the liking of France.

At the same time, however, and adding to the dilemma of the Gaillard government, more voices were being heard in France against the Good Offices Mission, including that, arguably inappropriate, of Marshal Alphonse Juin, who was still a serving military officer.

From both sides of the Atlantic there was mounting frustration at French institutional weakness. In Washington the leadership railed against the symptoms (witness Eisenhower who refused to be "blackmailed by French weakness"[72]) but still did not see how the French government could be made more decisive. In Paris more and more thinking was taking place on how to strengthen the government without losing the democratic system. In this context J.-R. Tournoux recalled what he termed "the pathetic appeal of M. Coty," in a speech given by the French president at Strasbourg:

Isn't it possible, following the example of other democracies, to reinforce the Executive without undermining the essential prerogatives of the Parliament? Are we going to have to wait indefinitely for this institutional reform, which is the key to all the reforms in our country, and of which our country has such a great need?[73]

At the conclusion of the Good Offices Mission, President Eisenhower sent a grave message to Prime Minister Gaillard. He did not state flatly what he wanted Gaillard to do, but he indicated the way. After having noted that the mission, "established by your Government and that of Tunisia," had explored all the aspects of its charge, and that the moment of decision could not be delayed much longer, Eisenhower came to the heart of the matter:

[I]t seems that the final word may now rest with France . . . [which] faces the question of whether or not it is consistent with France's own vital interests to accept the practical limits which seem to be imposed on the Tunisian Government by sentimental and even emotional ties, as well as geographical factors, which inescapably lead the people of Tunisia to sympathize with the aspirations of the Moslem nationalist elements in Algeria. . . . If the "Good Offices" mission fails to achieve at least a limited *modus vivendi* between France and Tunisia, larger aspects of the problem are almost sure to erupt violently . . . time is running out in the vital North African area . . . a military struggle in North Africa . . . could, despite our wishes, seriously undermine the strength and cohesion of the Atlantic Community . . . my estimate [is that there is a] . . . mounting danger to the West which looms in North Africa.[74]

The timing of this letter, April 10, was just two days before the Council of Ministers was scheduled to decide on the recommendations of Murphy and Beeley. The French government found itself in a virtually impossible position. It had had to submit to a degree of internationalization of the North African conflict by the very establishment of the Good Offices Mission. At the same time it had derived no advantage from this mission, other than the prospect, still problematic, of a resumption of bilateral talks with the Tunisians.

Finally, in order to avoid a further degree of internationalization through a reopening of the French complaint of February 14 to the United Nations, the Gaillard government, under strong pressure from Washington, decided on April 12 to accept the recommendations of the Murphy-Beeley mission. At the same time the government decided to submit the decision to the assembly in three days' time, in the form of a vote of confidence. It was also decided to put off a return to the United Nations.

With the increasingly negative statements such as Marshal Juin's in the background, an outburst of xenophobia seemed to take place among the parliamentarians during the weekend of April 12–13. The group of moderates in the National Assembly began to fear being overtaken by the right in the cantonal elections due to take place several weeks later. They constituted themselves as a delegation to the chief of state and expressed to him their concerns about the direction the mission was taking. Communist and pro–Mendès-France deputies stepped up their attacks against the Gaillard government as the hour for voting approached. Just after the vote, which went against the government, John Foster Dulles, as reported by *Le Monde*, vigorously denied rumors that the United States was seeking to replace France in North Africa. Nothing could be farther from the truth, he said.[75]

If Dulles thought that in making such a disclaimer he could still save the situation, he was wrong. At this point, public opinion in France was almost as suspicious of the Anglo-Saxons as it was of the communists and the Arab Nationalists. There was an underlying theme of a threat of withdrawal from NATO at each new failure of the Anglo-Saxons to support French policy in North Africa. The sentiment of going it alone (*la France seule*) was growing stronger, as another humiliation, growing out of the Good Offices Mission, seemed to be in the making. The disastrous failure-cum-farce of Suez was still fresh in the public mind, with its image of the British having given in to American pressure, on the pound and otherwise, and the Americans having failed to show Western solidarity when the Soviets threatened nuclear attack on London and Paris.

And so the Good Offices Mission did not succeed in bringing about a settlement between France and Tunisia: far from it. It did, however, contribute to the fall of what was to be the last government, in the traditional sense, of the Fourth Republic. (The new constitution ushering in the Fifth Republic was not approved by referendum until September 28, 1958.)

Most French observers of the time could not envisage real independence for the Maghreb. Either there would be association with France in a sort of Commonwealth-like arrangement, or the Maghreb would enter into another system— Soviet, American, or Nasserist.[76] Charles de Gaulle, however, had developed as early as February 1958 his own plan for Algerian self-determination, which he disclosed privately to his wartime colleague Maurice Schumann. The population would be asked to choose between three options: "francisation" (or what is today called integration), association with France, or secession, according to what Schumann related to Jean Lacouture.[77]

The formidable machine of "francisation," in its centralizing, republican, and Jacobin aspects, could not operate in the Algerian context because the scale was too large: 9 million Algerians with an economic and social status markedly inferior to the *colons* and their descendants. At the same time, these 9 million were inheritors of a different and distinctive religion that constitutes a way of life in itself. Thus "francisation" was doomed. In any event, the French population as a whole would not have agreed to accept 9 million Algerians as full-fledged French citizens.

Thus "association" came to be advocated as a substitute for "francisation." But association implies a liberty of choice. Indeed, a certain choice had been exercised early on by Morocco and Tunisia in refusing to participate as "associated states" in the assembly of the French Union. But later, once a full liberty of choice had been exercised by the French states of black Africa, beginning with Mali in September 1959, it became untenable not to permit this choice for Algeria—all the more so because the level of cultural life, by virtue of Islam and the Arab tradition, was more developed in the Maghreb than in black Africa.

Finally, putting the two other countries of the Maghreb in a different category and setting them on a path toward independence—all because of an accident of history—became utterly indefensible. It was not possible to sustain two different policies for the same people of North Africa. Neither "francisation" nor association was acceptable for the native population of Algeria. And so it became, of the three choices articulated by de Gaulle to Maurice Schumann, secession.

With the arrival of de Gaulle to power, it was the reversal: a new foreign policy was begun, as well as a profound change in France's institutions. Everything did not happen at once; it was necessary to await the year 1962. By this time the general had found, after many twists and turns, a solution to the Algerian problem, which was independence. And later in the same year France's institutional reforms were completed with the referendum on election of the president by universal suffrage.

It was a new and unfettered foreign policy—the implication of which was a more or less total decolonization and thus the destruction of the myth of association—plus the reform of France's institutions, which constitute the two poles of the reversal of 1958. It became apparent to the French political class that an *aggiornamento* was imperative; to accomplish this France had to have a strong government which would take the country's destiny into its own hands.

At first pleasing to the Americans, this French *aggiornamento* ended by being not completely to the liking of the great partner from across the Atlantic. To contain what now seemed to be emerging as untrammeled French nationalism, the imperium had some new ideas in mind, notably the Multilateral Force (MLF), which was essentially an effort to satisfy the Europeans' desire to participate in their own defense, while at the same time keeping these nations—and especially France—under control. It should not have been a surprise, then, that de Gaulle decided not to take part in the MLF. It was more of a surprise that he, in effect, scuttled it. The affair of the MLF (1960–65) is considered in the next chapter.

NOTES

1. *Le Monde*, January 30, 1991, 2 (the day after Minister of Defense Chevènement's resignation).

2. Jean Lacouture, *De Gaulle* (Paris: Seuil, 1985), 2:439.

3. *Le Monde*, February 11, 1958, 1.

4. Hervé Alphand, *L'étonnement d'être* (Paris: Fayard, 1977), 289.

5. *Le Monde*, February 11, 1958, 1.

6. Pierre Mélandri and Frédéric Bozo, "La France devant l'opinion américaine: le retour de de Gaulle début 1958–printemps 1959," *Relations Internationales*, no. 58 (Summer 1989): 195–96.

7. Ibid., 196.

8. From a lecture by Professor Ernest May, Harvard University, December 5, 1991, in the course entitled, "The Nuclear Revolution: Hiroshima to SALT-1, 1945–1972."

9. Words used by John J. McCloy in a memorandum to President Roosevelt, June 10, 1944. Franklin D. Roosevelt Presidential Library (FDRL), President's Secretary's File (PSF), Box 31, France: de Gaulle 1944–1945, 1.

10. Jean Chatelain, *La Nouvelle Constitution et le régime politique de la France* (Paris: Editions Berger-Levrault, 1959), 295.

11. Ibid., 300.

12. Ibid.

13. *Le Monde*, November 14–15, 1954, 3.

14. Ibid.

15. Chatelain, *La Nouvelle Constitution*, 303.

16. Jean Lacouture, *Pierre Mendès-France* (Paris: Seuil, 1981), 269.

17. Ibid., 282.

18. The words are those of President Eisenhower, in a letter to Prime Minister Félix Gaillard on April 10, 1958. Dwight D. Eisenhower Presidential Library (DDEL), Ann Whitman File, International Series, Box 11, France 1956–1960 (1): telegram 3782 of the Department of State to Paris, April 10, 1958, 4. See also p. 115.

19. Jean-Raymond Tournoux, *Secrets d'Etat* (Paris: Plon, 1960), 197.

20. Alastair Horne, *A Savage War of Peace* (Hong Kong: Elisabeth Sifton Books–Penguin Books, 1977), 167.

21. *Le Monde*, February 26, 1958, 1.

22. Horne, *Savage War of Peace*, 249.

23. Ibid.

24. *Le Monde*, February 11, 1958, 1.

25. Horne, *Savage War of Peace*, 250.

26. Lacouture, *De Gaulle*, 2:440.

27. Ibid., 445.

28. Ibid.

29. This is the opinion of Douglas Dillon. Interview with the author, October 15, 1990.

30. DDEL, Ann Whitman File, DDE Diaries Series, Box 19, DDE diary November 1956: Eisenhower note of meeting with Bourguiba.

31. Horne, *Savage War of Peace*, 85.

32. Ibid., 247.

33. Ibid.

34. DDEL, Ann Whitman File, International Series, Box 11, France 1956–1960: Journal of Eisenhower of November 14, 1957, 1.

35. Ibid., 2.

36. Ibid.

37. Ibid., Message from Eisenhower to Félix Gaillard on November 13, 1957, Telegram 1812 from the Department of State to Paris, 3.

38. Ibid., 4.

39. Ibid., Journal of Eisenhower of November 14, 1957, 3.

40. Ibid.

41. Ibid., 1.

42. Ibid.

43. DDEL, White House Central File (1953–1961), Confidential File, Subject series, Box 71, Department of State (April 1956): summary note on the meeting between Eisenhower and Valluy, April 2, 1956.

44. DDEL, White House Office File, Office of the Staff Secretary, Box 5, Department of State, February–April 1958: Good Offices Mission, note from Eisenhower to Dulles, March 3, 1958.

45. Horne, *Savage War of Peace*, 243.

46. Ibid.

47. DDEL, White House Office File, Office of the Staff Secretary, Box 2, Department of State, February–April 1958): letter from Eisenhower to King Idris, March 13, 1958.

48. *Le Monde*, February 21, 1958, 1.

49. Tournoux, *Secrets d'Etat*, 235.

50. Robert D. Murphy, *Diplomat among Warriors* (Garden City, N.Y.: Doubleday, 1964), 382.

51. Ibid.

52. Ibid., 395.

53. Ibid.

54. See p. 100.

55. DDEL, White House Office File, Office of the Staff Secretary, Box 5, Department of State, February–April 1958: Good Offices Mission, summary of developments number 3, February 26, 1958.

56. Ibid., summary of developments number 12, March 12, 1958.

57. Ibid., summary of developments number 3, February 26, 1958.

58. Ibid.

59. Ibid., summary of developments number 12, March 12, 1958.

60. Ibid., memorandum of the legal adviser of the State Department, March 14, 1958.

61. Ibid., summary of developments number 6, March 4, 1958.

62. Ibid., summary of developments number 9, March 7, 1958.

63. Jean Carpentier and François Lebrun, eds., *Histoire de France* (Paris: Seuil, 1987), 351.

64. Lacouture, *De Gaulle*, 2:447. (Napoleon took power on the 18th Brumaire in the revolutionary calendar. Thus the implication of Lacouture's term is that de Gaulle's takeover, while legal, was a near–coup d'etat).

65. *Le Monde*, April 13–14, 1958, 1.

66. DDEL, White House Office File, Office of the Staff Secretary, Box 5, Department of State, February–April 1958: Good Offices Mission, summary of developments number 11, March 11, 1958.

67. *Le Monde*, April 15, 1991, 2.

68. Ibid.

69. Eisenhower's words. See p. 109.

70. DDEL, Ann Whitman File, DDE Diaries Series, Box 30, DDE Dictation, February 1958: letter from Eisenhower to Hazlett, February 26, 1958, 5.

71. *Le Monde*, April 13–14, 1958, 1. According to *Le Monde*, the text of the French complaint mentioned "aid provided by Tunisia to the Algerian rebels."

72. See p. 109.

73. Tournoux, *Secrets d'Etat*, 205.

74. DDEL, Ann Whitman File, International Series, Box 11, France 1956–1960 (1): Eisenhower to Gaillard, Telegram 3782 of the Department of State to Paris, April 10, 1958, 2–4.

75. *Le Monde*, April 17, 1958, 3.

76. See Maurice Duverger, "L'Armée, la nation et le régime," *Le Monde*, February 26, 1958, 1.

77. Lacouture, *De Gaulle*, 2:439.

❖ 6 ❖

The Multilateral Force:
The Two Hegemons

Of course, life is life, in other words a combat, for a nation as for a man.

Charles de Gaulle[1]

In General de Gaulle's famous speech of November 3, 1959, before the classes of the French military schools, there is a passage very revealing of his line of thought:

The Government at all periods has had as a raison d'être the defense of the independence and the integrity of the territory. . . . In France in particular, all our regimes have come from that basis . . . there were always preoccupations or necessities regarding defense. Conversely, each invasion, each national disaster, has led infallibly to the fall of the existing regime. *If, therefore, a government had lost its essential responsibility it would lose, by the same token, its justification. Once peace came, it would be soon acknowledged that it had not fulfilled its objective.* (emphasis added)[2]

For de Gaulle, governing seemed to imply the necessity of a permanent joust. The essential function of the French state was to assure its defense. Put another way, among the affairs of state, primacy was given to defense. The tone of this passage (which contains a sort of subliminal ex post facto justification of his rebellion against Vichy) and of the passage at the beginning of this chapter suggest that de Gaulle saw himself as permanently at loggerheads with other states.

Charles Bohlen spoke of talks he had about de Gaulle with President Kennedy in Palm Beach, at the time when Bohlen was the American ambassador in Paris:

[When] I was Ambassador to France, every time I came home I would go down to Palm Beach where [Kennedy] was, and he would talk all the time about this angle or that angle of de Gaulle's personality, this policy or that policy—he was obviously groping around, trying to get something to satisfy him as an explanation for what is often very curious behavior on de Gaulle's part. I think he finally came to the conclusion that de Gaulle needed some form of friction with the United States for his own personal policies, domestic or otherwise, but Kennedy was equally determined that he was not going to oblige him on this.[3]

Eisenhower and Kennedy had a different attitude from the majority of American political leaders of their time about de Gaulle. They held him in respect, and in the case of Kennedy this respect bordered on admiration. But as has been noted by Michel Debré, the capable and polemical prime minister at the beginning of the Fifth Republic, there were limits to their lack of bias toward de Gaulle:

Admittedly, Eisenhower, then Kennedy, approved our firmness on Berlin in the face of the Soviet diplomatic offensive. . . . They had a great esteem for the work of decolonization and for the policy followed by the General toward Algeria. But the two Presidents, and their Secretaries of States, whether they were named Dulles, Herter, or Rusk, did not want to understand the French position, either regarding political independence or regarding the Common Market.[4]

Because de Gaulle had a profoundly bellicose temperament, and because he saw defense as the supreme mission of the state, it is not hard to understand why he appeared, in the eyes of other statesmen in general, as an interlocutor who was difficult and sometimes impossible. Very perspicacious and even rather noble in his views, but down deep, and to deal with, very difficult.

The subject of this chapter is the Multilateral Force (1960–65)—whose abbreviation in English (MLF) became habitual even in France—which André Fontaine called "a modest reprise of the European Defense Community of the 1950s."[5] In fact the MLF was a sort of EDC elevated to the nuclear level.

The MLF was first and foremost a way of integrating the nuclear problem into the Atlantic alliance, that is, how to manage a Western nuclear force on the continent of Europe. According to the point of view of Washington, the problem posed itself in the following terms: "how to develop a system by which our allies who wish to do so may participate with us in nuclear deterrent—without proliferation of national nuclear forces . . . and in a way which would tighten as well as strengthen the Alliance."[6]

The MLF was the way the United States would try to solve this problem. It was an exercise in trying to square the circle. Just as the Americans two hundred years earlier had found taxation without representation an unfair arrangement, so the Europeans, or those among them who felt sufficiently independent to say so, found that participation without proliferation (that is, without having a nuclear force of their own) was not an attractive proposition. And fundamentally because it was not attractive, except for those seeking rehabilitation, such as Germany and Italy, or those countries too small to challenge the U.S. theses, the MLF affair was to remain a preoccupation during three American presidencies—those of Eisenhower, Kennedy, and Johnson. The MLF began toward the end of the Eisenhower presidency and was terminated before the end of the Johnson presidency. Representing France was de Gaulle—de Gaulle alone.

The two protagonists, America and France, reacted to the problem presented by the MLF in a way that was opposed but parallel: as two hegemons. The Americans did not want to let go of their control over nuclear arms in Western Europe. De Gaulle's strategy was to gain time until the French nuclear weapon became operational. From that moment France would enjoy nuclear hegemony on the continent of Western Europe. Because it was a question of a hidden game, the French leader never completely revealed his cards, which was a source of irritation to Washington. A document of the period related: "Despite repeated urging from the United States and other NATO countries, France refused to sit down with her allies and make proposals for adapting NATO to meet special French concerns. Paris either ignored or turned aside efforts by others to draw de Gaulle out on this matter."[7]

At the high point of the debate on the MLF, during a meeting devoted to this subject on November 19, 1964, Assistant Secretary of State George Ball proposed "a public and serious approach to de Gaulle—an approach which would put to him the question: 'what do you want?' We should seriously make the point to him (in such fashion that it was understood publicly): 'We are not against you, but we don't know what troubles you, and we don't have proposals from you.' "[8]

This chapter develops the theme of the two hegemons as it recounts the history of the MLF.

THE RETURN OF DE GAULLE

Charles de Gaulle returned to power on June 1, 1958. It was a period of transition. The political figures on the scene were no longer those of the Fourth Republic. De Gaulle himself was a man totally different from those who had preceded him. The general's past was loaded with memories, sometimes bitter ones. As Alfred Grosser observed: "Forgetting offenses is not a Gaullist virtue. If, in June 1964, he did not go to Normandy to take part in ceremonies celebrating the twentieth anniversary of the landing, it was that the memory of the confrontations . . . [with the Allies] was still very present."[9]

With de Gaulle a whole generation of political leaders arrived on the scene who remembered with bitterness the stubborn refusal of the United States to recognize the Provisional Government until late in 1944. As Grosser put it, "A whole generation of new leaders would retain the conviction that such an acceptance was wrested from, was imposed upon, the Americans."[10]

General de Gaulle, as he indicated approximately eighteen months after his

return to power in a speech before the classes of the military schools (cited at
the beginning of this chapter), wanted to mark a divide between his regime and
those that had preceded it, in an epoch "when one could believe that the Free
World was faced with an imminent and unlimited threat, and when we had not
recovered our national personality."[11]

De Gaulle's Outsider View of the CCS[12]

Secretary of State John Foster Dulles met with de Gaulle in Paris on July 5,
1958, one month after the general's return to power. In the course of a meeting
with Eisenhower and several other senior officials two days earlier in Washington, Dulles took the position that it was necessary to support de Gaulle publicly,
as "there is some reason to think that he is all that stands between France and
chaos, or a popular front at least."[13]

Well before this first face-to-face meeting between the American leadership
and renascent Gaullism, there had been much discussion of "tripartism,"[14] or
tripartite discussions among the three Western allies of the war. The concept of
tripartism had been found wanting at the time of the disastrous affair of Suez.
But the idea in practical terms had scarcely existed at the strategic level, particularly since the French defeat in 1940.

For the French, after having undergone the terrible experience of the war,
especially the occupation, tripartism translated to a desire to be treated on an
equal footing with Great Britain. This feeling was expressed more and more
openly during the 1950s, as France began to recover from the war and was
catching up with Great Britain economically.

The reaction of General de Gaulle after this first high-level meeting on July
5, 1958, which apparently included an unsatisfactory exchange on nuclear weapons,[15] followed by that of Couve de Murville with Eisenhower on August 21,
was not long in coming. Noting that he had discussed defense problems with
Dulles on July 5,[16] de Gaulle launched on September 17 the famous "Memorandum on the Directory." The memorandum sketched out de Gaulle's concerns
in three areas: (1) NATO; (2) nuclear matters; and (3) tripartism—all intimately
linked, and all having to do with the rank and independence of France:

- [NATO:] which limits itself to the security of the North Atlantic, as if the indivisible
  responsibilities of France did not extend to Africa, to the Indian Ocean, and to the
  Pacific, as do, in the same way, those of Great Britain and the United States.

- [Nuclear weapons:] it is true that it had been acknowledged at the outset that atomic
  weapons, clearly of capital importance, would remain for a long time the monopoly of
  the U.S., which could appear to justify [the fact that] on a global level, decisions
  concerning defense would be practically delegated to the Government of Washington.
  But on this point too, it should be recognized that a similar situation taken as a given
  is now no longer valid in reality.[17]

- [Tripartism:] it . . . seems necessary [to France] that a worldwide organization should be created at the level of policy and strategy and that it should include the United States, Great Britain, and France. This organization would, on the one hand, make joint decisions on questions of policy involving world security, and on the other hand, establish and, if need be, execute strategic action plans, particularly as regards the use of nuclear weapons.[18]

In the memorandum, with its superb use of language and symbols, de Gaulle was aiming very high. As Raymond Aron said, de Gaulle only had words at his disposal; that is why he used them with such force.[19] But, as was his way, de Gaulle mixed in soothing words, especially on East-West issues, with very harsh assertions. This seemed to be part of his tactics. For example, in the preamble of the memorandum, he stated: "I can imagine how much the situation in the Far East can cause you concern, and I would like to assure you, on this occasion, of my sincere and confident friendship." In the memorandum itself, however, he complained sharply about the lack of consultation on the very issue of the Far East (and Middle East) and concluded that "the present organization of the Western Alliance is no longer responsive to the necessary conditions for the security of the Free World as a whole."[20] De Gaulle seemed to be aiming at nothing less than instituting tripartism, modeled, in his eyes, on the Combined Chiefs of Staff (CCS)—including, and above all, at the highest level, the nuclear level.

In reality, de Gaulle probably had a mistaken view of the CCS, or at least of its supposed continuing manifestations. This Anglo-American organization had functioned rather well during World War II, although it was dissolved immediately afterward. De Gaulle had observed from close up the functioning of the CCS (but only as an outsider), and it is likely he visualized the Anglo-American partnership as continuing in this model. With the CCS dismantled, however, little of this kind of consultation had continued once the war was over. Moreover, the United States had ended the agreement with the British on nuclear cooperation that had been drawn up during the war.

Given the ideas that de Gaulle probably had about the closeness of Anglo-American cooperation, any response from Washington, no matter what, could only disappoint him. Knowing the way he had been treated during the war, perhaps de Gaulle never expected a positive response, at least not from the Americans. (A similar letter to Harold MacMillan had been sent at the same time.)

Eisenhower's definitive reply (on October 20, 1958), which followed an anodine interim response (on October 2), was in effect a negative one. Eisenhower took pains to emphasize that decisions that affected NATO could not be made by a restricted group of only three of the countries of the alliance: "We cannot allow ourselves to adopt a system which would give to our allies, or to other countries of the Free World, the impression that fundamental decisions which affect their vital interests are being taken without their participation."[21]

Decidedly, the interests of the "Imperium" diverged from those of the "Nation,'' on this and other occasions. Eisenhower's reply in effect signed the death warrant of tripartism, if there ever had been any hope of reviving what would have been an avatar of World War I cooperation. It is also useful to set the memorandum in the context of the time, slightly less than two years after the Suez affair did lasting damage to American cooperation with its European partners and in particular with France.

In any event, the United States was in no way disposed to grant de Gaulle consultation rights on the use of American nuclear weapons. In this particular respect American policy was not basically different toward France than toward Great Britain. However, as will be discussed later, the Americans, at the time of the memorandum, had just signaled a change to the British: they would be willing to exchange nuclear information again.

The American reply to the request for a three-way consultation having been essentially negative, the general did not wait long to launch a counterresponse: the withdrawal of the French fleet in the Mediterranean from the integrated command of NATO, an action he explained in an official letter to Eisenhower on May 25, 1959.[22]

THE NUCLEAR CONUNDRUM

For the Americans, the concept of integration was the paramount necessity for the defense of the Western world. The stakes were so important, the possibilities of miscalculation, with disastrous, even apocalyptic consequences, so evident, that centralization of defense through an integrated command became the Americans' supreme requirement. According to a note of May 22, 1964, prepared by the administration for Congress, "US policy for NATO over 15 years has been to build a tight alliance with a closely integrated military power— not a loose association. We believe the nuclear defense of the West is indivisible."[23]

Although most Europeans recognized and accepted this as a strategic imperative, they were often confused by the political choices of the United States. European hesitations and doubts about American political judgments mounted, especially during the Vietnam War. Some estimated that the military choices of the United States were based on erroneous assessments, particularly regarding the menace of international communism in Southeast Asia. Paradoxically, as confidence in the wisdom and moderation of American foreign policy waned during the 1960s, the impulse toward European solidarity waned also.

The European Objection: Raymond Aron

Raymond Aron, the most prominent of the liberal (in the European sense) and non-Marxist thinkers in postwar France, neatly summed up the contradiction between the American desire for efficiency and security regarding nuclear weapons ("integration") and the desire of the Europeans to have a say in what concerned their life and death. It was in the course of a conversation in Paris on April 7, 1962, with Alain Enthoven of the Defense Department. The following is an excerpt of the latter's account:

Aron believes that U.S. military policy regarding Europe is based on technical considerations rather than an understanding of European political realities.

Aron stated that the U.S. and the Soviet Union have in effect an unwritten agreement, the most stable agreement of the cold war, not to permit the spread of nuclear weapons technology and to avoid any situation which would result in attacks on each other's territory. This unwritten agreement perfectly suits Soviet interests, particularly as regards China, but the arrangement is absurd as far as the United States' European allies are concerned. These nations have the technology, manpower, and wealth to develop modern armaments and thus make an enormous contribution to Western defense which would help stabilize the world. The U.S. refuses to permit them to develop this capability.

[From Aron's point of view] the development of a European nuclear capability is the only practical solution in view of the present U.S.-Soviet accord. At the moment the British and the French are developing national nuclear forces but a more practical solution for the long range is a European force which could defend Western European interests.[24]

Two months later, in an article in *Le Figaro*, Aron queried whether a solution to the problem could not be found in the application of the formula of the European Defense Community to the area of nuclear weapons. He asserted that there were two routes open to the European states, one that led to numerous small nuclear forces, the other to two forces, European and American, closely linked. Aron's preference was for the latter solution. He dismissed as out of the question a NATO nuclear force, which would be unsatisfactory to the French.[25]

What has actually happened in the thirty years since Aron's article falls into neither of his two options: not a European nuclear force, but not numerous national forces either. Instead, two national nuclear forces have been created in Europe, in Britain and France, and this too has created imbalances and tensions. As Aron himself put it at the time, "if France is to be given atomic weapons, why not Italy and Federal Germany?"[26]

The American Objection: Admiral Rickover

At the opposite pole from Raymond Aron was the figure of Admiral Hyman Rickover, the father of the American nuclear submarine, whose views were very "technical," to recall Aron's phrase. In an oral history interview, Rickover recounted to Professor Arthur M. Schlesinger, Jr., his impressions of a meeting he had with President Kennedy in February 1963. Kennedy solicited his opinion on the idea of a multilateral force comprised of nuclear submarines equipped with Polaris missiles. Rickover succeeded in convincing Kennedy not to use nuclear submarines but surface ships instead. (As it turned out, the choice came down to merchant ships.[27])

I pointed out that it is not necessary for members of an alliance to know the details of each other's military secrets. . . . In fact, the existence of an alliance had never been a convincing argument for inducing a nation with superior weapons to share with allies the secret of their design or manufacture. I said that I could not agree with the novel concept urged by proponents of the MLF that entry into an alliance requires disclosure of all military secrets. . . . In my opinion, these people [who supported the MLF] were not sufficiently knowledgeable technically to understand the value of this information, the strenuous efforts being made by foreign nations to obtain it, or how quickly it would leak to the Russians and jeopardize our national security.[28]

IN SEARCH OF GAULLIST INTENTIONS

As noted above, the solution Aron favored was that the Europeans should equip themselves with their own nuclear force, which would be closely linked with that of the Americans. Clearly, this solution would not have met with approval in Washington. The United States insisted on an integrated command—under its control—where the coordination would be complete and the possibility of a war started by a "national" nuclear force would be definitely ruled out.

A European nuclear force such as that advocated by Aron would have been just as unacceptable to Charles de Gaulle. The general seemed to want a nuclear monopoly on the continent. In this regard he had caused to be cancelled the beginnings of nuclear cooperation among France, West Germany, and Italy, which was started in the years just preceding his return to power. De Gaulle was able to shut this off even before he came back to power, thanks to his influence over the Minister of Defense at the time, Jacques Chaban-Delmas.[29]

It appears that, for de Gaulle, any nuclear force on the continent of Western Europe had to be under the hegemony of France, and he preferred that there exist only one such nuclear force: the French *force de frappe*. For de Gaulle, such a monopoly seemed to represent at the same time a ticket of admission to the club of the great powers and the means of subordinating the former conqueror of France in 1940: Germany, which was already handicapped by the constitutional limitation concerning the development of nuclear weapons on its soil, and which remained cut off from its *laenders* to the east.

For the Americans, de Gaulle's pretension was "incredible": "It seems incredible that de Gaulle could have envisaged a West Germany that would be subordinate to France in international affairs when the relative strength and power (with the exception of nuclear matters) is examined."[30]

De Gaulle's reasoning appears to have been the following: Obviously, he knew he could not prevent the emergence of Great Britain as a nuclear power (aided by the United States, of course). On the other hand he thought he could establish nuclear hegemony hold over the rest of the continent of Western Europe by virtue of: (1) the suppression of the Multilateral Force, which would have put nuclear weapons in the hands of continental powers; and (2) the exclusion of Great Britain, a nuclear power, from a continental grouping by his veto of British entry into the Common Market.

General de Gaulle aimed at both objectives in one fell swoop—during his famous press conference of January 14, 1963, the first dramatic juncture in the MLF affair—less than a month after the Anglo-American accord at Nassau. By the Nassau agreement, President Kennedy gave in to the insistent entreaties of Prime Minister Harold MacMillan, not quite recovered from the U.S. cancellation of the Skybolt missile, by consenting to sell the British Polaris missiles for British nuclear warheads, to be launched from submarines the British would build.[31] At the same time Great Britain accepted becoming a part of the MLF, but with a clause that gave it the right to withdraw its forces if its national interests were suddenly in danger. In de Gaulle's eyes, this proof of loyalty toward the American ally, and this gesture of reserve toward Europe (in accepting the American-built Polaris missile), publicly justified the notion that Great Britain would not be a fit member of the Common Market.

From the moment of that press conference, when de Gaulle refused at the same time the MLF, in turning down a similar offer of Polaris missiles for France (whose hollowness was evident from the fact that France at the time had neither the warheads nor the submarines to go with them), as well as British entry into the Common Market, the general could develop his own nuclear strike force in tranquility—on the condition that neither the Multilateral Force nor a variant thereof come into being. It is interesting to note that each time in the two ensuing years (1963–65), whenever it appeared that the United States was about to create a bilateral (with the Germans) or a trilateral nuclear force (with the Germans and the British), tension mounted in Paris. This was particularly the case in November 1964, which was the second dramatic juncture in the MLF affair. The main objective seemed always to be that no other continental power in Western Europe get its hands on nuclear weapons.

In this context it is interesting to note de Gaulle's words in the January 14, 1963, press conference. He admitted that France could have used the same escape mechanism as Great Britain—that is, the possibility of withdrawing the French element in the MLF in a case where its national interests were threatened, as for example in its overseas territories. But de Gaulle stressed that it would be very difficult from an operational point of view to remove French elements from the MLF and use them for France.

General de Gaulle later was to reach the heights of operational infeasibility when, in 1966, he refused the Americans the principle of "right of return" to the ex-NATO bases in France in an emergency; this could only be granted after a French declaration of war![32] But operational infeasibility was not the central issue with de Gaulle, who probably figured that the American strategic nuclear force would be sufficient in any case to deter the Soviets. The central concern was not to let any foreign power gain control over French nuclear capability, not to allow French sovereignty to become compromised in any way, and indeed not to allow any nonnuclear power on the continent of Western Europe to gain a nuclear weapons capability.

This policy of nuclear hegemony is very well described in a telegram from

Ambassador Bohlen in Paris, dated January 5, 1965. Bohlen stated outright that the goal of France's nuclear policy, though very rarely admitted, was to maintain hegemony for France on the continent of Western Europe:

From the nature of the objections which the French have brought forward to the MLF, it would appear to me that the real French objection is the recognition that any form of NATO (or outside NATO) nuclear force in which some continental Europeans would participate would inevitably do away with the French monopoly of European nuclear weapons and would, in de Gaulle's view, subject European defense to American veto and American control rather than French. The French undoubtedly feel that given the difficulties which the Germans would encounter (the WEU treaties, the lack of place of test, shortage of raw material), France could easily retain in the future under any circumstances the advance she has over Germany in this field. . . .

This central aim of French policy has rarely been enunciated and does not figure among the public chief objections to the MLF, but it is what lies behind the charge that the MLF is divisive.[33]

De Gaulle himself, during a long conversation with Secretary of State Dean Rusk on December 14, 1964, revealed something of his real intentions—that is, his desire to obtain nuclear hegemony on the Continent. After having recognized that the United States would keep control over the MLF's nuclear weapons and that it was the United States's decision alone in regard to their use, de Gaulle observed that nevertheless the MLF would give the appearance of German participation in the use of nuclear weapons. And he added, according to the telegram of the American Embassy in Paris, that

the MLF will not eliminate the German appetite [for nuclear weapons] but in all probability will increase it. . . . He said even more importantly it changed the entire texture of the organization of the Alliance which had been based upon the proposition of the equality of European countries under the protection of the U.S., and this would give the Germans a privileged position. The MLF would be disastrous for NATO.[34]

In other words the MLF, in French eyes, was "divisive" to the alliance in the sense that if Germany came to have nuclear weapons it would then outweigh France significantly. Consequently, within the alliance system in Europe, the "equality" referred to by de Gaulle (better read as "equilibrium") would be lost. Put another way, the MLF violated Lord Ismay's dictum that one of the objectives of NATO was to "keep Germany down."

Clearly, de Gaulle was playing his own game for France, and this meant gaining time. During the 1960s he awaited the moment when the French nuclear weapon would become operational, all the time doing his best to prevent the emergence of a Western European nuclear capability. In the same conversation with Rusk on December 14, 1964, de Gaulle, as was often his wont, partially revealed his game:

De Gaulle agreed that at some time in the future there would have to be discussion on the coordination of nuclear weapons in time of war. He said they would be ready to discuss this in 1967 or 1968 at which time they would be ready to take up the changes in the organization of the Alliance if there was no drama or crisis at that time.[35]

At the end of this period, during which he had "left time to time,"[36] the French nuclear arm was operational, the French were out of the military structure of NATO, and the general had arrived at his goal of nuclear hegemony over the continent of Western Europe, as the Americans had renounced the MLF. Moreover, and indirectly serving his aim of nuclear hegemony, the United States had succeeded in putting into effect the treaty of nonproliferation, signed on July 1, 1968 (to which France did not adhere until 1991).

After de Gaulle's death the British entered the Common Market and thus continental Europe, but by this time it mattered less in terms of Gaullist intentions: France had achieved strategic parity with Great Britain. And in a posthumous coronation of de Gaulle's nuclear policy, the national nuclear forces of France and Great Britain were recognized by NATO during the Ottawa Conference of 1974 as making a contribution to the overall strategy of the alliance (which is the subject of the next chapter).

FRENCH AND AMERICAN NUCLEAR DIVERGENCES

During the numerous discussions that took place within the North Atlantic Council, there were three fundamental questions concerning nuclear relations between the United States and its allies, all closely linked:

- Provision by the U.S. of nuclear weapons information to NATO.
- Assurances of the U.S. that it will maintain [an] adequate nuclear capability at the disposal of the alliance.
- Guidelines for the use of nuclear weapons.[37]

The question of the sharing of nuclear information among the three principal Western Allies of World War II constituted an apple of discord in varying ways until the 1970s. By the McMahon Act of 1946 the United States in effect renounced the wartime cooperation with Great Britain in what had been called "alloy tubes" (the code name for the atomic bomb).[38] The law was categoric:

until Congress declares by joint resolution that effective and enforceable international safeguards against the use of atomic energy for destructive purposes have been established, there shall be no exchange of information with other nations with respect to the use of atomic energy for industrial purposes.[39]

During the 1950s and the presidency of General Eisenhower, it seemed to some contradictory, and especially to Ike himself, not to be able to share with the Allies what the Soviets already knew. At least Eisenhower and a few others in the administration seemed conscious of the contradiction noted by Raymond Aron.[40] Congress, on the other hand, generally did not want to divulge such information.

A modification of the McMahon Law came into effect on August 30, 1954 (the date, incidentally, of the rejection of the EDC by the French National Assembly). In a new law, called the Atomic Energy Act of 1954, the president was authorized to convey "restricted data," that is, information on atomic energy, in certain areas exclusive of those that had to do with the design or manufacture of atomic weapons. Specifically, the 1954 law authorized the president to make the decision to cooperate with another nation or with a regional defense organization (e.g., NATO) and to communicate data on: (1) the development of defense plans; (2) the training of personnel in the employment of and defense against atomic weapons; and (3) the evaluation of the capabilities of potential enemies in the employment of atomic weapons. However, such cooperation could not involve "the communication of Restricted Data relating to the design or fabrication of atomic weapons."[41]

For General Lauris Norstad, the SACEUR, a modification of the McMahon Act along these lines did not go far enough. Conveying testimony to Congress on June 4, 1958, concerning possible amendments to the 1954 act, Norstad admitted that the latter had allowed NATO forces to make some progress, but that "the restrictions imposed by this Act still prevent NATO forces from training on a fully realistic basis or developing the operational capability and readiness status required, particularly in view of the many types of modern atomic weapons which are now becoming available."[42]

Finally, on July 2, 1958 (two months before the "Memorandum on the Directory"), a new law added another category of information to exchange with another nation or regional defense organization beyond the three in the 1954 act: the development of compatible delivery systems for atomic weapons. Additionally, the new law permitted cooperation with another nation in terms of communicating restricted data on atomic weapons provided such information was necessary to improve its capability in this area and "*provided that nation has made substantial progress in the development of nuclear weapons*" (emphasis added).[43] A further clause mandated

that the proposed cooperation . . . will promote and will not constitute an unreasonable risk to the common defense and security, while such other nation is participating with the United States pursuant to an international arrangement by substantial and material contributions to the mutual defense and security.[44]

The clause cited immediately above meant, inter alia, that the candidate nation for cooperation had to meet certain security standards.

Clearly, the 1958 act harked back to the close relations that had existed in the past between Great Britain and the United States in the nuclear field. Coming less than two years after the Suez debacle, it helped to close the parenthesis on that unfortunate chapter in relations between London and Washington.

Because of several factors, one being the widespread suspicion that the French government was infiltrated by the Soviets, due in part to the significant presence of a Communist Party in France,[45] the 1958 act was phrased in such a way that the Americans could cooperate with the British in the nuclear field but not with the French. This was clear through the innocuous-sounding formula of "substantial progress." France, not yet at this stage, was not included. The 1958 act, besides admitting Great Britain to the "club," was essentially a means of excluding France without naming her. At the other end of the tunnel—if France did make "substantial progress"—there would always be the difficulty of getting Congress to accept the idea that French "security" was adequate. Finally, the language referring to a nation "participating with the United States pursuant to an international arrangement" constituted in effect a bar to assistance for a French *national* nuclear deterrent. In short, France was blocked from all sides, and this situation was to prevail essentially until the 1970s and the "Year of Europe."

This intention to exclude France from the American-led nuclear "club" is clear through documents of the period. General Norstad, who was not among those who favored nuclear sharing with France, made the point with a seeming touch of satisfaction (emphasis added):

[I]t may finally have been brought home to the authorities here [in Paris] that there is an American law and that this law clearly excludes them from any further benefits as far as weapons or technical information for national purposes are concerned, unless it is changed or unless there is a new interpretation of "substantial progress" which would be acceptable to Congress, *although contrary to their original intent.* It may now occur to some of the responsible people here in Paris that a policy of negativism and non-cooperation provides no basis for hope of a changed attitude on the Hill.[46]

Toward the end of the 1950s, the salient issue between France and the United States on nuclear matters became that of assistance in the development of French nuclear submarines. This originated with a speech by John Foster Dulles in December 1957 at a NATO Council meeting, at which he said that the United States intended to share more nuclear information with its allies and specifically mentioned atomic submarines. He said the U.S. government would seek new legislation to this effect.[47] There followed the new Atomic Energy Act of July 2, 1958, which did not however fulfill the expectations of Dulles's speech of the previous December, as only the British were given an overall entree to atomic energy information, including that for nuclear submarines.

Ensuing developments further complicated the situation. As a follow-on to the law, the U.S. government concluded in the Fall of 1958 that the French Atomic Energy Commission (*Commissariat à l'ènergie atomique*, CEA) was not politically reliable.[48] Then, in the spring of 1959, de Gaulle withdrew the

French Mediterranean fleet from the integrated command of NATO, causing Washington to break off nuclear negotiations with the French Navy, which it had been conducting separately from those with the CEA.

The outcome, less than satisfactory to the French, was an "Agreement for Cooperation with France for Mutual Defense Purposes," signed on May 7, 1959. It consisted of a fuel supply agreement with the CEA on enriched uranium. The agreement excluded the provision of restricted data, introduced safeguards to ensure that the fuel would be used only in a land-based prototype nuclear submarine plant, and limited the fuel supply to ten years.[49]

According to American records, there were no discussions with the French on whether they intended to develop a nuclear submarine of the Polaris type, to be used as a launching platform for nuclear weapons. Washington was "operating largely on the presumption that the ultimate goal of the cooperation would be the development by France independently, except for the use of U.S. enriched uranium, of a capability to build hunter-killer type submarines."[50]

What complicated the situation further was that the United States, having developed its own Polaris-type submarine (SSBN), now became conscious of the need for protecting this technology, particularly in view of the difficulties the Soviets were having in developing a nuclear submarine.[51] Responses to the French, therefore, were "sharply limited to exclude assistance in SSBN's."[52]

De Gaulle himself visited the United States from April 22 to 26, 1960. He was well aware of U.S. hesitancy on nuclear sharing with France. Almost a year earlier, in his letter to Eisenhower on May 25, 1959, explaining his reasons for withdrawing the French Mediterranean fleet from NATO command, he observed:

Clearly the question [of the use of atomic weapons] would be quite otherwise if you had acted in such a way that we could have taken advantage of your advances [in this field]. But America intends to guard its secrets vis-à-vis France. This impels us to discover them ourselves, at a very high cost.[53]

Before the April 1960 talks with de Gaulle in Washington, a briefing note had been prepared for Eisenhower on a gamut of subjects, including nuclear matters:

• If de Gaulle asks for liberalization of the Atomic Energy Act or an interpretation that France, like the UK, has made "substantial progress," we cannot hold out much hope of favorable action.
• It would be useful to point out the benefits of the NATO stockpile concept and the possible long-term advantages of a multilateral weapons capability as against the costly national program.
• The US and France are cooperating in the nuclear field. In addition to cooperating in peaceful uses we are currently negotiating a third party stockpile agreement for French forces in Germany and an agreement to permit the training of these troops.[54]

Clearly, this was not at all responsive to the objectives of General de Gaulle. As for the participation of French forces in the atomic stockpile in Germany, de Gaulle had from the beginning refused to countenance the idea of a similar atomic stockpile in France dedicated to NATO. And already, the idea of a multilateral force was in gestation, as is evident from this briefing note.

De Gaulle's visit to the United States followed shortly on the French atomic explosion in the Algerian Sahara, on February 13, 1960. Following this success, the question of nuclear cooperation with France surfaced anew in Washington. In the summer of 1960 a series of meetings was held during which the Joint Chiefs of Staff advocated a more flexible position toward France. Secretary of Defense Thomas Gates, in a meeting on August 24, 1960, suggested that the 1958 act "be interpreted by making a finding that the French had made substantial progress and thus permitting nuclear sharing without legislation."[55] This position was opposed by the SACEUR, General Norstad, who was supported by CIA Director John McCone, and the proposition was dropped. Norstad's argument, which had been put forth in a meeting earlier that month, was the following:

• If the U.S. creates another nuclear power, it will make it much more difficult for the future Germany to resist getting into the field also. Germany is as much a "great power" as France in terms of population and gross national product.

• It is also very difficult to explain to Italy that France should have a special status.

• Sharing nuclear weapons information with the French will not "buy" any better French cooperation in NATO. Prestige is the real French motive for desiring an independent nuclear capability. There is nothing to be gained from the U.S. point of view in helping them attain an independent capability more quickly than they will by their own efforts.[56]

Against a background of a constant reserve on the part of Washington toward nuclear sharing with France, and on the French side a feeling of bitterness over the issue, in December 1960, at the end of the Eisenhower presidency, the United States launched the idea of a Multilateral Force with nuclear weapons.

GENESIS OF THE MULTILATERAL FORCE

This plan [of the Multilateral Force] seeks to reply via a military gimmick to a question that is political in all respects: how to correct the fantastic inequality among the different members [of the Alliance], who are theoretically equal; to wit, the fact that one of them has complete freedom of control over practically the entire nuclear potential of the said Alliance, without the others having a say.[57]

Toward the end of 1964, which, as noted above, was a critical juncture in the debate over the MLF, André Fontaine wrote a historical overview of the subject in *Le Monde*.[58] The second in this series was "In Which a Harvard Professor, after the Rejection of the Polaris by France, Invents the MLF."

Fontaine was referring to Robert Bowie, the former head of the Policy Planning Staff of the Department of State. In a conversation of December 1990,[59] Bowie recounted his role in the genesis of this idea, which never came to fruition.

In December 1959 in Paris, at the time of the annual meeting of the North Atlantic Council, Secretary of State Christian Herter, the successor to John Foster Dulles who had died seven months earlier, came out in favor of a "ten-year plan" for NATO. Upon returning to Washington, Herter, who had only a vague idea of what he had in mind in making the proposal, assigned Gerald Smith, then chief of the Policy Planning Staff, to draw up such a plan. Smith suggested that Bowie, who had been his predecessor in the Policy Planning Staff between 1953 and 1957, and who had returned to Harvard, come back to Washington at the head of a small working group charged with the conception and drafting of this plan.

The Bowie Report, as it came to be known, dealt essentially with two problems. First was the necessity to increase conventional forces within the Atlantic alliance. This was the precursor of the concept of "flexible response," but not yet known under that name. It was a reaction to the significant increase in Soviet nuclear power, which had the resulting effect of putting the conventional forces of NATO in a weakened and exposed position.

Second, was a clear feeling in Washington that something should be done for the Europeans, who felt excluded from discussions on strategy, including and especially the use of nuclear weapons. It was at a moment when the Soviets, having practically attained strategic parity, were in a position potentially to threaten American cities. For the Europeans, this meant that the U.S. commitment to defend Europe could be called into question. Were the Americans prepared to sacrifice their cities for European cities? Certain French strategic thinkers, such as General Pierre Gallois and a number of British parliamentarians (during a debate in the House of Commons at the time), expressed strong doubts.

And yet the European continent depended entirely on the protection of the United States—the so-called American nuclear umbrella. The proposal for a Multilateral Force (MLF) was therefore a way of deflecting the feeling of non-participation the Europeans were experiencing. Associating them in the development and operation of medium-range ballistic missiles (MRBMs), which could be launched from Europe against targets in the Soviet Union, was a way of overcoming this sense of impotence.

The Bowie Plan was borne out of an idea launched by the SACEUR, General Norstad: a NATO nuclear force consisting of mobile nuclear missiles mounted on trucks which would move around on roads.[60] Bowie, as a result of visits to SHAPE, was aware of Norstad's idea and respected his views; however, Bowie realized the political impracticality of missiles being moved around on roads. He was nevertheless in agreement with Norstad that the Europeans were beginning to doubt the reliability of the American nuclear umbrella. In Europe voices were being heard in favor of national nuclear forces on the grounds that the Americans were ultimately not a reliable partner. The Suez affair, at one point during which the Soviets held out the threat of bombing London and Paris if the operation continued, was cited as an example of the lack of credibility of the American nuclear deterrent. At that point, according to the account of the French Ambassador to Washington, France asked for a declaration that in such an event the United States would bomb Moscow. No answer had been received by the time the cease-fire intervened.[61]

That such doubts existed about the reliability of American deterrence were undeniable, but they also served the ends of those leaders who had to justify the enormous sums spent in achieving a national nuclear deterrent. On the other hand, in Bowie's view, the British and French insistence on their own national means could only increase the insecurity of the other Europeans, in the first place the Germans. In Washington there was great receptivity to this line of reasoning. At a meeting on the MLF on April 10, 1964, Assistant Secretary of State George Ball discussed the rationale of the MLF concept, "stressing the danger of perpetuating German discrimination."[62]

Bowie had three aims in mind behind his proposal on the MLF: a means of dissuasion against national nuclear forces; a way to increase the German feeling of security; and a step toward the integration of Europe.

Regarding the latter aim, it was always in the mind of Bowie and those he called the "integrationists" in Washington (that is, the supporters of the integration of Europe, the European Community, and a European "defense pillar") that once a real political authority had been established in Europe, the Americans would abandon their right of veto over the use of nuclear weapons, and the control over the MLF would be transferred to this European authority. But this long-range intention was far from meeting with unanimous approval in Washington. The integrationists ran into the opposition of those in the State Department and elsewhere in the administration described by Bowie as the "Atlanticists." For the latter, whose model was NATO, there could be no question of transfer of control by the United States, however far into the future.

For Bowie and his allies, the model to follow was the European Economic Community (EEC) and Jean Monnet's vision of European integration. In Bowie's view, de Gaulle was right in the sense that it was necessary that Europe acquire the means to defend itself. But the tactic the general employed to arrive at this goal—all-out nationalism—led to the opposite effect.

The MLF, whose conception came to evolve over the years, comprised in theory at its apogee (1961–63) nuclear submarines equipped with Polaris missiles. The control over this force was to remain in the hands of the SACEUR. By virtue of this command arrangement the Europeans would not be in control. Moreover, in the rules of engagement of the MLF's nuclear weapons, there was a provision for "advance use agreed upon," that is, a procedure for automatic response, based on NATO plans, in case of a surprise nuclear attack. In all other cases the launching of nuclear weapons was based on a decision by an inter-governmental council of MLF participants, with the United States retaining in all situations its right of veto over use.

Some American officials made much of the fact that the SACEUR was supposed to respond to orders from the participating MLF countries and not to the orders of the president of the United States. But few could doubt the primary loyalty of the SACEUR to his commander-in-chief, the president.

Bowie admitted that the concept of the MLF was a better-than-nothing solution, a little like the EDC of the previous decade. Bowie thought that, just as for the EDC, there was nothing else in view which seemed better than the MLF concept.

In contrast to the EDC, the exclusive weapon of the MLF was to be nuclear.[63] Also, and again in contrast to the EDC, the Americans and the British were to participate in the MLF. In his heart of hearts, Bowie thought that, militarily speaking, the alliance did not need this new force; the American strategic deterrent was much stronger and therefore sufficient. But from this political point of view the MLF would have given to Europeans the impression that they had a finger on the nuclear trigger. Moreover, as noted above, the MLF in Bowie's vision was to evolve into an independent instrument once European unity had been achieved.

Clearly, the creation of the MLF is explainable in large part by the fact that the British already had the nuclear weapon and the French were preparing to have one. One of Bowie's avowed objectives in proposing the MLF was to prevent the coming into being of national nuclear forces,[64] which in practical terms meant primarily the French. Indeed the French national nuclear deterrent and the MLF were to develop intimately linked to each other.

These national nuclear forces in varying stages of coming into being symbolized for Bowie a lack of confidence in the common strategy of NATO. They constituted a factor of division, especially for the Germans, whose feeling of insecurity increased as the British and French nuclear forces continued to develop. ''It was important not to give the Germans the impression of being naked,'' said Bowie.

MUTATIONS OF THE MLF DURING THREE AMERICAN PRESIDENCIES

At the outset of the Bowie Plan its author thought the Germans, the Dutch, and the Italians would quickly subscribe to it. The pressure could then be put on the British, and it would eventually be successful. With time, the French would be obliged to adhere. It was not known what the reaction of the French would be, but an all-out opposition by de Gaulle was not expected.

Bowie finished his report on a ten-year plan for NATO in August 1960 and the following month presented it to President Eisenhower in the company of General Andrew Goodpaster. Ike was intrigued by it and ordered that the

SACEUR, General Norstad, receive a briefing, which was done several weeks later. At the time there was an idea that a conventional element could be added to the MLF, but Eisenhower did not want this. However, he was very interested in the MLF concept.

It was during the annual NATO ministerial meeting in December 1960 that the idea of the MLF was officially launched by Secretary of State Herter. The American objective was clear: American control of nuclear weapons with European "participation." Said Herter:

We believe that creation of additional national nuclear weapons capabilities would have a marked divisive effect on the Alliance. It would mean duplication of effort and diversion of resources, tend to stimulate competition within the Alliance in the nuclear weapons field, and increase the possibilities of nuclear war through miscalculation or accident.[65]

The remarks were pointed first and foremost at the French nuclear weapons program, then in gestation, and given the Gaullist objectives, Herter's initiative represented a major danger for the French policy of nuclear independence. Although there were half-hearted American attempts during the MLF affair to do away with the British nuclear force (as when the British were pressed to enter the MLF but managed to insert an escape clause for national use of their force in an emergency), the French *force de frappe* was the constant target of the American MLF initiative. Also, the development of nuclear weapons in Great Britain was much more advanced than in France, thanks in part to American assistance. For the British, it was essentially a question of a delivery vehicle, Britain having already exploded an atomic bomb and a thermonuclear bomb in the 1950s. Only in February 1960 had the French conducted their first nuclear explosion, and they were thus well behind the British.

The main lines of the MLF proposal as it was presented by Herter in December 1960 were the following:

A nuclear force that would be truly multilateral, with multilateral ownership, financing and control, and to include mixed manning to the extent considered operationally feasible by SACEUR.

As an initial step, and to meet SACEUR's MRBM requirements for 1963, the U.S. Government would commit to NATO before the end of 1963, as an interim MRBM force, five Polaris submarines having a combined capability of firing eighty missiles.

The U.S. Government would expect that other members of NATO would be prepared to contribute approximately 100 missiles to meet SACEUR's MRBM requirements through 1964, under the multilateral framework. The US would be prepared to facilitate NATO procurement by sale of Polaris missiles.[66]

A force that would be "truly multilateral" (Herter's own words[67]) did not however mean that the United States intended to lose control over the nuclear weapons of NATO. Subsequently, Congress was assured that:

The US has made absolutely clear that its positive concurrence [is] necessary to release the weapons for firing.

This is accepted willingly and understandingly by all the participating nations.

They understand it would be senseless to think of using small numbers of MLF weapons, except in concert with the great number of US weapons.

Beyond this, voting arrangements for release are essentially for the Europeans to decide.[68]

It is obvious from the foregoing that the Europeans would be able to vote on very little of consequence. It should also be noted that the idea of eventual European autonomy in the MLF context, an idea Bowie, Jean Monnet, and others of similar outlook espoused, seems never to have been taken seriously by Washington. This idea, known as the "European clause," was spelled out in a briefing to Congress:

The German and Italian governments wish to keep open the possibility that at some future time the Force might evolve into a European nuclear force—possibly without a US veto. We will make no commitment.

However, we do not object to recognizing this possibility, particularly if it is related to progress toward European unity and the evolution of the Atlantic Community, as long as it is clear that our consent (including Congressional approval) would be needed for any such change in the [projected] Charter [of the MLF].[69]

National Security Adviser McGeorge Bundy, who became in the course of time lukewarm about the MLF, noted, in a memorandum to President Kennedy on June 15, 1963:

Only among the passionate pro-Europeans like Monnet is there real sentiment for the MLF, and this sentiment itself is conditional upon a clear offer to abandon the [U.S.] veto at an early stage if a genuinely European force becomes practicable. While I believe in making this offer, I am more and more clear that it is a debating trick, for the present.[70]

In fact, the U.S. had an ultimate hedge to the invoking of the "European clause":

It is . . . important . . . that we not highlight the "European clause" of the charter in a manner that will convey the impression we would consider any evolution that would add an additional independent capability to the world without the melding into the MLF of at least one of the existing national capabilities.[71]

This would seem to have been a fail-safe formula for justifying never giving nuclear autonomy to the MLF, as the French were not expected to join the MLF in any event, at least not in the political lifetime of de Gaulle, and the British, if they joined, would do so only with such reservations that it would not be a true melding of their national deterrent into the MLF. If the British really melded their deterrent with the MLF, this presumably would have given Washington the confidence to invoke the European clause. But this question never arose. The British at no point showed a willingness to drop their insistence on a veto, and Washington did not press them.

In fact, the British insistence on their right of veto over the use of nuclear weapons by the MLF complicated all the various efforts of the United States to bring the concept into reality. With the French out of the picture of their own volition and with the British poised to enjoy special exemptions (withdrawal of their forces from the MLF in case of national emergency, right of veto over use of nuclear weapons), how could the others, especially the Germans, feel they were participating as equals in this cooperative venture?

The speech by Christian Herter proposing the MLF, delivered to the NATO Council in December 1960, represented only a willingness on the part of the United States to contribute to the MLF if the European Allies were interested in the idea. The French expressed reserves from the outset, and in Washington a change of administration was imminent: the inauguration of John F. Kennedy was to take place in January 1961. And so the matter was left in suspense. The new Kennedy administration undertook an in-depth examination of the MLF while at the same time conducting talks with the Allies on the subject. As with each new American presidency, a pause set in while the governing team weighed what its policies should be.

In May 1961, four months after his inauguration, President Kennedy renewed the MLF proposal in a speech in Ottawa. The offer again surfaced during the December 1962 conference between Kennedy and Harold MacMillan in Nassau. What was the explanation for this long delay? Walt Rostow, who was in the Kennedy administration and later became national security adviser to President Johnson, described this period:

The MLF was low key in those days. We were on a nice pre-Nassau long slow track with the MLF. We had the Smith-Lee mission. We were getting these concepts known and explored at working diplomatic and military levels. Our policy was grossly out of balance; but I couldn't do much about it. Monnet, Ball, Mac [McGeorge Bundy], EUR [the State Department's European Bureau], the whole Atlantic Establishment took the view: first get the British into the Common Market; then political union; then the nuclear question. It is a major regret of mine that Monnet came so late to understand the critical power and influence of the nuclear question. . . . I couldn't see a Common Market settlement while the UK remained a national nuclear power, specially linked to the U.S. . . . But . . . [there was] the obsession with the Monnet sequence.[72]

Charles de Gaulle, who, in contrast to Monnet, believed that nuclear weapons were supreme in defense, and defense in turn was the supreme instrument of the state, rejected the MLF. As we have seen, this took place at his famous press conference on January 14, 1963, when he refused an offer by Kennedy of Polaris missiles for France as well as Great Britain.

Notwithstanding this refusal, in early 1963 President Kennedy appointed a negotiating team whose mission would be to discuss the MLF project with the other NATO partners. The team of Ambassador Merchant, Mr. Smith, and Admiral Lee then conducted talks in Europe. (The latter two had held exploratory discussions in Europe during 1962). In June 1963 President Kennedy and Chancellor Adenauer issued a joint communiqué recommending that the "best efforts" be made to establish the MLF.[73]

Talks resumed in the fall with the formation of a Working Group, which held its first meeting in Paris in October. As of January 1964, eight nations were represented in this group: the United States, West Germany, Italy, Greece, Turkey, the Netherlands, Belgium, and Great Britain. The latter two had joined on a "no commitment" basis.[74]

The assassination of President Kennedy in November 1963 and his replacement by Lyndon B. Johnson did not slow down much the elaboration of the MLF project, because the same team running foreign affairs and national security under Kennedy remained in the Johnson administration. In May 1964 a report by the administration to Congress summed up the characteristics of the MLF in the following terms:

- A naval fleet of approximately 25 vessels with specially built merchant-type hulls, armed with 8 Polaris A-3 missiles each (200 total) . . .

- No member's participation to exceed 40 percent.

- Under the direction of a board composed of representatives of the participating nations . . .

- Each ship to have men from at least 3 nations. No nation to have over 40 percent of personnel on any ship . . .

- Control and release of weapons for firing would be by decision of US and an agreed number of participants. US concurrence mandatory.

- The Fleet to be assigned to SACEUR for targetting and firing pursuant to NATO plans.[75]

Thus the concept had evolved from MRBM missiles on trucks to Polaris missiles on submarines (rejected on the recommendation of Admiral Rickover) to Polaris missiles on merchant-type ships. And yet there was a uniform insistence that the MLF project continued to be worthwhile from the military point of view. Within the military subcommittee of the MLF Working Group in Paris it was judged that "the merchant-type vessel mode would be the most practical for the MLF . . . [it was] a very satisfactory combination of low cost and high effectiveness."[76]

According to the briefing prepared for Congress in May 1964, the hope was that a charter or agreement on the MLF could be finalized by the end of the year, so that the national governments and their legislatures could take up the question early in 1965.[77] A month later, in June 1964, President Johnson and

Chancellor Erhard issued a joint communiqué of support for the MLF, expressing the hope that this timetable would be followed.

In American official circles a radical change in the French position toward the MLF was noted, starting in October 1964. According to the American Embassy in Paris, the French attitude had been clear from the beginning, from the moment the MLF had been presented as an idea to France and the other members of NATO:

The French said to us on a number of occasions, and told the same to other members of the Alliance, that France would not participate presumably because all of its resources in this regard were fully utilized by its own *force de dissuasion*, but it had no objection to the project as outlined nor any objection to any other member of the Alliance participating.[78]

Starting in October 1964 this seemingly inoffensive French attitude changed sharply, as stated in a telegram from the American Embassy in Paris in January 1965:

In October 1964, this attitude changed radically. While the exact cause is speculation, the French themselves tell us that initially they did not believe the idea would ever approach reality, but it is probable that Erhard's press conference, and particularly his reference to the possibility of a German-American bilateral arrangement in this field, was what triggered off the new French opposition.[79]

THE END OF THE MLF

At the beginning of 1965 the MLF issue was at an impasse. In the face of the new and determined opposition of France, the original concept had to be abandoned. On the suggestion of the British, a new name was proposed, the ANF (Atlantic Nuclear Force), without, however, the critical question of a British veto having been resolved. Such a veto would destroy the hopes of the other participating members, first and foremost the Germans, of being treated on an equal basis. Sources at the American Embassy in Paris described de Gaulle's state of mind at this juncture:

Foreign Office believes General de Gaulle currently quite optimistic because of apparent collapse original MLF concept and failure to date replace it with anything acceptable to any group of countries, i.e., what is acceptable to Germans is anathema to British and vice versa. Given current lack agreement on any specific formula, French feel they have gained considerable time, perhaps entire year 1965.[80]

Meanwhile, another problem much larger than the MLF had already begun to cast a shadow over the overall future of NATO: the destiny of Gaullist France within the alliance. After the fact, a document of the Department of State gave this version of the French-NATO problem of the late 1960s:

[T]he France-NATO question constituted the most acute test of the Johnson Administration's European and Atlantic policies. A combination of US firmness and restraint resolved the crisis in a manner that minimized the damage to US and Western interests, and provided a basis for new initiatives to strengthen NATO.[81]

The fact is, nevertheless, that the United States had to give ground almost all along the line: first and foremost, French forces were able to remain in Germany without the French having to make any concessions politically and in spite of American desires to the contrary; France was able to remain in the alliance without having to submit to the orders of the NATO integrated command; and France retained a presence in two subcommittees of the Defense Planning Committee, of which it was no longer a member: the intelligence and communications subcommittees (which, however, were of minor importance).[82]

Paradoxically, the French withdrawal from the integrated military structure of NATO gave new breathing space to the Germans. This took place through the creation of a subcommittee within the Defense Planning Committee known as the Nuclear Planning Group, with West Germany and Italy as members along with a small number of other NATO countries. This led Secretary of Defense Robert McNamara to observe to the National Security Council at the end of 1966, after the most critical moment of the France-NATO crisis had passed: "The Nuclear Planning Group, which we are developing, meets the needs of our allies, especially Germany. It will more closely tie in Germany with the U.S. and the U.K. in the nuclear field. It will end talk of the Multilateral Force."[83]

RETROSPECTIVE

Looking back over the lengthy time span since the event, it can be said that the American idea of the MLF was doomed at the outset, due to the fateful decision of the United States in the summer of 1958 to, in effect, exclude France from what was to be an exclusive Anglo-American nuclear club. This decision and the repeated and futile efforts of de Gaulle to reverse it poisoned French-American relations during the entire period of de Gaulle's presidency and beyond. What is more, it was following the rejection of the French request in this supreme area of nuclear weapons that the Americans launched the idea of the MLF, a major aim of which was to block the route to nuclear independence for France.

In its fundamental sense, the MLF was aimed at overcoming what André Fontaine characterized as the enormous disparity between Europeans and Americans in terms of power and decision making in the nuclear area. From both sides there was an effort to cope with this disparity, and from the side of continental Europe, the French were the most persistent and energetic. For the French, the key was independence: how to accede by their own means to a portion of this formidable nuclear arm.

For the Americans, on the other hand, the focus was on not alienating Germany, this very important member of the alliance that was unable to possess nuclear weapons, and to a lesser degree Italy, both former enemies of the United States. On the American side, the belief was that remaining with the strategic status quo meant relegating the Germans to second-class status, which seemed to the Americans (perhaps fallaciously) to be less and less acceptable to the Germans.

The stock of Adenauer was so high with the U.S. leadership (as was Erhard's later on) that Washington felt impelled to make the MLF succeed, principally as a favor to the Germans. They were the most exposed to the Soviet threat, and in the eyes particularly of George Ball, Robert Bowie, and other supporters of the MLF, the objective of having the Germans participate in the strategic decision-making process, because their lives were the most at stake, became all-important. Beyond this it should be noted, though it was rarely admitted in American statements of the time, that the MLF was also a means of pulling Germany away from France in the struggle during this period between America and France for German loyalty.

Even supposing the status quo was untenable for the Germans (which is not at all proven), the MLF was basically impracticable. The fundamental reason was the American position that nuclear defense of the West was indivisible and must remain in American hands. The lack of credibility of the "European clause" (an eventually independent MLF free of the U.S. veto) turned the whole project into a sort of trompe l'oeil.

In addition, in a manner parallel to the EDC, the United States felt compelled to go along with the British exemption. Once the British had been given the Polaris missile system in Nassau, and at the same time were granted the possibility of withdrawing their MLF component if their national interests were at stake, the concept then and there became invalid. The question of a British veto was never resolved, and with the British exemption in force, the MLF edifice was meaningless to the Germans—not to speak of what the MLF thus represented to the French, who felt that once more, as in the case of the EDC, they were in effect classed with a "club of defeated nations" of the Continent. In sum the United States, in order primarily to bolster German morale, conceived a European strategic entity in which British participation was provisional. The net effect, as far as France was concerned, was to deny its national strategic interests once more.

As Alfred Grosser has pointed out, the French conventional arm was not powerful enough to make itself felt throughout the world, whereas the French nuclear arm was too powerful to be used against weak countries.[84] The inescapable conclusion from this formulation was that French military force used not in concert with other Western powers was of little consequence. But the paramount goals of France were in the psychological domain—in the areas of independence, rank, prestige—and these were achieved, largely through France's nuclear policy. In the final analysis both Americans and Europeans came

to realize that a Western alliance without France left much to be desired. Therefore, with the passage of time and a transition to new leaderships in France and
in America, an eventual compromise on the question of the French national
nuclear deterrent had to be, and was, found. This is the subject of the next
chapter.

NOTES

1. Charles de Gaulle, in a television broadcast from the Elysée Palace on December
31, 1964. Quoted in *Discours et Messages* (Geneva: Editions Edito-Service, 1970), 6:
319.

2. Ibid., 5: 126.

3. John F. Kennedy Presidential Library (JFKL), Oral History series, interview of
Charles E. Bohlen with Professor Arthur M. Schlesinger, Jr., May 21, 1964, 21.

4. Michel Debré, *Trois républiques pour la France: Mémoires 3: Gouverner, 1958–
1962* (Paris: Albin Michel, 1988), 3: 408.

5. André Fontaine, *Un seul lit pour deux rêves: Histoire de la "détente" 1962–1981*
(Paris: Fayard, 1982), 73.

6. Lyndon Baines Johnson Presidential Library (LBJL), National Security File (NSF),
Multilateral Force (General), vols. 1–3 (NATO), Box 22, Outline for Congressional Committee briefings, May 22, 1964, 8.

7. Ibid., Administrative History of the Department of State, vol. 1, chap. 3 (Europe),
section B, U.S. Relations with NATO, pt. 5 (French Withdrawal and NATO Counter-
Measures), 2.

8. Ibid., NSF, Memoranda to the President, Box 2, vol. 7 (2): account of a meeting
in the Oval Office, November 19, 1964, 3.

9. Alfred Grosser, *Affaires extérieures: la politique de la France 1944–1989* (Paris:
Flammarion, 1989), 158.

10. Ibid., 23.

11. Charles de Gaulle, *Discours et Messages* 5: 127.

12. Combined Chiefs of Staff, the Anglo-American war planning dyarchy of World
War II.

13. Dwight D. Eisenhower Presidential Library (DDEL), White House Office File,
Office of the Staff Secretary, Box 3, Department of State, May–August 1958: account
of a meeting with the President, July 3, 1958, 1.

14. The term should not be confused with the concept of tripartism (Communists,
MRP, SFIO) in French internal politics following the departure of de Gaulle in January
1946 (discussed in chapter 3).

15. In Dulles's account, the secretary observed that the Germans and Italians were
likely to be very jealous of the French (presumably—though this is not stated in this
heavily excised account—because of the French intent to acquire atomic weapons).
DDEL, White House Office File, Office of the Staff Secretary, Box 3, Department of
State, May–August 1958: Dulles's memorandum of conversation with General de Gaulle,
July 5, 1958, 2.

16. DDEL, Ann Whitman File, International Series, Box 11, France 1956–1960: note
from Christian Herter, Acting Secretary of State, to President Eisenhower regarding a

meeting of the latter with French Foreign Minister Maurice Couve de Murville on August 21, 1958.

17. A year and a half after the "Memorandum on the Directory," on February 13, 1960, France conducted its first atomic explosion, at Reggane in the Sahara.

18. DDEL, Ann Whitman File, International Series, Box 11, France 1956–1960: Letter from de Gaulle to Eisenhower (known as the "Memorandum on the Directory"), September 17, 1958, 2–3. (Translation by the author.)

19. LBJL, NSF, France, Box 173, Cables, vol. 10, 10/66–1/67: Paris A-1163, January 26, 1967, 3 (report of a talk by Raymond Aron to the "Association Française de Science Politique").

20. DDEL, Ann Whitman File, International Series, Box 11, France 1956–60 (1): Memorandum on the Directory, September 17, 1958, preambular letter.

21. Ibid., Box 12, De Gaulle June 1958–October 30, 1959 (3): letter of Eisenhower to de Gaulle, October 20, 1958, telegram 1392 of the Department of State to Paris, 3.

22. Ibid., Box 11, France 1956–60 (1): letter of de Gaulle to Eisenhower, May 25, 1959.

23. LBJL, NSF Multilateral Force (General), vols. 1–3 NATO, Box 22, outline for Congressional Committee briefings, May 22, 1964, 7.

24. DDEL, Lauris Norstad Papers, Box 85, Atom-Nuclear Policy: 1962 (2), Paris telegram A-1870, April 7, 1962, 1–2.

25. Ibid., Paris telegram A-2302, June 9, 1962 (containing a report on this article), 1–2.

26. From an article of September 1, 1960, in *Le Figaro* entitled, as reported by the American Embassy, "A Nuclear Force for Poor Countries." DDEL, Norstad Papers, Box 48, France 1960–62.

27. See p. 142.

28. JFKL, Oral History Series, Interview of Hyman Rickover by Arthur M. Schlesinger, Jr., 4–5.

29. This is the hypothesis of General Pierre Gallois, who made his remarks during a colloquium at the Institut de France on June 22, 1990, on the subject of this tripartite relationship in the nuclear area, known as FIG (an acronym standing for France, Italy, and Germany).

30. LBJL, NSF, Europe and USSR, Box 169, Finland and France: France, telegrams, vol. 5, 12/64–2/65, Paris telegram 3893, January 8, 1965, section 1, 5.

31. Interview of Professor Richard E. Neustadt with the author, December 18, 1991.

32. "[The French position was that] there could not be occupation nor reutilization of any French base before there was a declaration of war by France. The United States could not accept this position." LBJL, Administrative History of the Department of State, vol. 1, chap. 3 (Europe), section D, Bilateral relations with Europe, pt. 3 (France), 9.

33. LBJL, NSF, Europe and USSR, Box 170, France: vol. 5, 12/64–2/65, Paris telegram 3798, January 5, 1965, section 2, 1–2.

34. LBJL, MLF Cables, Box 24, vol. 3 (1): Paris telegram SECTO 12, December 14, 1964, section 3, p. 2.

35. Ibid., 3.

36. "Laisser du temps au temps" is one of the favorite expressions of de Gaulle's successor and rival, François Mitterrand. See also the article by Jacques Almaric, "M. Mitterrand, le temps et l'Histoire," *Le Monde*, August 27, 1991, 1.

37. DDEL, Norstad Papers, Box 85, Atom-Nuclear Policy: 1962 (2), telegram TOPOL 1579 from Washington to Paris, London, Brussels, and Bonn, April 17, 1962, 1.

38. "On August 19, 1943 at Quebec, an agreement on cooperation in the atomic field was signed between the United States and Great Britain. Canada became associated with the implementation of the agreement, although not a signatory to the treaty." Bertrand Goldschmidt, *Le complexe atomique* (Paris: Fayard, 1980), 62.

39. Public Laws, 79th Congress, Chapter 724, Atomic Energy Act of 1946 (McMahon Act), 766.

40. See pp. 126–27.

41. Public Law 703, August 30, 1954, 942.

42. DDEL, Norstad Papers, Box 85, Atom-Nuclear Policy: 1957–1959 (1), Message ALO 8–939, June 4, 1958, from SHAPE to the Department of the Army, transmitting the text of a letter from General Norstad to Senator Pastore, 1.

43. Public Law 85–479, July 2, 1958, 278–79.

44. Ibid.

45. "With more than a million members, five ministers in the Government, [and] 160 members elected to the Constituent Assembly, the Communist Party dominated French political life." Georgette Elgey, *Histoire de la IVe République* (Paris: Fayard, 1965), 1: 15. (This was in 1946, but the memory of the times was still vivid.)

46. DDEL, Norstad Papers, Box 87, France Problems: 1960–62 (4), letter of Norstad to Eisenhower, January 19, 1960, 3.

47. LBJL, NSF, Committee on Nuclear Proliferation, Box 5, France: "Review of Negotiating History of Mutual Defense Agreement with France of 1959," 1.

48. It should be recalled that during the early years of the CEA, its head was Frédéric Joliot-Curie, who was at the same time a member of the Politbureau of the French Communist Party and who had brought with him to the CEA a number of his scientific colleagues.

49. LBJL, NSF, Committee on Nuclear Proliferation, Box 5, France: "Review of Negotiating History of Mutual Defense Agreement with France of 1959," 1–2.

50. Ibid., 3–4.

51. Ibid., 3.

52. Ibid., 5.

53. DDEL, Ann Whitman File, International Series, Box 11, France 1956–60 (3): de Gaulle letter to Eisenhower, May 25, 1959, 3. (Translation by the author.)

54. Ibid., Box 12, De Gaulle Visit to U.S., April 22–26, 1960 (5): talking points prepared for President Eisenhower for the visit of de Gaulle.

55. DDEL, Norstad Papers, Box 85, Atom–Nuclear Policy: 1960 (2), memorandum of conversation on nuclear sharing, August 24, 1960, 2.

56. Ibid., memorandum of conversation of a meeting on nuclear sharing, August 2, 1960, 2. In this regard it is worth noting that France had refused to participate in the Norstad Plan to create an atomic stockpile, inter alia, in France. See also p. 134.

57. Fontaine, *Un seul lit pour deux rêves*, 69.

58. Five articles in *Le Monde*, on November 15–16, 17, 18, 19, and 20, 1964.

59. Interview with the author. N.B., Robert Bowie conceived the idea of the MLF toward the end of the Eisenhower presidency, well before the refusal by France of the Polaris offer made by President Kennedy in the immediate aftermath of the Nassau Conference, December 1962.

60. This was during the same period that Norstad conceived and implemented a plan

for storing nuclear weapons in Europe ("atomic stockpile"), which de Gaulle refused for France. See also p. 134 and note 56, above.

61. LBJL, NSF, France, Box 173, Cables, vol. 10, 10/66–1/67: memorandum of a conversation between Alphand and Rostow, December 20, 1966, 3.

62. LBJL, Multilateral Force (General), vols. 1–3 NATO, Box 22, discussion on the MLF at the White House, April 11, 1964, 1.

63. At the beginning of the project there was a question of including a conventional arm in the MLF, but Eisenhower was not in favor of it. See p. 139.

64. See p. 137.

65. DDEL, Christian A. Herter Papers, Box 18, NATO, December 1960: Herter statement at NATO Ministerial, political-military section, 2–3.

66. DDEL, Norstad Papers, Box 85, Atom-Nuclear Policy: 1960 (1), Washington telegram 1024 to Paris, December 10, 1960, 2–3.

67. Ibid.

68. LBJL, NSF Multilateral Force (General), vols. 1–3 (NATO), outline for Congressional Committee briefings, May 22, 1964, 15–16. In a related document entitled, "Essentials of a Charter," May 6, 1964, several voting options for release were advanced on the basis of different percentages of participation in the MLF, all of which, because of significant U.S. participation, guaranteed a U.S. veto. The question of a U.K. veto was mentioned only in the sense that the United Kingdom had declared it must have one.

69. Ibid., 16.

70. LBJL, NSF, Memoranda to the President, Box 2, vol. 7 (2): memorandum from McGeorge Bundy to President Kennedy, June 15, 1963.

71. LBJL, Multilateral Force (General), vols. 1–3 (NATO), Box 22, memorandum from Adrian Fisher, Acting Director of the Arms Control and Disarmament Agency, to the Secretary of State, June 15, 1964, 4.

72. JFKL, Oral History series, interview of Walt Rostow by Professor Richard E. Neustadt, April 11, 1964, 133–34. N.B., the Smith-Lee mission was sent by Washington to European capitals to explore means of implementing the MLF concept. (In this regard see also p. 141.)

73. LBJL, NSF Multilateral Force (General), vols. 1–3 (NATO), Box 22, outline for Congressional Committee briefings, May 22, 1964, 4.

74. Ibid., 5.

75. Ibid., 2–3.

76. Ibid., letter from Ambassador Livingston Merchant to Eisenhower, February 29, 1964, 1.

77. Ibid., outline for Congressional Committee briefings, May 22, 1964, 5.

78. LBJL, NSF, Committee on Nuclear Proliferation, Box 5, France: Paris telegram 3798, January 5, 1965, section 1, 4.

79. Ibid., 4–5.

80. LBJL, NSF, Europe and USSR, Box 169, Finland and France: France, telegrams, vol. 5, 12/64–2/65, Paris telegram 3802, January 5, 1965, 1.

81. LBJL, Administrative History of the Department of State, vol. 1, chap. 3 (Europe), section B, U.S. Relations with NATO, pt. 5 (French Withdrawal and NATO Countermeasures), 14.

82. Ibid., 10–11.

83. LBJL, NSF, National Security Council Meetings, Box 2, vol. 4, tab 48: summary report, NSC Meeting 566, December 13, 1966, 1.

84. Grosser, *Affaires extérieures*, 196.

$$\diamondsuit \ 7 \ \diamondsuit$$

Posthumous Coronation and Détente: The Year of Europe

In the 1950s and the 1960s the United States had totally dominated Europe. After that the situation changed. We had no objection to Europe unifying itself and that it assert itself more. Our objective was to give a new emotional content to the Atlantic alliance. At the beginning of our initiative, we expected this would lead to a summit in several months' time. We were not expecting an esoteric and theological drafting exercise which would last a year and a half.

Henry A. Kissinger on the Year of Europe.[1]

THE PERSONALITIES

The year 1973 marked a transition and a departure from the period of détente between the two superpowers ("under the sign of détente, destabilization gained little by little, resulting in a new cold war"[2]), and also a period of adjustment in relations within the Western camp.

After a period of total incomprehension between Lyndon Johnson and Charles de Gaulle which saw the withdrawal of France from the NATO-integrated command, the American administration, represented by the tandem of Richard Nixon and Henry Kissinger, was reputed to be better disposed toward Europe and especially France. On the French side Georges Pompidou had come to the Elysée Palace hardly several months after Nixon was installed in the White House. It was discontinuity within continuity: down deep, Georges Pompidou did not want to hear of Charles de Gaulle, but he had need of the Gaullist "barons."

In 1965, in the middle of a decade marked overall by stormy relations between Washington and Paris, Henry Kissinger wrote a book on the Atlantic alliance, *The Troubled Partnership*. In it is a chapter devoted to France. Without knowing that he himself would have a ''great design'' to propose eight years later, Kissinger made the following observation:

A society which has suffered severe shocks cannot find fulfillment in the Grand Design of others without risking its identity. Before it can decide what it wishes to become, it has to rediscover what it is. Far from being based on an excessive estimate of France's strength, de Gaulle's policy reflects, above all, a deep awareness of the suffering of his people over the span of more than a generation.[3]

Peter Rodman, who was to become one of Kissinger's closest assistants during the Nixon presidency and who specialized in European-American relations, described in similar terms the Kissinger perspective as reflected in the latter's book:

Kissinger wrote that France was healthy. Gaullism represented something. France needed to be cured of the trauma of 1940. She needed to recover her own identity. It was all the more significant that the French were aware of this and had arrived at this conclusion independently. At heart de Gaulle was a man of the West, and in a crisis he was with us. He [Kissinger] took this all very seriously.[4]

Richard Nixon, according to Rodman, came into office with much the same viewpoint as Kissinger, and he was critical of the maladroit policy of the Johnson administration toward de Gaulle.[5] Johnson and de Gaulle had the lugubrious distinction of meeting each other only at funerals: those of Kennedy, Adenauer, and Eisenhower. They never met in the role of chiefs of state who exchange official visits to each others' capitals. One of the reasons was that the issue of the venue of a possible meeting was apparently never resolved between them.

Rodman emphasized that for Nixon and Kissinger, it was absolutely essential to try to restore cordial relations with France. Accordingly, shortly after his inauguration, Nixon paid a visit to de Gaulle (February 28–March 2, 1969). Admiral François Flohic, de Gaulle's aide-de-camp, recounted that the visit marked a new era in the bilateral relationship: ''not only did Nixon accept the policy of France, but he stated that he understood that she would want to equip herself with an independent nuclear force. At the end of the visit, he invited de Gaulle to come to Washington.''[6]

Shortly thereafter de Gaulle had the ill-chosen idea of testing his popularity with the French people by organizing a referendum on basically tangential issues—reform of the senate and regionalization. The loss of this referendum of April 1969, and with it the loss of face for de Gaulle, ineluctably brought about his resignation. Nixon had assumed office only three months earlier.

It is quite possible that Nixon would have had an easier time of it with France had de Gaulle remained. There was a relationship of mutual esteem between the two men which probably survived the American bombing of Cambodia in the spring of 1970. De Gaulle died in November of the same year. Kissinger described Nixon's "gallant gesture of announcing immediately his attendance at de Gaulle's funeral, thus setting a protocol level all other countries had to emulate."[7] Michel Jobert, who was to become the Minister of Foreign Affairs in the last year of Pompidou's presidency, noted "the ancient debt [of Nixon] with regard to the clairvoyance of General de Gaulle, who had perceived early on the presidential sign on him."[8]

In any event, at the outset of the Nixon presidency, French-American relations immediately started to get better. The group of passionate "Europeans" sympathetic to Jean Monnet, such as George Ball and Robert Bowie, and the various denigrators of Gaullism from the old Eastern establishment, no longer held the levers of power in Washington. However, Pompidou was not de Gaulle, and moreover relations between the general and his former prime minister had sharply deteriorated since the May 1968 crisis in France. At times, in the years that followed the death of de Gaulle, Kissinger seemed to want to restrain Nixon in the latter's praise of de Gaulle in front of Pompidou, because this was having the opposite effect of what Nixon desired. According to Kissinger, "Nixon never fully understood that panegyrics on de Gaulle tended to irritate Pompidou more than reassure him. . . . After all, de Gaulle had dismissed Pompidou as Prime Minister, and only his unexpected resignation had saved Pompidou from oblivion."[9]

Pompidou, although well acquainted with the world of international finance thanks to his long service with the Rothschild banking enterprises, was much less at ease with the outside world than was his predecessor. There was nevertheless at least one point of commonality between Nixon and Pompidou, as noted by Kissinger: "Pompidou was leery of potential German nationalism; Nixon was uneasy about Willy Brandt—operationally the attitudes merged."[10]

In all there was some optimism in Washington when the change in the spring of 1969 took place in France. There was a feeling that the worst excesses of the Gaullist period were now over, the nadir having been reached with France's withdrawal from the integrated NATO military command and the subsequent departure of Allied troops from French soil. Pompidou, who was not part of the Gaullist movement during World War II and therefore not a real Gaullist "baron," was, in principle at least, likely to adopt a more reasonable approach.

And so against a background of a shared distrust of the *Ostpolitik* of Willy Brandt, Nixon and Pompidou, again according to Kissinger, "were akin in their unsentimental recognition of the importance of the balance of power . . . [and] they shared a skeptical assessment of Soviet motivations."[11] Thus, Kissinger asserted, during the first Nixon Administration "relations between the United States and France flourished."[12]

During this period of the first Nixon administration, Kissinger had frequent dealings with his French counterpart, Michel Jobert. "We remembered him as a mousy, efficient little man who was secretary general at the Elysée," Kissinger recalled.[13] Jobert had worked for a long time under Georges Pompidou, where he had been the deputy cabinet director, then the cabinet director in the Prime

Minister's office. It was only later, Kissinger noted, that "Jobert became popular. He began to appear on television, etc."[14]

Jobert had helped in arranging the official and secret contacts between Kissinger and the North Vietnamese in Paris, with the express approval of Pompidou. Jobert and Kissinger had established good relations, based on the helpfulness of the French in these secret talks, the analogous functions of the two men, and their mutual taste for oratorical banter. "They were buddies," observed Peter Rodman.[15] "I rather liked Jobert," is Kissinger's feeling, even today.[16]

At the summit level, on the other hand, it seems that the chemistry was never there between Nixon and Pompidou. What is worse, the atmosphere turned distinctly sour because of an unfortunate experience Pompidou had during his first official visit to the United States in February–March 1970. It was one year after Nixon had come to office. Kissinger may well assert that during the first Nixon administration relations between France and the United States flourished;[17] but the White House seems to have underestimated the disastrous effects of this visit. In Chicago President and Madame Pompidou were jostled, insulted, and even spat upon by pro-Israeli demonstrators.[18] The police appear to have been either incompetent or overwhelmed. Given the absence of a large French colony (like Chicago's Polish community) to counter-demonstrate, the French visitors found themselves very much alone.

Pompidou, sensitive about anything affecting his wife because of an underhanded operation mounted against her during de Gaulle's presidency when Pompidou was the front-runner to replace him, never forgot the Chicago incident. Although Nixon made amends, arriving unscheduled in New York for a dinner in honor of Pompidou, the French president resolved never again to meet his American counterpart on U.S. soil. "The fallout from this visit . . . was dreadful for subsequent Franco-American relations," wrote Jobert, who had accompanied Pompidou and advised him against visiting cities in the hinterland of the United States.[19] Kissinger's opinion does not differ from this: "Pompidou never got over the attack on his wife in Chicago."[20]

The Pompidou visit, quite apart from the poor preparation, seems from this distance to have been premature. De Gaulle was still alive, and the differences that existed during his tenure still persisted in the mind of the American people. Pompidou was scarcely known as yet in the United States, and he had to take on himself all the rancors of the American people toward de Gaulle, including and especially those of the Jewish community, still furious at de Gaulle's angry words (and actions) at the time of the Israeli-Arab Six Day War, when he described the Jewish people as "an elite people, sure of itself and dominating." From de Gaulle's vantage point, this was not a totally critical observation, but for a people having been subjected to the most dreadful experience in history, it was a remark with the cruelest irony. The sale of Mirage aircraft to Libya shortly before Pompidou's visit did anything but calm the atmosphere.

In the monetary and commercial area there were also growing differences between Europe and the United States. On August 15, 1971, finding itself no longer able to defend the dollar in world financial markets, the United States unilaterally abolished convertibility of dollars to gold and at the same time decreed a 10 percent surtax on all imports to the United States. An aggressive policy was put into execution, led by Treasury Secretary John Connally. Kissinger, who had not been consulted before this policy was launched, observed that

Connally had started the fight. Then I was chosen as negotiator. The problem was that I absolutely did not know the dossier. I went to see Pompidou, and I told him that. I said I did not have an alternate solution to propose because I didn't know enough of the background to defend it. In the final analysis this turned out to be a good negotiating tactic.[21]

The result was the Smithsonian Agreement (following on the Azores Summit between Nixon and Pompidou on December 13–14, 1971), where France, as the representative of the EEC, accepted a moderate devaluation of the dollar (less then 10 percent) on condition that the United States cancel the import surtax. Professor Pierre Mélandri had the following comment on the Smithsonian Conference:

Pending the monetary reform that was going to be undertaken, a return to the convertibility of gold was not envisaged. . . . From the American point of view, the advantages of the past system were retained. The United States currency continued to benefit from the position of being the standard of money, whereas the foundation of this position, the commitment made at the end of 1947 by its Secretary of the Treasury to exchange gold for all dollars presented, was abrogated.[22]

The Smithsonian Agreement was in turn overtaken by a second unilateral devaluation of the dollar, announced by the United States on February 12, 1973.

In spite of differences on monetary and commercial matters, Kissinger maintained that, up to a certain point, relations between France and the Nixon administration were good: "We had good relations with France, except in the last year of Pompidou."[23]

Another development of capital importance that took place at the start of the Year of Europe was the entry of Great Britain, Ireland, and Denmark into the European Economic Community (EEC). The Americans began to realize increasingly that the community could indeed amount to something. According to Stanley Hoffmann, Kissinger wanted to get control over this phenomenon before it was too late.[24]

In fact, the Year of Europe could not have begun in worse circumstances for the White House. First and foremost, the creeping cloud of Watergate was beginning to damage slowly the authority and image of President Nixon. His standing, in particular with his European interlocutors, had started to suffer.

Second, Nixon and Kissinger were confronted by leaders in the principal Allied countries who were not favorable to American ambitions in Europe: Willy Brandt did not want the "American connection" of the Federal Republic to prevent his rapprochement with the Soviet Union, which he judged to be beneficial; Edward Heath was concerned that the suspicion of a special relationship between Britain and the United States would impede the smooth entry of his country into the Common Market; and the unfortunate Georges Pompidou, gravely ill, seemed to barricade himself in his last months behind hard-line, Gaullist positions.

It was particularly in Great Britain where the situation was unusual and, from the American point of view, prejudicial. As Kissinger explained it, "With a 'normal' British prime minister, it would not have been difficult—if Lord Home had been prime minister, for example. Heath was the only British prime minister in my experience who either did not like Americans or treated them cooly."[25] All the leaders in the equation, Kissinger noted, had difficulties at the time— Nixon, Heath, Pompidou, Brandt—and so the bureaucrats played a larger role than otherwise might have been the case.[26]

In this spring of 1973 Georges Pompidou had only one year to live and knew it. So did Michel Jobert, his faithful aide of many years. Toward the end of his life Pompidou seemed to turn bitter, and he balked more and more at American initiatives. In April 1973 he replaced his foreign minister, Maurice Schumann, who had lost his assembly seat in an election the month before and who had never been one of his men, with Jobert. Pompidou left considerable room for maneuver to Jobert.

Jobert, in taking over at the Quai d'Orsay, seemed to change. He became a strident supporter of the foreign policy of Pompidou, then having entered his twilight phase. From that point on Jobert's relations with the United States, which meant for the most part Henry Kissinger, seemed to change as well. Gone were the days of jovial complicity. Kissinger stated his perplexity:

Before the year was out, we found ourselves embroiled with France in the same sort of nasty confrontation for which we had criticized our predecessors. The reasons for it are not fully clear to me even today. . . . The principal cause of our disappointment, in my view, was the ascendency of Michel Jobert, coinciding with the physical decline of Pompidou and the political collapse of Nixon at home. . . . What Michel Jobert lacked was neither intelligence nor analytical ability but a sense of proportion.[27]

As for Jobert, he seems to have had a rather detached view of his American counterpart (and antagonist). While describing him as an "intrusive" (*envahissant*) personality who tried to be in on everything, he also characterized Kissinger as possessed of "a certain Cartesian logic" tempered with a prudence not to push this logic to the end.[28]

But it was exactly this "intrusive" quality that provoked the French government's allergic reaction in this Year of Europe. France, having left the integrated military command of NATO in 1966, now saw itself being forced by Nixon and Kissinger to give a new definition of its position toward the alliance.

What gave the Year of Europe its uniqueness in the French-American context was the atypical situation in which the principal actors found themselves: the French president was gravely ill and doing his best to conceal it; the American president was beginning his political agony. Thus the sword of the ''intruder'' was passably blunted, whereas the victim resembled a man flayed alive.

Putting aside the verbal jousting in which both Kissinger and Jobert seemed to take such pleasure, the two governments brushed close to the line of incivility in the year Jobert had the leading role over French foreign policy. Though Kissinger asserted that ''I liked him enormously through all our conflicts,''[29] a serious incident came close to taking place. Kissinger noted that, after the death of Pompidou forced Jobert out of the Foreign Ministry, ''for the rest of the decade Franco-American quarrels vanished like a puff of smoke.''[30]

François de Rose, French Ambassador to NATO at the time—termed by Jobert a ''fanatical Atlantist''[31] and by Kissinger a ''splendid Ambassador''[32]— had this to say about the Jobert-Kissinger relationship:

Henry told me two things about Jobert. First, he said that ''of all my colleagues, Jobert is the one with whom I would most have liked to keep good relations.'' But he also said that ''it was a good thing that Jobert did not stay as Minister of Foreign Affairs. Otherwise, the relations between France and the United States would really have turned sour, and it would not have been we Americans who would have suffered the most.''[33]

The Year of Europe, reduced to its simplest manifestations, began with Kissinger's speech launching the idea publicly in April 1973 and ended with the ultimate response to this initiative: the Ottawa declaration of June 1974, signed later the same month by the NATO heads of government in Brussels. In between these two dates there was a series of sharp skirmishes between the United States and its European partners, which meant essentially France.

THE DISCOURSE

From the beginning of Nixon's term in office he and Kissinger sought most of all to put an end to the war in Vietnam and establish a relationship of détente with the Soviet Union. They thought they had attained these two goals with the first SALT Agreement (SALT I) on May 26, 1972, and with the agreement with North Vietnam on January 27, 1963. Kissinger recalled:

It was always our idea that, once the Vietnam War was over, we would turn our attention to European relations. We often told ourselves that our generation could be the last to concentrate on European problems. Those who followed might be more interested in other parts of the world.[34]

On December 10, 1972, six months after the SALT I Agreement, and with a solution to the interminable Vietnam conflict in sight, Henry Kissinger met with President Pompidou at the Elysée Palace. Referring to the Vietnam War, Kissinger's host observed, "In my view you are condemned to succeed." Then he added, "And afterwards, what will be the center of gravity of your policy?" Kissinger's account is as follows:

I said that after the war was over we intended to give more emphasis to Atlantic relationships. Europe and North America had made no serious effort in two decades to chart their larger common purposes. A suitably prepared summit meeting of the leaders of the Atlantic community might do so. Pompidou was avuncularly encouraging.[35]

Several days later, in an interview with James Reston appearing in the *New York Times*, came the confirmation: Pompidou told Reston that he would favor a consultation "at the highest level" sometime in 1973 for the purpose of clarifying the economic and particularly the political relations among the democracies, as the larger political and philosophical questions had been neglected during recent years.[36] Kissinger had the following commentary: "It was a farsighted comment. In light of the controversies to which it later gave rise between France and the United States, there is no little irony in the fact that the ill-fated Year of Europe was born in the office of the President of the French Republic."[37] "Born" is perhaps an overstatement, as Kissinger himself had mentioned the term "Year of Europe" in an earlier interview with the *Times* on November 27, 1972.[38]

And so it was in apparent innocence that Kissinger, during the speech he gave in April 1973 announcing the Year of Europe, credited Pompidou with giving a benediction to the idea. Whether or not Pompidou indeed had lent his "avuncular" encouragement, the Elysée's point of view, in the aftermath of the April 1973 initiative, seemed markedly different. Or at least Jobert, in an acid passage in his *Mémoires*, so indicated:

[Kissinger] claimed to have also sounded Georges Pompidou, during his last visit to Paris, and to have found him receptive: the idea of preparing a new "Atlantic Charter" before the end of the year, the very lack of sensitivity [*la brutalité même*] of the proposal, on the contrary gave rise within him to a cold determination not to associate himself with a gesture that was maladroit in form, and that did not attach much importance to our interests. We had not over the years justified our policy by the refusal of blocs to then accept a process establishing American hegemony over the Western world, with which Kissinger's plan artificially associated Japan.[39]

The April 1973 speech was for Kissinger a first of its kind, as he had until that time remained relatively anonymous in the White House. With this speech Kissinger, who did not become Secretary of State until September, emerged as the new pontiff of American foreign policy. But overall, Kissinger's declaration represented essentially an analysis of the problem without presuming to suggest a remedy: "In Europe, a new generation to whom war and its dislocations are not personal experiences takes stability for granted. But it is less committed to the unity that made peace possible and to the effort required to maintain it."[40] But neither was the United States spared in the somber analysis of Kissinger: "In the United States, decades of global burdens have fostered, and the frustrations of the war in Southeast Asia have accentuated, a reluctance to maintain global involvements on the basis of preponderant American responsibility."[41]

The Kissinger speech was intended to mark the return of primary American interest to Western Europe. He suggested a new Atlantic charter for this alliance that had reached the age of twenty-five years. Peter Rodman, Kissinger's close assistant, admitted that the term "Atlantic charter" could have offended French sensitivities.[42]

In his speech Kissinger included two elements that for some Europeans were disquieting. He wanted to find a role for Japan—"artificially" (*par amalgame*), said Jobert[43]—in the strategic councils of the West, and in all ill-fated phrase, he ascribed to the Europeans a regional role only:

Diplomacy is the result of frequent consultations but is essentially being conducted by nation-states. The United States has global interests and responsibilities. Our European allies have regional interests. These are not necessarily in conflict, but in the new era neither are they automatically identical.[44]

It was a turn of phrase Kissinger was quickly to regret.[45] Two close assistants had drafted the speech, Peter Rodman and William Hyland. According to the former, Kissinger did not reject a global role for the Europeans; rather, he was deploring that their role had remained essentially regional.[46]

But the heart of the initiative in the Year of Europe lay in the defense area. Here again, Kissinger seemed to have only an analysis to offer in his speech of April 23, 1973: "The East-West strategic military balance has shifted from American preponderance to near-equality, bringing with it the necessity for a new understanding of the requirements of our common security."[47]

The Kissinger speech—to his and Washington's surprise—went unanswered. As regards its defense and security aspects, however, Jobert's speech at the opening of the Conference on Security and Cooperation in Europe (CSCE), on July 4, 1973, can be considered an indirect reply. Jobert put his emphasis on the nation, all nations large and small, whose duty it was to defend their own security by themselves. It was the antithesis of the world of superpowers warily observing each other from behind nuclear arsenals. It was a speech replete with "Third Worldism" (*tiersmondisme*). Jobert himself remarked that his speech "was a sharp departure from the others because it transgressed the laws of the genre."[48] His golden rule—freedom and security for each nation, provided they defend themselves—seemed also to be applicable to Europe. And the April Kissinger speech seemed to be the target of his warnings. Jobert spoke of Europe, for a long time the passive stake of great international confrontations, from now on committed by nine States, acting in solidarity, to the affirmation of its destiny. . . . For Europe cannot be this special area, this racetrack where external forces find their equilibrium, a place chosen for these rivalries. Those who think this are deceiving themselves in their analysis, because sooner or later this is no longer going to be tolerated: at that point when the peoples of Europe will have understood the danger of their passivity.[49]

In Henry Kissinger's memoirs, this figure having come from Europe and thus less imbued with the external American optimism, there appears a feeling of having been deceived by his French counterpart and at the same time a tinge of regret at not having been able to maintain a cordial working relationship with Jobert.

Unfortunately for Kissinger, his vision of the Year of Europe, a rather vague concept in itself, went against the objectives of the leadership in Paris. Jobert (and his president, then in the last stages of his illness) were concerned that a redefinition of the Atlantic charter would result in a more political role for NATO—coming at a time when the European Economic Community, constituting itself into a new entity of nine countries on January 1, 1973, was groping for its own political identity. Suddenly, and in part because of the redefinition sought by Nixon and Kissinger, the conflict between Atlantic unity and European identity seemed to gain in intensity.

Paradoxically, it was precisely Kissinger, this "pro-French" American figure ("Nixon and I were both very pro-French"[50]), who wanted to compensate for the recent lack of American attention toward Europe and wanted to calm European fears of a Soviet-American condominium. It was Kissinger who was willing to grant considerable leeway to France. This was the country of the center, without which the other nations of Western Europe were reluctant to follow American initiatives. As Kissinger put it,

We were quite prepared to come to a prior understanding with the French leaders about the Year of Europe; in fact, we preferred it that way. We were convinced that France's unsentimental conception of the national interest would lead it to the same conclusion that we had reached: that Western solidarity was crucial to European security and freedom. This assessment turned out to be badly mistaken.[51]

According to François de Rose, "America accepted that France assume the leadership of Europe. But [it was] in the framework of cooperation with the United States. However, the French saw things differently. For them, it was a question of independence and therefore of being in opposition to the United States."[52]

The battle plans were drawn.

THE EVENTS

The Declaration on the Prevention of Nuclear War

Shortly after the Kissinger speech of April 1973, in which a return of American attention toward Europe was announced with fanfare, a new event took place that for many Europeans came as an unpleasant surprise: the Declaration on the Prevention of Nuclear War, the result of the second Nixon-Brezhnev summit of June 18–25, 1973. The origins of this affair went back to the first summit between these two leaders a year earlier, during which the Soviets made an obvious attempt to isolate and intimidate China. According to Helmut Sonnenfeldt, a close assistant of Kissinger's during this period, Brezhnev had suggested, in effect, an alliance of the Soviet Union and the United States against China:[53] "Nixon had chosen not to reject outright the Soviet proposal. He wanted in effect to raise false hopes with Brezhnev for reasons that were related to Vietnam."[54]

Over the ensuing months American diplomatic efforts succeeded in transforming Brezhnev's proposal little by little into an anodine declaration. Sonnenfeldt emphasized that, looking back on it, the declaration could be said to have confirmed what was already an established doctrine of NATO, namely that nuclear weapons could be used in the event of an all-out conventional attack by enemy forces.

However, the declaration mandated consultations between the two superpowers in the event that a nuclear conflict seemed possible. During the negotiations special emissaries were sent by Washington to explain this provision on consultations, as well as the rest of the declaration, to the British, the French, and the Germans. Sonnenfeldt himself put Jobert in the picture in September 1972, in a briefing that took place in Munich.[55] This notwithstanding, Jobert chose to take public issue with the declaration, notably at the time of the NATO Council meeting in December 1973.[56] Jobert's annoyance, which was more or less inevitable given the context of the negotiation, comes through in his *Mémoires*:

When power is thus concentrated in the hands of two great countries, what could be more natural than that they try to avoid confrontation? But what could be more natural also than that everyone in the world [would] worry about this entente and the sense of arbitration that it presupposes? . . . The facts . . . had already revealed [a condominium], but not yet treaties themselves since the dividing up at Yalta.[57]

What particularly disturbed the Europeans was the provision on consultation, although this had been briefed to the Allies by Sonnenfeldt and other emissaries. It is contained in Article IV of the declaration of June 22, 1973:

If at any time relations between the Parties or between either Party and other countries appear to involve the risk of a nuclear conflict, or if relations between countries not parties to this Agreement appear to involve the risk of nuclear war between the United States of America and the Union of Soviet Socialist Republics or between either Party and other countries, the United States and the Soviet Union, acting in accordance with the provisions of this Agreement, shall immediately enter into urgent consultations with each other and make every effort to avert his risk.[58]

Behind this astonishing display of peaceful intentions, some saw the possibility of the United States refraining from taking part in a war in Europe in a situation in which European interests were threatened. The specter of Suez (concerning which Kissinger had been critical of American policy[59]) would simply not go away. Notwithstanding the success of Washington's diplomacy in softening the text of the declaration, U.S. leadership had in the final analysis given way in the face of Brezhnev's pressures, and Kissinger himself seemed to regret it: ''the result was too subtle; the negotiations too secret; the effort too long; and the necessary explanations to the Allies and to China too complex to have the desired effect.''[60]

Several days after the Declaration on the Prevention of Nuclear War, Jobert made a visit to San Clemente, California, on June 29–30, 1973. This visit had been arranged between Pompidou and Nixon at the Reykjavik summit (May 31–June 1). In the meantime the declaration had appeared. Already the Europeans, and particularly the French, had become disturbed by it, feeling themselves out of the game and more or less at the mercy of the superpowers. Neither the explanations given to Jobert at San Clemente nor those of the Soviets, given by Brezhnev to Pompidou at Rambouillet on the return trip from the United States, succeeded in calming these feelings.

The Burgeoning of the Charters

At San Clemente Kissinger gave Jobert two proposed drafts of a new Atlantic charter (which he had proposed in his Year of Europe speech), one drawn up by himself and his assistants, the other by the State Department. It was agreed between them that Jobert would not only comment on these drafts but also try them out on the smaller EEC countries. As it turned out, Jobert found both drafts unsatisfactory,[61] and Washington was so informed on July 16, 1973.

Then, at an EEC meeting in Copenhagen on July 18, Jobert proposed to the nine that a Defense Committee of the Western European Union (WEU) be reactivated. Almost at the same time was born the idea of another charter: one that would define relations between the United States and the EEC and be presented to Washington by a single spokesman of the EEC countries. In the meantime other drafts appeared, as Kissinger put it, ''like pollen in the Spring air.''[62] At the end of the summer, Kissinger felt betrayed: ''Jobert had ruthlessly used our effort to conciliate France as a device to isolate us. It was at Jobert's request that we had resisted the importuning of the smaller countries for a formal proposal or a wider forum.''[63]

For not having consulted with the EEC members apart from the Big Three, but rather having left this function largely to France, Nixon and Kissinger found themselves confronted by a group of allied countries that did not want to deal with the United States except as a bloc—and in this case through the representative of the country that held the presidency of the EEC by rotation. For matters concerning relations between the United States and Europe, Washington could deal only with the representative of Denmark!

On September 24, 1973, Danish Foreign Prime Minister Anderson found himself in the unenviable position of presenting to the authorities in Washington the response of the EEC to the April Kissinger speech as well as the position of the EEC vis-à-vis the United States, in a document Kissinger described as ''feeble.''[64]

[The document] stressed the separate identities of the European Community and the United States; the United States was specifically asked to recognize the European Community as a ''distinct entity'' in world affairs, a wounding proposition that implied we might otherwise oppose what owed so much to American initiatives.[65]

That this absurd situation was the Machiavellian creation of Jobert, as Kissinger appeared to believe, is far from proven. Perhaps it was the outcome of two Machiavellis occupying the same positions in their respective countries, in which case the mix became too explosive. Whatever the case, there was something inevitable in the fact that a bloc of countries seeking cohesion thought of speaking with a single voice, especially in the opening burst of optimism following the creation of the community of the nine at the beginning of 1973.

Jobert chose this moment of extreme confusion to make a new start: On September 25, 1973, he presented to Kissinger a draft declaration on the Atlantic alliance that the latter found more constructive than any previously presented by other ministers.[66] In fact, Jobert had apparently decided to divide the problem in two: recognize the competence of the alliance in security matters but deny it a political role. This distinction was not lost on Kissinger:

On the Atlantic Alliance Declaration Jobert was so forthcoming and on the European Community one so ruthlessly obstinate because in his mind success in the Alliance and failure in Europe were two sides of the same coin. Jobert wanted America fully committed to defend Europe but he wished to reduce our political links to Europe to the greatest extent possible. It was vintage Gaullism.[67]

François de Rose recounted the story, as seen by him, of the draft Jobert presented to Kissinger on September 25, 1973:

Jobert convoked me and told me, ''We are going to have great differences with the United States on the relations between the U.S. and the [European Economic] Community, and I will not yield on this. On the other hand, I am willing to give them more than they probably expect in the area of the Alliance. I have asked the Foreign Ministry to draft a declaration for the occasion of the twenty-fifth anniversary of the Alliance. What they have sent me until this point does not meet my requirements. You have twenty-four hours to send me something good, because I have to go soon to China to meet Monsieur Pompidou, and I want to take this declaration with me.''[68]

De Rose came up with a draft that seemed to please Jobert. The foreign minister then asked him to come up with an English version, which de Rose wrote by hand. Jobert, then Pompidou approved the document with minor alterations. The foreign minister then took it to Kissinger who, according to de Rose,[69] recognized his handwriting immediately. Kissinger approved the text without hesitation.[70]

The document Jobert had asked de Rose to draft became the basis of the Declaration of Ottawa the following year, a declaration that marked the end of the Year of Europe. In this document is found for the first time NATO endorsement of the idea that the national nuclear forces of Britain and France contribute to the overall deterrent posture of the Atlantic alliance. This affirmation was not completely to the liking of certain other NATO members. ''The northern countries, particularly the Netherlands,'' said de Rose, ''did not want to admit that the French and British deterrent forces added to the overall Alliance deterrent.''[71] But basically Nixon and Kissinger did not object, and so the document won overall approval. Said Kissinger: ''My opinion was that it was not a bad idea that France have its own nuclear force. I thought that a situation in which the United States alone possessed nuclear weapons was not completely healthy.''[72]

And so what had been rejected by the United States for many years, namely the validity of the French *force de frappe*, was accepted by the NATO Council in a document written by a Frenchman and originally requested by Kissinger.

The October War

Suddenly the October 1973 War followed by the oil crisis burst upon the scene to perturb further relations between the United States and Europe. Although the American presidency was in a state of progressive decomposition because of the Watergate affair, this time the United States seemed to come out of the situation well. Kissinger obtained a cease-fire based on a precarious equilibrium between the forces on the ground with, finally, the acquiescence of the Soviets. The vulnerability of Europe's oil supplies was particularly exposed, and the understanding shown by most of the European countries during the war toward the predicament of the Arabs did not seem to bring these countries any special benefits.

At the end of the year, while the new Atlantic charter proceeded laboriously toward its conclusion, Kissinger decided to launch the idea of forming a group of oil-consumer countries, in a speech before the Society of Pilgrims in London on December 13. However, the French wanted the oil-producer countries also to join in this association. In other words, France wanted to continue with the pro-Arab orientation laid down by de Gaulle in 1967. On several occasions Pompidou had made clear his intention not to "become associated with a front of consuming countries against a front of countries producing oil or any other raw material."[73] (The French counterproposal was for a meeting between the European countries and the Arab countries, as advanced by Jobert, although Kissinger believed, according to Jobert, that such a meeting "could only undermine the efforts he was making to bring peace to the Near East!"[74] The French proposal was accepted in principle by the nine in March 1974.[75])

The Washington Conference

The Kissinger speech before the Society of Pilgrims in London[76] resulted in the Washington Conference on energy in February 1974. When the United States issued the invitations for this conference, at which the issue was the establishment of an association of oil-consumer countries, Washington found itself, at least in the area of energy, in a strong position. As Pierre Mélandri put it, "The quadrupling of oil prices had put the United States henceforth in a position of force and thus more able to 'isolate' the French."[77]

In the end the French government decided to be represented by Jobert. This was on the basis of a coordinated mandate of the nine, decided on in Brussels on February 5, which, according to Jobert, comprised the following main points: "the Washington Conference could not resolve concrete questions in the absence of the producing countries; it could not transform itself into an organ of permanent consultation; and the [EEC] . . . must retain complete freedom for negotiating and contracting with the oil producing countries."[78]

Once the delegates arrived in Washington, this clearly stated consensus evaporated. Once more France (perhaps largely Jobert?) chose confrontation. In this he lost, and admitted it, deploring that the solid front of Europe had cracked. Upon returning to Paris, Jobert told Radio France-Inter:

This conference conceived, announced, and convoked on the 12th of January on the problem of energy by the Untied States government, absolutely did not have energy as the objective. It was aimed simply at reinserting, in a certain conception of the organization of the Atlantic world, the European countries and also Japan, which is not a European country (but for good measure they put it there too). I have been saying this for the last month.[79]

The Washington Conference marked the apogee of "Jobert's comet." From then on he began to disappear rapidly from the scene. In Kissinger's view: "Jobert did not have the nerves necessary to carry out his policy. He would begin by attacking me, and when I resisted him, he completely lost control."[80]

Apart from the personal setback for Jobert, the Washington Conference brought home to the Europeans that they could not go it alone in the energy area without the United States. The International Energy Agency of oil-consumer countries was formed, without France.[81] And by a turn of fate the leaders of Great Britain, France, and West Germany, who had become "non-partners" of the United States, disappeared shortly thereafter from the international scene. Nixon also was forced to leave the White House, to avoid impeachment, before the end of the summer. Only Kissinger remained.

The Death of Pompidou

Georges Pompidou died on April 2, 1974, after having suffered terribly from bone cancer. Some of Kissinger's assistants had heard from French officials that Jobert was entertaining the hope of succeeding as president.[82] Kissinger himself mentioned in his memoirs that some members of Pompidou's entourage also believed that Jobert held such ambitions.[83] Whatever hopes Jobert may have harbored, the idea that he could have succeeded Pompidou seems far-fetched. Jobert's background was as a civil servant; he had no party experience behind him.

With Pompidou's death there were no Gaullist candidates of great stature, and in the first round of the ensuing presidential elections the conservative vote in France went massively in favor of Valéry Giscard d'Estaing, a centrist in the "European" tradition, and against the Gaullist Jacques Chaban-Delmas. With the victory of Giscard in the second and decisive round against the Socialists' François Mitterrand, a turning point had set in, for with Georges Pompidou also died the effort to assure the continuity of Gaullist power. Under Pompidou there was a chance of arriving at a synthesis between the "barons" of Gaullism, of whom Pompidou was not a part, and French capitalism, a milieu in which Pompidou was at ease. In other words, there was a possibility that a moderate capitalism, with a popular, Gaullist base, could find root in France as a majority party. Outside of Pompidou there was no one who could incarnate this synthesis. Jobert's hope concerning "the serene determination of France. I hoped that with . . . [the] death [of Pompidou], it would not be lost"[84] would turn out to be disappointed.

As president, Valéry Giscard d'Estaing emerged rapidly as a man who sought to please and as someone who wanted to put an end to the persistent transatlantic quarrels. Although representing only a minority of the conservative forces—the centrists with a European outlook—he seemed to incarnate best the right half of the French electorate. In Washington there was visible relief.

The Ottawa Conference

In June 1974 the Conference of the Atlantic Alliance took place in Ottawa. On June 19 the new foreign minister, Jean Sauvagnargues, put his signature on the Ottawa Declaration, described by André Fontaine as a "document in 14 points whereby the signatories buried the old Franco-American quarrel."[85] Later in the same month, the chiefs of state of the alliance signed this document in Brussels.

As regards the Declaration on the Prevention of Nuclear War of the previous June, Article VII of the Ottawa Declaration addressed this problem with a statement that pledged that the United States and its Allies would "maintain forces in Europe at the level required to sustain the credibility of the strategy of deterrence and to maintain the capacity to defend the North Atlantic area should deterrence fail."[86]

The most significant part of the Ottawa Declaration was Article VI, which emphasized the importance of European military capabilities, including in the nuclear area. The key portion is the following:

The European members who provide three-quarters of the conventional strength of the Alliance in Europe, and two of whom possess nuclear forces capable of playing a deterrent role of their own contributing to the overall strengthening of the deterrence of the Alliance, undertake to make the necessary contribution necessary to maintain the common defence at a level capable of deterring and if necessary repelling all actions directed against the independance and territorial integrity of the members of the Alliance.[87]

This major concession regarding the French and British nuclear forces was accompanied by a recognition of the key and continuing role of North American forces in Europe. After having noted (Article IV) that there had been an evolution toward a situation of near strategic equilibrium between the United States and the Soviet Union, and that as a result the problems that the defense of Europe posed for the alliance "have assumed a different and more distinct character," Article V declared that that had not changed anything fundamentally, and that therefore U.S. nuclear forces based in Europe and the United States, as well as the presence of North American forces in Europe, remained indispensable.[88]

In this context it should be noted that overall—except with respect to the "legitimation" of the British and French nuclear forces—the Year of Europe did not produce a new defense or security concept. There was only the reaffirmation in Ottawa that the American and Canadian forces in Europe were important and should remain.

On the strategic plane the Ottawa Conference can be said to represent a sort of posthumous coronation of the policy of nuclear independence of Charles de Gaulle. Also, and more fundamentally, with the recognition of the contribution of the national nuclear forces of Britain and France, there ensued a thaw in strategic relations between France and the United States. Although Kissinger would write, perhaps with a touch of rancor, that "by then [June 1974], it [the new Declaration of Atlantic Relations] had been drained of its moral and psychological significance by a year of bickering,"[89] he agrees today that a significant step was made toward harmonizing French and American strategic views in the supremely important nuclear area.[90]

And though Kissinger deplored the lack of vision of the Europeans ("the obsession with tactics deprived the politics of the democracies of moral suste- nance"[91]), it was exactly this insistence on a vision that many Europeans found intrusive. For the Europeans the Year of Europe, which began with the entry of Great Britain, Ireland, and Denmark into the Common Market, should rightly have been the year of the nine. The apparent efforts of Kissinger to get on this train already underway were perceived by many Europeans as unwelcome and ill-timed.

OTHER ADVANCES

As his close colleague Helmut Sonnenfeldt noted,[92] there were under Kissin- ger's aegis a number of other significant advances during this Year of Europe. There was the increased role of what is known as the Quad. This involved the evolution of a long-standing custom within NATO whereby the four countries dealing with Berlin—the United States, Britain, France, and the Federal Repub- lic—would have separate meetings on this subject at the time of NATO gath- erings. As Kissinger noted, "Since the Berlin agreement of 1971, there has not been much Berlin business; what there is can be disposed of in a few minutes. The remainder of the time is devoted to a review of the international situa- tion."[93]

In the 1970s the Quad took on added importance. Its meetings were no longer tied to the NATO Council meetings but were held at regular intervals in the four capitals, by rotation. According to Sonnenfeldt, the enhanced role of the Quad (literally the Quadripartite Meeting of the Ministers of Foreign Affairs) was a direct consequence of the Year of Europe. It is a subject on which even now a certain discretion is observed, although a number of participants, now in retirement, have written about it. "We were all part of this gang of conspira- tors," said Sonnenfeldt, who was in charge of the Quad meetings on the Amer- ican side, at the working level. "We surrounded the Quad with all the mystery and secrecy that Henry appreciated so much."[94] It was particularly important to short-circuit the NATO structures in Brussels, where Secretary General Joseph Luns did not like the idea of activities taking place within NATO's orbit of which he was not aware. "Even today, the Quad is treated with a certain deli- cacy," said Sonnenfeldt, who added, "it is not exactly the Directory, but there are in it some of its qualities."[95]

There was also an advance during the Year of Europe in the area of exchange on nuclear matters between the United States and France. This began, according to Kissinger,[96] with the summit meeting between Nixon and Pompidou at Reyk- javik, May 31–June 1, 1973. It was followed up in meetings between Kissinger and Jobert at San Clemente, June 29–30. According to Sonnenfeldt, Kissinger envisaged this increased exchange on nuclear matters as a means of getting a hold on the French: "Henry was in favor of a certain calibration. He wanted to have some instruments, some tools, in his diplomatic arsenal in order to produce political effects, as he had done with the Soviets."[97]

Sonnenfeldt recounted that, after Jobert's visit to San Clemente, where he and Kissinger discussed cooperation in the nuclear area, Defense Minister Robert Galley in turn arrived in San Clemente in the course of the summer of 1973. Finally, Jean-Laurens Delpech, Delegate-General for Armaments in the Defense Ministry and a confidant of President Giscard d'Estaing, was put in charge of the dossier on the French side. On the American side the principal contact was John E. ("Johnny") Foster. This was the process of "negative guidance" described by Professor Richard Ullman,[98] in which French specialists made known their progress and their American counterparts told them whether they were on the right track or not.

However, Jobert denied the value and even the existence of such an exchange in the nuclear field between the United States and France. Perhaps this was because the activity did not really reach the take-off stage until after he had left the Quai d'Orsay. Whatever the case may be, Jobert maintained:

We received no satisfaction from the Year of Europe, [neither] with monetary policy [nor] with atomic policy. It is clear that the promises of Kissinger were little lies. And he was [later] put to the wall at the time we were told that the McMahon Law forbade that to us: "Cher Ami, you made some suggestions to us and you already knew that the McMahon Law prohibited going in that direction. So you took me for an idiot."[99]

On the other hand the view of Giscard d'Estaing on this exchange is essentially positive. In July 1974 Giscard, the newly elected president of France, learned from Kissinger in a meeting at the Elysée Palace about the existence of the exchange. Asked whether he wanted it to continue, Giscard feigned knowledge of it and said he would get back to him. Then Giscard made an inquiry of French officials:

The Delegate-General for Armaments confirmed to me that these exchanges were of interest. They were helpful to our progress in three areas, which were moreover linked, and on which we needed to make rapid advances: that of the miniaturization of nuclear weapons; that of the technology of multiple warheads; and that of the hardening of our nuclear warheads in the face of electronic countermeasures. These contacts had already helped us avoid going off in sterile directions.[100]

Giscard in essence confirmed the procedure of "negative guidance" described by Richard Ullman. According to Giscard, "[It] consisted for the Americans, when our specialists took the initiative to describe a program of research, to indicate to them the routes that would lead to failure, which allowed [us] to gain time and economize on resources. The Americans never 'gave' us intelligence."[101]

Subsequently, at Martinique in December 1974, in the greatest secrecy, Giscard confirmed to Kissinger and to Nixon's successor, Gerald Ford, his agreement to continue the exchange. Giscard's overall appraisal of the exchange was: "The judgment of those in charge of our armaments [program] confirmed to me periodically the usefulness of our cooperation. At no moment did [this cooperation] call into question the independence of our move and our decisions."[102]

The balance sheet of this arrangement on nuclear exchange seems to have been positive but not really crucial for France in its development of nuclear weapons. This is also essentially the viewpoint of Kissinger,[103] who was at the origin of this exchange and who had knowledge of it, in general terms, until the end of his mandate as Secretary of State at the time the Ford presidency ended in January 1977.

RETROSPECTIVE

In the course of the Year of Europe, which lasted in effect from December 1972 (the Pompidou-Kissinger meeting) until June 1974 (the Ottawa Declaration of Atlantic Relations), the Europeans, principally the French, balked each time they perceived their interests were being slighted, first with the Kissinger speech on the Year of Europe in April 1973 which appeared to relegate them to a regional role. But that was essentially a surface reaction. More serious was the Declaration on the Prevention of Nuclear War, which seemed to revive the old fears of U.S. abandonment of Europe. Still more disturbing was the position taken by the United States during the October War. The unilateral alert decided upon by Washington in the face of Soviet threats demonstrated anew the impotence of the Europeans in moments of world crisis; but it was especially Washington's actions favoring Israel that upset the European governments, or most of them, because such perceived one-sidedness went against both their convictions and their interests.

Looking back on it, Kissinger's judgment on the Year of Europe, especially in his memoirs, seems too severe. This man with a supposedly monumental ego seems to have made too harsh a judgment on himself. It is worth asking the question of what might have happened if Kissinger had not shaken up the Europeans during this year of the gestation of the nine; what distances might the nine have taken from their transatlantic partner had another less worldly and less adept team been in charge in the White House.

The Year of Europe, which seemed to have been a fiasco, can be considered twenty years later as having accomplished something. The task of this initiative was made particularly difficult because of the personalities in charge at the time—not just with respect to France and the United States but also Heath and Brandt. In the French-American context there was the unfortunate combination of Jobert and Kissinger, both sensitive and both passably Machiavellian. Although Kissinger asserted in his memoirs that he enjoyed his relationship and his exchanges with Jobert—both being masters of words—there shows through, beneath the brilliance of the text, his exasperation.

First and foremost, the Year of Europe ended by producing something very important—a more or less acceptable solution, albeit partial, to the dilemma the leaders of the Atlantic alliance had been unable to resolve satisfactorily for years: how to reconcile the enormous preponderance of the United States, in terms not only of nuclear weapons but the decision to use them, with the fact that Western Europe, taken together, represented more economic power than its American partner. The 1974 compromise consisted in recognizing the European (read British and French) contribution to the West's nuclear deterrence, while at the same time reaffirming the indispensable role of the United States in Europe's defense, both on the conventional and nuclear plane. Gone were the days, officially, of deprecation of the British and particularly the French deterrents as insignificant or dangerous or both.

Thus one difficult bone of contention between France and the United States was settled, at least in the sense that France's decision to go it alone in the nuclear area was applauded after the fact. But the question of who's in charge of Europe's defense has yet to be settled in a permanent fashion satisfactory to all.

It is interesting to note that in the Year of Europe, it was a man with a "European" perspective (Kissinger) who largely directed the moves from the American side. That a compromise could be found in the end was due additionally to the fact that the Europe of the nine was only beginning to feel its weight, while at the same time the American government was in a position of relative weakness because of Watergate.

Essentially Nixon and Kissinger produced the Year of Europe compromise; they were able to break with the demons of the past, especially the old quarrel with France. From the time of his arrival in the White House Nixon had sought to put an end to this quarrel, and immediately met with some positive results. And when the moment came for the U.S. government, in 1973, to turn its attention to Europe, Kissinger was ready to confide the task of a redefinition of the Atlantic alliance to the most nationalist country on the Continent: France.

The Year of Europe also produced a response, in some degree, to the old French request for the creation of a Directory of the major Western powers, by enhancing the role of the Quad discussions involving the United States, Great Britain, France, and West Germany. This increased Western consultation was exemplified by other institutions created during the 1970s, starting with the initiative of Giscard d'Estaing, shortly after becoming president, in favor of summit meetings of the seven leading industrialized countries. This summit structure in turn gave birth to regular meetings of the finance ministers of the seven (the G7).

In a certain sense Giscard's initiative had a relationship to the Year of Europe, since Japan had figured in the Kissinger speech of April 1973 as a country that should be associated with the great decisions of the West. (In fact, when he formulated his proposal for a summit of industrialized countries, Giscard did not have the intention of including Japan but then acquiesced.)

The Year of Europe also brought about a more satisfactory exchange on nuclear matters between France and the United States, an area that for a long time had been a subject of discord between the two countries.

In the internal French ("franco-français") context it should be recalled that, because of the premature death of Georges Pompidou and the departure of Michel Jobert from the political scene, the Year of Europe marked the end of traditional Gaullism in France. It was in the Gaullist movement that the resentment originating from the policies of the Roosevelt administration toward the Free French movement during World War II was centered. One can say that the Year of Europe represented the last spasm of the Gaullist movement in its traditional form, as the continuity of Gaullist rule was broken with the death of Pompidou.

All this is not to say that the misunderstandings have ended between France and the United States; far from it. Differences persist in many areas, sometimes increasing in intensity, such as in the commercial area, particularly over the issue of the Common Agricultural Policy (CAP) of the EEC. And defense has returned to the scene as a burning issue with the breakup of the Soviet Empire and with the potentially competing roles that have resulted between NATO and the Western European Union (a subject to be dealt with in the next chapter). But all the same a certain step had been accomplished with the new Declaration of Atlantic Relations, followed by the institution of the G7 Summit and finance ministers meetings. The post-Gaullist era had begun.

NOTES

1. Interview with the author, November 7, 1991.
2. Maurice Vaïsse, *Les relations internationales depuis 1945* (Paris: Armand Colin, 1990), 106.
3. Henry A. Kissinger, *The Troubled Partnership* (New York: McGraw-Hill, 1965), 42.
4. Interview with the author, January 17, 1991.
5. Interview with the author.
6. François Flohic, *Souvenirs d'Outre-Gaulle* (Paris: Plon, 1979), 103–104.
7. Henry A. Kissinger, *Years of Upheaval* (Boston: Little, Brown, 1982), 129.
8. Michel Jobert, *Mémoires d'avenir* (Paris: Grasset, 1974), 178.
9. Kissinger, *Years of Upheaval*, 180.
10. Ibid., 129.
11. Ibid.
12. Ibid.
13. Interview with the author.
14. Interview with the author.
15. Interview with the author.
16. Interview with the author.
17. See p. 153.
18. Jobert, *Mémoires d'avenir*, 190.
19. Ibid., 189.

20. Interview with the author.

21. Interview with the author.

22. Pierre Mélandri, *Une incertaine alliance: les Etats-Unis et l'Europe, 1973–1983* (Paris: Publications de la Sorbonne, 1988), 68.

23. Interview with the author.

24. Lecture of Professor Hoffmann, Harvard University, November 7, 1990, in the course entitled, "Europe 1945–1990: From Division to Unity."

25. Interview with the author.

26. Interview with the author.

27. Kissinger, *Years of Upheaval*, 163–66.

28. Jobert, *Mémoires d'avenir*, 309–310 (excerpt from an interview of Jobert on Radio Luxembourg, December 11, 1973).

29. Kissinger, *Years of Upheaval*, 164.

30. Ibid., 165.

31. Interview with the author, November 22, 1990.

32. Kissinger, *Years of Upheaval*, 705.

33. Interview with the author, November 21, 1990.

34. Interview with the author.

35. Kissinger, *Years of Upheaval*, 130.

36. Ibid.

37. Ibid., 130–31.

38. Mélandri, *Une incertaine alliance*, 71.

39. Jobert, *Mémoires d'avenir*, 259–60.

40. Kissinger, *Years of Upheaval*, 152.

41. Ibid.

42. Interview with the author. See also pp. 2–3.

43. See p. 158.

44. Kissinger, *Years of Upheaval*, 153.

45. Ibid., 152.

46. Interview with the author.

47. Kissinger, *Years of Upheaval*, 152.

48. Jobert, *Mémoires d'avenir*, 275.

49. Ibid., 277.

50. Interview with the author.

51. Kissinger, *Years of Upheaval*, 163.

52. Interview with the author.

53. Interview with the author, December 17, 1990.

54. Interview with the author.

55. Interview with the author. It should be recalled that the negotiations on this declaration were conducted in great secrecy. The Ministries of Foreign Affairs, including the State Department, were largely kept out of the picture.

56. Jobert, *Mémoires d'avenir*, 307.

57. Ibid., 270.

58. Kissinger, *Years of Upheaval*, 1235.

59. Ibid., 708.

60. Ibid., 285–86.

61. Ibid., 187–88.

62. Ibid., 187.

63. Ibid., 189.

64. Ibid., 703.

65. Ibid., 704.

66. Ibid., 705.

67. Ibid., 706.

68. Fletcher School of Law and Diplomacy (FSLD), Oral History Series, François de Rose.

69. Ibid.

70. Ibid. N.B., Kissinger confirmed that he recognized de Rose's handwriting when Jobert presented him the document (interview with the author).

71. Ibid.

72. Interview with the author.

73. Jobert, *Mémoires d'avenir*, 316.

74. Ibid., 323. The exclamation point is Jobert's.

75. Ibid., 329.

76. See p. 164.

77. Mélandri, *Une incertaine alliance*, 98.

78. Jobert, *Mémoires d'avenir*, 322.

79. Ibid., 326. Before a more restricted audience, the Foreign Affairs Commission of the French National Assembly, Jobert made an official report, in which he dropped the remark "Hello traitors" (*Bonjour les traîtres*) in reference to his European colleagues at the conference (ibid.).

80. Interview with the author.

81. France finally decided to join the IEA in 1992.

82. Interview with Peter M. Rodman, January 17, 1991.

83. Kissinger, *Years of Upheaval*, 165–66.

84. Jobert, *Mémoires d'avenir*, 325.

85. André Fontaine, *Un seul lit pour deux rêves: Histoire de la "détente" 1962–1981* (Paris: Fayard, 1982), p. 338.

86. *Texts of Final Communiqués Issued by the Ministerial Sessions of the North Atlantic Council, the Defence Planning Committee and the Nuclear Planning Group, 1949–1974* (Brussels: NATO Information Service, 1976), 319.

87. Ibid.

88. Ibid., 318–19.

89. Kissinger, *Years of Upheaval*, 193.

90. Interview with the author.

91. Interview with the author.

92. Interview with the author.

93. Kissinger, *Years of Upheaval*, 722–23.

94. Interview with the author.

95. Interview with the author. N.B., this is a reference to a Directory of the leading Western powers which de Gaulle proposed, unsuccessfully, in 1958.

96. Interview with the author.

97. Interview with the author.

98. Richard H. Ullman, "The Covert French Connection," *Foreign Policy*, no. 75 (Summer 1989), 9–13.

99. Interview with the author.

100. Valéry Giscard d'Estaing, *Le Pouvoir et la vie* (Paris: Editions Compagnie 12, 1991), 2:190–91.

101. Ibid., 188–89.

102. Ibid., 191.

103. Interview with the author.

❖ 8 ❖

Euro-Corps: Return of the Ambivalences

All throughout these years, France's defense policy was characterized by a remarkable continuity and the perpetuation of her difference, made easier and encouraged by a national consensus, which allowed her to modernise her [nuclear] deterrent force. With the revolutions of 1990–1991, the *aggiornamento* was ineluctable: the moment of choice had come.[1]

THE END OF THE FEARFUL, BUT STABLE, COLD WAR

On November 10, 1989, the wall dividing East and West Berlin ceased to be a barrier between the same people. The date, in both symbolic and real terms, can be taken as the end of the Cold War, or the beginning of the end of the Cold War in its previous stark form. Mikhail Gorbachev was on the way to permitting the unification of Germany: he had refused to allow Soviet troops to back up the failing regime in East Germany. As Robert M. Gates, director of U.S. Central Intelligence put it, "Whatever one may think of Gorbachev—and I have criticized him strongly in the past—without his sense of humanity, the end of the Cold War would not have come about in this way."[2]

On November 28 Chancellor Helmut Kohl announced—unilaterally—his own plan for a rapid reunification of Germany. The West, and in particular France, was not prepared for this swift dénouement. German unification had been expected to result from an orderly process in which France would have been one of the major participants.

It was a moment of hesitation in Paris. François Mitterrand overreacted by flying to Kiev to meet with Gorbachev on December 9, 1989. The meeting left the impression that Mitterrand was not in favor of German reunification, and that he was trying to slow it down or at least control it by evoking the symbols of the historic Franco-Russian alliance. Later in the same month, on December 20–22, he made another ill-chosen trip, this time to East Berlin to visit the tottering regime of the German Democratic Republic (GDR). Only after elections swept the Communist Party out of power the following spring did Mitterrand realize, as Stanley Hoffmann put it, "that German unity was a *fait accompli* for all practical purposes; the problem for France was accommodation, not prevention."[3]

The "revolutions" referred to at the beginning of this chapter stretched roughly from the fall of the Berlin Wall in November 1989 to the failed *putsch* in Moscow in August 1991 and its aftermath. It was precisely in this time period that a related change was taking place in the world of NATO and European defense, culminating in the NATO summit in Rome in November 1991 and the Maastricht declaration of the European Community (EC) countries the following month. As a result of these two meetings, the defense of Europe as an entity was recognized, in theory at least, by all the Western powers. The ambiguities and tensions that have resulted from this "*aggiornamento* in the West," to paraphrase the words of Maurice Vaïsse at the beginning of this chapter—tensions embodied in the Euro-Corps—are the subject of this chapter.

France, by its unilateral and harsh withdrawal from the integrated NATO military command in 1966, had signalled its unwillingness—at least politically if not operationally—to recognize American predominance in Europe. Though France had thrown down a marker, it was in no position to make its desires a reality with the Cold War still in full swing. The 1966 withdrawal from NATO's military structure simply put off a debate that was bound to return in the future. Now, as 1989 drew to a close and the end of the Cold War was evident, a redefinition of the strategy of the Western alliance was inevitable. With the frozen (and stable) atmosphere of the Cold War now a thing of the past, the long-postponed question of "who's in charge here" (in Europe) returned in force.

For the "Europeanists" (1990s style), the reform of NATO was preferably to proceed in the direction of less integration in the command structure and not more: the eventual strategic goal would be an essentially bilateral relationship between a European defense identity on the one hand and the United States on the other.[4] For the "Atlanticists," on the other hand, the conjurer's trick for demonstrating the continuing validity of the alliance was finding more missions for NATO's involvement rather than fewer. These two conceptions were to contest each other.

Perhaps the most persistent critic of the attempt to extend NATO's role was President François Mitterrand. And perhaps his sharpest criticism came in a speech on January 10, 1992, at which time the French president registered his satisfaction at the Maastricht declaration of the previous month but noted that the EC had largely lacked a common approach to foreign policy in the past:

[T]he countries of the Community appeared [to feel] they had to accept without batting an eyelid the proposals of M. Reagan suggesting consideration . . . of Japan's entry into the Atlantic Alliance, and a whole series of ludicrous proposals. . . . It was also a question, regarding the concept of the Atlantic Pact, and its geographical area, of the possibility of being drawn into a series of common actions well beyond what had been foreseen, and of being used as an auxiliary in many political actions bearing no relationship to our interests.[5]

For France, extending the zone of NATO's competence for intervention meant extending the zone of American domination, via NATO's integrated command, to other areas besides Western Europe.

During the forty-odd years of the Cold War, and in the perspective of international relations, the United States can be said to have created a hegemonic power in Europe through the integrated military command of NATO. It was parallel to the command system the Soviets had in force in Eastern Europe, less coercive of course, but nevertheless real. In this perspective what took place in 1989–91 was perceived at the time by some as a double dissolution of empires— the one in the East and the one in the West. As President Mitterrand put it in understated fashion in the fall of 1991 after the failed coup in Moscow, "We have just witnessed the deposition of the last empire on our continent. There is no longer an imposed order. Europe now is master of its choices, or it can be."[6]

While motivations of revenge for past humiliations were certainly never absent from French thinking toward the United States as the Cold War drew to a close, there had been all along a certain logic to French policy which the more pragmatic Americans found difficult to discern, much less accept. Frédéric Bozo has described the long-term strategic objective of France as a unified whole represented by the concept of a "European strategic identity," a seeming synthesis of the Gaullist vision of a Europe of nationalities and the supranational thesis of Jean Monnet: "The affirmation of a European strategic identity has in effect represented for forty years the constant ambition of the diplomatic and strategic action of France, which legitimately considers the European upheavals of 1989 to have increased both the necessity and the possibility."[7]

As the Cold War faded away, French spokesmen were adamant that the U.S. veto power—related symbiotically to NATO's integrated command structure— could not be allowed to perpetuate itself: "the Americans must understand that all right of veto on their part regarding European political or military decisions is excluded because it is contrary to the very nature of the plan [for a European strategic identity]."[8]

NATO AND THE EC: THE RACE AGAINST THE CLOCK

The first major disagreement of the post–Cold War era between France and the United States took place at the NATO Summit in London on July 5–6, 1990, seven months after the fall of the Berlin Wall. One month earlier, in a parallel development in response to the revolutions in Eastern Europe, the twelve nations of the European Community had agreed to work toward a "political union," including the progressive unification of their foreign and security policies.[9] Like most EC initiatives, this was originated by the Franco-German "locomotive." The new "European Union" was proposed by François Mitterrand and Chancellor Helmut Kohl in a joint letter to their EC colleagues on April 19, 1990. In their letter the two leaders suggested the holding of a conference on Political Union—including a common foreign and security policy—in parallel with the EC's Economic and Monetary Union Conference.[10]

On the same date as that of the Kohl-Mitterrand letter the French president and President Bush met at a bilateral summit in Key Largo, Florida. At such French-American summits, particularly between these two men and particularly in the early years of the Bush presidency, the atmosphere was generally favorable, certainly more favorable than most of the meetings at lower levels between the two governments.

Mitterrand returned from Key Largo apparently believing he had extracted a commitment from U.S. officials not to press the matter of a new strategic doctrine for NATO until they had had a chance for further discussions. This was against a background of various NATO organs having been actively considering, since the fall of the Berlin Wall, a new strategic concept, including nuclear strategy; a more politically oriented alliance; and new initiatives of friendship toward Eastern Europe.[11]

Three months after the Key Largo meeting, at the London NATO Summit in July 1990, the United States went ahead and obtained a statement on new major principles for NATO which included the following key points: a significantly reduced role for very short-range, tactical nuclear weapons including, depending on Soviet reciprocity, the elimination of all of NATO's nuclear artillery shells from Europe; the development of a new nuclear strategy making nuclear weapons truly weapons of the last resort; a move away from "forward defense;" and a modification of the concept of "flexible response" to take account of the reduced reliance on nuclear weapons.[12]

France disassociated itself from the section of the London communiqué dealing with the revision of NATO's strategic concept.[13] Mitterrand was obviously stung at this denigration of nuclear deterrence, which had been the cornerstone of French defense policy since de Gaulle. In a press conference of his own in London on July 6, Mitterrand issued a sharply worded demurrer:

France does not share the strategic conceptions of the Alliance, neither those of yesterday nor those of today: those of yesterday concerning flexible defense and the forward battle, those of today on [the use of] nuclear weapons [only] as a last resort. . . . Deterrence was created to prevent a war, indeed to prohibit it, and not to win it. Therefore any idea which gives the impression that there are degrees in the use of nuclear artillery, that there could be a long process of conventional war which could in a last resort turn into a nuclear war, all this appears to us completely in contradiction with the reality of things.

... As we desire that there not be a war, if each one knows that everything is in play from the moment of departure, there will not be one.

They announce that nuclear weapons will not be used except after the fact, after a conventional war. . . . This seems to me completely antinomic with French strategy, which is not to take the initiative to resort to force, but which keeps the option to use all of its forces at the desired moment, the latter having as much as possible to precede the opening of the conflict.[14]

There is a kind of logic displaced from reality in this and similar French pronouncements on nuclear strategy. Based partly and quite legitimately on the reality of Europe's geographic position, these constructions nonetheless exhibit a kind of Alice-in-Wonderland quality. Professor Maurice Vaïsse comes close to evoking a sort of frozen assurance that recalls the France of the 1930s, transmuted to the late twentieth century:

Nobody dares to touch the military policy inherited from General de Gaulle. But to remain really faithful to his ideas, France—faced with the changes in international strategy—should not put its "diplomacy at the service of its defense," but quite to the contrary retain as a principle that armies are there to maintain the security of states. The political leaders should think over this observation, taken from [de Gaulle's] "The Edge of the Sword": "Our country has too often in the past lulled itself to sleep in the false security of beautiful constructs of the mind which appear irrefutable until the moment when the shock of reality blows them to bits."[15]

But Mitterrand went further in his critique at the London Summit, counterattacking at a vulnerable point: the Allied troop presence in Germany at a time when the Germans needed the stability of that presence to ease the way for a Soviet withdrawal from all of Germany.[16] In elliptical but unmistakable terms Mitterrand brandished the threat of French troop withdrawal from Germany and hinted that it would be advisable for the other Allies to do likewise:

When Germany is united and sovereign, we will discuss . . . [French troop presence] with our other partners present militarily in Germany and, of course, with the German Government. . . . We do not have the intention of carrying out a power play, but it would seem logical that the French Army would return to its country once the role of the "Four" is over.[17]

Whether wittingly or not, Mitterrand had helped open the way for the creation of a Franco-German Corps. From the German point of view this would be one way to prevent the departure of French troops from Germany, certainly not a desirable event with Russian troops still present in the former GDR.[18]

Seen through the eyes of American military planners associated with NATO restructuring, France was now attempting to weaken NATO by co-opting German forces into an organization outside NATO. Once again France and the

United States were competing, in their historic postwar roles, for the loyalty of Germany. And once again, Germany had an interest in pleasing both.

Like it or not, the two communities of NATO and the EC were now engaged in a sort of race against the clock. The EC was headed toward twin conferences on the Economic and Monetary Union and on the Political Union, in December 1990. And NATO, at its London Summit in July 1990, had set in motion a revision of the alliance's strategic concept and force structures.

THE EFFECT OF THE GULF WAR

Though Mitterrand had taken an aggressive position at the London Summit, he was compelled to moderate his rhetoric following the Iraqi invasion of Kuwait on the night of August 1–2, 1990, and the crisis that resulted. Mitterrand found himself forced to go along with the world's one remaining superpower— partly for reasons of rank and specifically so as not to call into question France's UN Security Council seat; and partly in order to have a presence at the table in the peace arrangements that would follow.[19]

The fact of French nuclear (and conventional) power was reflected during the Gulf War, despite the fact that France's contribution was limited and not on the same technical level as that of the United States. The fact was nevertheless registered, and what took place in geopolitical terms, if not in real power terms, was the first application, posthumously, of what de Gaulle had proposed in 1958: a "tridominium" of the United States, Great Britain, and France to regulate the strategic problems of the world.[20]

This "tridominium" concept, because it does not function in terms of real power, is fleeting. It was operational during the war against Saddam Hussein but fell apart in the incompleted peace that followed. Once again, the French found themselves shut out of U.S. plans and intentions in the aftermath of the Gulf War in early 1991. A blunt letter of February 23, 1991, from U.S. Under Secretary of State for Security Affairs Reginald Bartholomew, warning European governments not to disrupt the role of NATO,[21] served to increase the sense of bitterness and distrust in Paris. As Frédéric Bozo put it, "American precipitousness in pushing through a reform of NATO which offered only a facade of Europeanization could only be interpreted as a will to 'preempt' the European objectives of France."[22]

In fact, the "tridominium" of the Gulf War, operating under the larger umbrella of the UN, had bypassed NATO, the EC, and the resurgent Western European Union (WEU). Essentially due to French objections, NATO was not authorized to operate outside the radius of action of the Atlantic alliance, that is, in defense of the territories of the member countries, and the WEU, expected to play the role of military arm of the EC, was far from becoming a functioning reality. Still, on the levels of operational planning and logistics, NATO was important in the background during the Gulf War, as its assets and plans were brought into play in the Middle Eastern theater. Also, the WEU's planning mechanisms were activated during the crisis: on August 21, 1990, the WEU's foreign and defense ministers met in Paris to work out guidelines for cooperation in the Gulf, and a week later the WEU's chiefs of defense staff began to meet for the first time.[23] American military planners, however, considered these activities as an unhelpful and unnecessary complication which only served to muddle things.

THE REORGANIZATION OF NATO: THE STRATEGIC DIALOGUE

Though Mitterrand had registered strong opposition to the strategic line the June 1990 London Summit had taken, the French asked to be included as an observer in the ad hoc Strategy Review Group (SRG) headed by Michael Legge, a Briton on the International Staff of NATO. The SRG was formed by NATO later in July 1990 to elaborate the line laid out in the London Summit and thus develop a ''new Strategic Concept.'' With France in the SRG became a committee of sixteen NATO nations, not fifteen.

However, the French did not officially participate in the first three drafting sessions of the SRG that lasted from August 1990 to March 1991. Then Ambassador Gabriel Robin, the French Permanent Representative to NATO, announced that France would formally participate in future deliberations of the group. On March 15, 1991, the French joined in the debate on the proposed fourth draft and became major players in the remaining drafting sessions leading to the presentation of the ''new Strategic Concept'' at the NATO Summit in Rome on November 7–8, 1991.

Although French participation in the SRG led to immediate hopes that France was in the process of returning to the NATO fold, Ambassador Robin made clear at the time he announced his country's participation that under no circumstances would France consider returning to the NATO military structure.

During those SRG meetings in which the French formally participated, major concessions were wrung from the United States, according to American officials familiar with the talks, who became dismayed with what they saw as the French and Germans carving out a new role for Europe and in the process downgrading the importance of NATO. Initially, as these officials related it, the United States had considered that an enhanced European identity and defense role would be welcome, as it would mean that Europe would pay relatively more (the familiar ''burden-sharing'' theme)—just as long as it remained clear that the strengthened ''European pillar'' would be locked firmly into NATO.

As early as the ministerial meeting of the North Atlantic Council (NAC) in Copenhagen on June 6–7, 1991, attended by the foreign ministers of the alliance,[24] the presence of the French in strategic deliberations could already be felt. As Le Monde commented, the Copenhagen meeting would ''remain in the annals as the one in which NATO explicitly recognized in the Europe of the Twelve the right to look after its security.''[25] The council's communiqué hailed the progress by the EC countries "towards the goal of political union, including the development of a common foreign and security policy."[26]

But the communiqué also stated that the adaptation of NATO and the development of a European security identity were "mutually reinforcing" and that the Atlantic alliance remained the "essential forum" for matters "bearing on the security and defence commitments of its Allies under the Washington Treaty." Furthermore, the integrated military structure for the Allied countries participating in NATO's collective defense system must be maintained.[27]

The Rome NATO Summit declaration of November 8, 1991, reaffirmed what it termed "the consensus in Copenhagen," endorsing the development of a European security and defense role while also reaffirming the alliance as the essential forum for consultations of the Allies on defense matters under the Washington treaty of 1949. At the same time, and perhaps reflecting the influence of the "Europeanists" anxious to establish a double vocation for the WEU, the Rome communiqué also welcomed the reinforcement of the WEU as the defense component of European unification and recognized the "different nature of its [the WEU's] relations with the Alliance and with the European Political Union."[28]

The Rome declaration also noted that the alliance's "new Strategic Concept," published the day before, reaffirmed NATO's "core functions,"[29] and mandated new peacetime roles for the Allied forces, which could

contribute to the maintenance of the stability and equilibrium in Europe . . . bring a contribution to dialogue and cooperation in Europe as a whole, in participating in confidence-building measures, including those that increase transparency and improve communication, as well as the verification of arms control agreements . . . be called upon to contribute to peace and stability in the world by furnishing forces for missions of the United Nations.[30]

The widening of NATO had thus been decreed, and this was certainly not to the liking of the "Europeanists." The new attributions of NATO, particularly the establishment of defense liaisons with some of the former Eastern Bloc countries, with implied guarantees of security; the environmental and nuclear security initiatives in the East; and the possibility of peace-keeping missions outside the zone of the Washington Treaty have been criticized by French officials, including Jacques Andréani, the French Ambassador to Washington: "We don't much like all this. One is losing completely the idea of an alliance, which implies a community of values and common political and economic structures."[31]

Though the widening of the Atlantic alliance had been set in motion, however, the zone of NATO military operations per se remained, in the strict juridical sense, the same as had been originally laid out in the Washington Treaty: the defense of the territorial security of the alliance members.

Although technically the French did not disturb the consensus around the "new Strategic Concept," they made plain through public statements at the time of the Rome Summit that they disagreed with aspects of it, particularly the widening of NATO and also the use of nuclear weapons only as a last resort, which, as noted earlier, had the effect of undermining the French nuclear doctrine. Nevertheless, and most importantly for the "Europeanists," the principle of a defense and security role for Europe as such had been recognized by NATO at the summit level.

THE REORGANIZATION OF NATO: THE MILITARY DIALOGUE

Parallel to the Strategy Review Group (SRG) meetings, in which NATO's "new Strategic Concept" was drafted, informal meetings were held in Brussels among the Secretary General and the Permanent Representatives. These were termed "brainstorming meetings." One of the items on the "informal" agenda was a proposal for a European SACEUR.[32] American officials familiar with the talks were disappointed that the United States did not scotch this idea immediately, because from their point of view, it spread confusion among the smaller powers that were anxious to preserve the U.S. anchor in Europe represented by an American SACEUR. Eventually the United States stated that it would not consider a change from an American SACEUR, and the matter was dropped from the agenda. At the end of May 1991 Defense Secretary Dick Cheney reaffirmed this decision publicly.[33]

While discussions were continuing at the SRG level, the Defense Planning Committee (DPC)[34] of the alliance was proceeding with its own planning for a restructuring of NATO based on the concept, enunciated at the July 1990 London Summit, of multinational forces.

Part of the developing problem was structural, and here France was at a disadvantage: although France was part of the ad hoc SRG, it did not belong to the military organs of NATO (the DPC, the Military Committee, including the Chiefs of Defense Staff, and the Nuclear Planning Group), which continued to meet regularly. Part of the problem was one of approach. The French position was that military planning should take place only as a follow-on to a reconceptualization of the alliance. By contrast, the American approach, decidedly pragmatic, was to develop a military structure based on an approximation of scenarios deemed likely to happen. Behind this genuine difference of approach was a leaven of opportunism and cynicism on both sides: the Americans in seeking to lock in quickly a readapted NATO military apparatus still under the integrated NATO command structure; and the French in not wanting to let the opportunity pass to get Europe out from under the American yoke in matters of strategy and defense—an opportunity that had not been there as long as the potential of nuclear conflict posed by the Cold War was real (and, as it appears to have turned out, an opportunity that was fleeting given the "Euro-pessimism" that set in following the formulation of the Maastricht Treaty and the continuing failure of will over Yugoslavia).

It soon became apparent to the French that, on the military level, the swiftly engaged reform of NATO was not going in the direction of less integration. Furthermore, the military restructuring was focussing on the creation of a Rapid Reaction Corps with implied future missions outside the NATO zone.

Eventually, the DPC came around to presenting its recommendations officially. As announced following a meeting of the DPC and the Nuclear Planning Group on May 27–28, 1991, the core of the proposals was a new force structure consisting of Main Defense Forces, Reaction Forces, and Augmentation Forces, based generally on a multinational principle.[35] According to Le Monde, the Main Defense Forces would be made up of seven army corps, six of which would be multinational (the seventh being a German corps based in the former East Germany).[36]

The Reaction Forces were made up of immediate and rapid reaction forces. The core element in the immediate reaction forces is the five thousand-man Allied Command Europe (ACE) Mobile Force, which has been in existence since the 1960s but was used operationally for the first time in the Gulf War, when it was deployed to Turkey.

The Rapid Reaction Corps was new. Essentially a European force, it would comprise some seventy thousand men, made up of two British divisions, one mixed division (German-Dutch-Belgian-British), and one Italian division (with Turkish and Greek supporting elements). It would be under British command with a multinational headquarters.

The British, stealing a march on their other European partners, had offered their 1st Corps, in reduced strength, as the nucleus of NATO's Rapid Reaction Corps. The corps naturally would be commanded by a Briton. Not the least taken aback by this was Germany, the primary land power in Western Europe. The United States, while supporting the British proposal, made efforts to placate the Germans by offering them more posts within the NATO command.

THE "OCTOBER SURPRISE" OF MITTERRAND AND KOHL

The announcement on May 29, 1991, of the plan for a NATO Rapid Reaction Corps to be functioning by 1995[37] caused a reaction of consternation and near-panic in the Elysée Palace. The French had all along made clear in the SRG meetings that they did not accept the multinational concept for NATO. There soon followed another burst of activism by the French, this time aided and abetted by the Germans, who, as noted above, were not pleased at the idea of a British commander at the head of the Rapid Reaction Corps. By the autumn of 1991, under Chancellor Kohl's impulsion and helped by able staff work by the number two official at the German Embassy in Paris, Wolfgang Hichinger, the French and German answer to the NATO Rapid Reaction Corps was ready:

a similar force for the WEU/EC, called the European Corps or Euro-Corps, with the 4,200-man Franco-German brigade, created in 1987, serving as its nucleus. This brigade had been placed under the orders of the Franco-German Defense Council, created in 1988 under the rubric of the Elysée Treaty of 1963. The Euro-Corps would comprise some thirty-five thousand men—hardly a negligible force.

The presentation of this fait accompli was made on October 14, 1991, in a joint statement by President Mitterrand and Chancellor Kohl on foreign policy and European defense, to which they attached proposed texts for a common foreign and security policy for the European Union, to be considered by the Maastricht EC Summit on December 9–10. Describing the WEU as "an integral part of the process of European union," the two leaders called for the "development of a clear organic relationship between the WEU and the [European] Union, and the operational organization of the WEU acting in conformity with the directives of the Union."[38]

At the end of the proposed texts, tacked on almost as an afterthought, was the following *petite surprise*:

Pour mémoire: French-German military cooperation will be strengthened beyond the existing brigade. The augmented Franco-German units could thus become the nucleus of a European Corps that could include forces from other members states of the WEU. This new structure could also become the model for closer military cooperation among member states of the WEU.[39]

The Franco-German initiative had been prepared in strict secrecy. Involved essentially on the French side were Mitterrand, Roland Dumas, Defense Minister Pierre Joxe, and Armed Forces Chief of Staff Admiral Jacques Lanxade. On the German side were mainly Kohl, Foreign Minister Hans-Dietrich Genscher, and Chief of Defense Staff Admiral Dieter Wellershof.

Earlier, on October 4, 1991, an Anglo-Italian initiative, presented as a compromise proposal but likely intended, at least by the British, as a preemptive move, suggested that a European rapid reaction force could be created to act where NATO could not go. The Anglo-Italian text recommended over the long term "a common defense policy compatible with the common defense policy we already have with our Allies in NATO."[40]

Mitterrand and Kohl had gone ahead and presented their "October surprise" without a discussion of the merits of the Anglo-Italian proposal, except to pay perfunctory tribute, in their October 14 statement, to "various contributions, of which the latest is the Anglo-Italian joint declaration."[41]

According to U.S. officials, the German rationale for this development seemingly in contradiction with NATO's Rapid Reaction Corps was that both they and the French needed the European Corps as a justification for keeping French forces in Germany. The Germans also claimed to see the corps as a way of drawing the French closer to NATO.

The position of U.S. officials, on the other hand, was that for the first time the "leak-proof vessel"—Germany's undivided participation in NATO—was beginning to malfunction. As they saw it, there were two problems: unless the Euro-Corps were clearly linked to NATO, and unless the first priority of the German troops assigned therein was to NATO, this would be unacceptable and not in keeping with either the spirit of NATO or WEU-EC declarations. (The German element in the Franco-German brigade has been composed of German territorial troops not part of the NATO force structure. Hence this problem had not arisen prior to the announcement of the Euro-Corps.)

THE CREATION OF EUROPEAN DEFENSE: MAASTRICHT

The European defense identity was made explicit at the EC Summit in Maastricht on December 9–10, 1991, in the declaration instituting a common foreign and defense policy for the twelve, of which the key sentence is the following: "The common foreign and security policy shall include all questions related to the security of the European Union, including the eventual framing of a common defense policy, which might in time lead to a common defense."[42]

The question of the autonomy of this European defense entity was left vague, largely due to the fact that the likely authority to direct it, the WEU, remains in a form of tutelage under NATO. According to the modified Brussels Treaty which created the WEU in 1954, the latter is supposed to "rely on the appropriate Military Authorities of NATO for information and advice on military matters."[43]

Thus, on the one hand, the Maastricht Treaty stated that the WEU was "an integral part of the development of the European Union," and should "elaborate and implement decisions and actions of the Union which have defense implications."[44] But, on the other hand, the Maastricht Treaty stated that the policy of the European Union—the new name for the EC with the entry into effect of the treaty—would "respect the obligations of certain member states under the North Atlantic Treaty and be compatible with the common security and defense policy established under that framework."[45]

In a still further refinement, the Maastricht Treaty mandated that the article on common foreign and security policy "shall not prevent development of closer cooperation between two or more member states on a bilateral level, in the framework of the WEU and the Atlantic Alliance."[46]

Despite all the studied ambiguities and compromises in the process that had led to the paired declarations of the Rome Summit (NATO) and the Maastricht Summit (EC), the terrain was decidedly different than before: a defense identity for Europe as such had been recognized by NATO, meaning in the first instance the United States, and at the summit level. In Rome this identity was "reflected in the further strengthening of the European pillar within the Alliance."[47] In Maastricht the formulation was nuanced further into Europe's eventually framing a "common defense policy."[48] Fundamentally, a "common defense policy" could only imply greater autonomy for Europe in the area of defense.

For the "Europeanists," it had been an effort stretching back to the 1980s to gain acceptance of the principle of a European defense identity, centered around a reactivated WEU, described by the latter's Ministerial Council on June 12, 1984 as "the only European organization that is by treaty competent in defense and security matters."[49] This action was reinforced three years later, in light of the intervening signing of the Single European Act and the intention to create a European Union by the "platform statement" of the WEU Council at The Hague on October 27, 1987, which stated that the integration of Europe must extend to defense, and that the Franco-German position was "aimed at making the WEU an organ of the [European] political Union."[50]

French (and to a lesser extent German) intentions, even at that early date, could not have been more clear. Five years later, in Rome and Maastricht, the first chapter in a subtle struggle of the "Europeanists" to get out from under American tutelage in matters of defense ended. The "struggle for the heart of Germany" goes on, as was evident in the declaration of the subsequent NATO Summit in Oslo (June 4, 1992), in which the U.S. effort to nail down the status of German forces—the heretofore "leak-proof vessel"[51]—was clearly apparent:

[A]s the transformation of the Alliance proceeds, we intend to preserve the operational coherence we now have and on which our defence depends. We stress the importance of maintaining Allies' existing obligations and commitments of forces to NATO, and we emphasise in this regard that the primary responsibility of forces answerable to the WEU will remain NATO's collective defense under the Washington Treaty.[52]

Germany, clearly the "swing state" in this dialectical process, has been subjected also to other than public pressures. American officials have spoken their mind in letters to German counterparts, including an especially frank one from State Department Counsellor Robert Zoelleck on the eve of the Franco-German Defense and Security Council meeting at La Rochelle (May 22, 1992). However, the Mitterrand-Kohl joint statement at the end of this meeting, which constituted the official launching of the Euro-Corps, continued to emphasize that the latter "will contribute to the strengthening of the Atlantic alliance."[53]

Finally, the French yielded ground: in order to lessen the ambiguity behind the existence of the Euro-Corps, in which the two participating countries had differing relationships with NATO, on January 21, 1993, France agreed that in case of a crisis the French units in the corps would be placed under the operational command of NATO[54] (as would, of course, the German units).

At the time of the official launching of the Euro-Corps, Mitterrand and Kohl invited other WEU member states to join. The responses were slow in coming, but finally, in June 1993, Belgium agreed to join, and as of early 1994 French officials were hopeful that Spain would as well. As of October 1, 1993, the

Euro-Corps had its first commander, Gen. Helmut Willmann, who will serve for three years and then be replaced by an officer from one of the other participating countries. The Euro-Corps Headquarters in Strasbourg was officially activated on November 5, 1993, in a ceremony attended by the defense ministers of the three participating countries. The corps was to be operational by October 1995 at the latest.[55]

THE AMBIGUOUS ROLE OF THE WEU

The WEU, dormant until the 1980s, is a purely European organization. Although the United States favored and sponsored its creation, Washington was not a signatory to the modified Brussels Treaty of 1954 that gave birth to the WEU; and, if at some point in the future, the WEU desires to transform itself exclusively into the military arm of the European Union, the United States has ultimately to acquiesce—although there is an "interlocking" contradiction: the obligations to NATO that apply to those WEU states belonging to NATO's military structure remain in force.

Because of this contradiction, and because of the WEU's position of semi-tutelage under NATO, noted previously in this chapter, the "Europeanists" may seek not to entangle the Euro-Corps too closely with the WEU. There was some evidence of this post-Maastricht, in view of the fact that Maastricht conferred a defense identity on the European Union per se. In this regard the Mitterrand-Kohl joint declaration of La Rochelle on May 22, 1992, which launched the Euro-Corps, of which the following is an excerpt, may be instructive: "the [Franco-German Defense] Council has decided to create a large unit with a European mission. . . . Putting this Corps into operation will contribute to giving the European Union its own military capability."[56]

Other than the fact that the other WEU states were invited to join the corps, there was no mention of the WEU in this communiqué as having any authority over the corps. Rather, it was the Franco-German Defense Council.

The Brussels Treaty comes up for renewal in 1998, at which time the WEU could conceivably decide to change its statutes so as to alter its relationship with NATO, or, for that matter, dissolve itself into the European Union. (The British, the Dutch, and other WEU members would have to be heard on this subject, however.) It should be noted that the Maastricht Treaty text paves the way for possible changes in the WEU–European Union relationship come 1998:

With a view to furthering the objective of this Treaty, and having in view the date of 1998 in the context of Article 12 of the Brussels Treaty, the provisions of this Article [on the common foreign and security policy—CFSP] may be revised . . . on the basis of a report to be presented in 1996 by the [CFSP] Council to the European [Union] Council, which shall include an evaluation of the progress made and the experience gained until then.[57]

In other words, there is a mechanism in the Maastricht Treaty to alter the section dealing with the common foreign and security policy—in light of possible parallel revisions in the Brussels Treaty itself as the latter's renewal date of 1998 approaches. Therefore, by that date the relationship between the WEU and the European Union is to be made precise.

NEW ANOMALIES

With the Maastricht Treaty instituting a common foreign policy and eventually a common defense for Europe, at least two anomalies became obvious. The first is the integrated (i.e., American) command structure of NATO, and the second is the French nuclear monopoly on the continent of Western Europe.

The American-commanded military structure of NATO is becoming an anomaly in a world where a European defense identity is now recognized, at least in theory, and in which Europe, if and as it becomes increasingly unified, will constitute a more important economic entity than the United States. An American military commander for Europe was a logical arrangement when the West was faced with an overarching nuclear and conventional threat from the Soviets. In historical terms the end of the Cold War, the reunification of Germany, and the collapse of the Soviet Empire have greatly lessened the role of NATO's strategic deterrent.

Yet threats remain, especially of ethnic conflict, in Eastern Europe and elsewhere. The need for a system of control of nuclear weapons worldwide has intensified. In these and other areas, therefore, NATO has potential uses, but in its present form—that of an American-commanded military structure in Europe—it is potentially, at least, outmoded.

The U.S. reluctance to intervene with American troops in Yugoslavia underscores the potential inappropriateness of an American-commanded NATO in crisis situations in which Allied forces are called upon to be sent out of the NATO area. In the long run, and if it develops credibility and force entities, the WEU may become the appropriate framework authority for such crises, at least in Central and Eastern Europe. Not only may there be situations in which use of American troops would be more unpalatable than the use of European troops, but the American public may not be willing to support such faraway interventions not affecting American vital interests. At present, however, the WEU is simply a shell or, in Mitterrand's own word, a "coterie" (*cénacle*).[58] It cannot accomplish a major force projection without American technological, intelligence, and logistical support.

It is difficult to visualize a non-American commander of Supreme Headquarters Allied Powers Europe (SHAPE) as long as there is a U.S. military presence in Europe. This has never been in the American tradition. However, the day is likely to come when the United States will no longer be the vital element in coping with threats to Europe. In terms of sheer numbers the United States cannot expect to maintain the leading role in the defense of Europe as its troop commitment continues to decline to 100,000 by the mid-1990s. Thus a rotation of command may in time become the pattern, although this would in turn introduce a new element of competition and dissension among the principal European countries.

If indeed the integrated command of NATO were modified into some form of rotating Supreme Allied Commander Europe (SACEUR), it should theoretically make for easier relations between the United States and France—relations which were disturbed almost continuously in the 1950s and 1960s over U.S. attempts to impose multilateral instruments on France while retaining for itself the benefits of the integrated command structure—through such devices as the European Defense Community (notwithstanding that the EDC was originally a French idea) and the Multilateral Force. As of early 1994 a new attempt at resolving the dilemma between efficacy and independence was underway, in the form of a U.S. proposal whereby the European security and defense identity (essentially the WEU) would intervene in situations inappropriate for NATO but appropriate for a coalition of European countries. The United States specifically proposed the creation of flexible "Combined Joint Task Forces" that would be embedded in the major subordinate commands of NATO but that would in all cases be capable of operating outside the integrated NATO command structure. This is the formula of "separable but not separate." In this way, NATO's infrastructure could be put at the disposition of operations that were purely European. This arrangement, while effective for the short run, is unlikely over time to satisfy those whose ambition is to create a purely European defense identity.

A second anomaly brought into relief by the Maastricht Treaty is the imbalance between France and Germany in the nuclear area. France, aspiring to be among the leaders of a European defense identity, will likely be called upon to make sacrifices regarding its national nuclear deterrent, and the process had already begun in the early 1990s. The possession of the "ultimate weapon" by France alone on the continent of Western Europe is bound to become more and more contested.

The rationale for France's independent nuclear deterrent rested on the postulate that the United States might not use its nuclear weapons in the event of a Soviet attack against Western Europe. If the United States, by prudence or by weakness, decided not to intervene in Europe with nuclear weapons at the crucial moment, and if France were threatened with attack, the French president could at that moment launch the process of final warning that in the event the Soviets persisted, could lead eventually to the obliteration of as many Soviets as there are Frenchmen, that is, some 60 million persons on each side. This is the essence of the French doctrine of deterrence, aimed at protecting the "sanctuary" of France.

Because this French deterrence doctrine, however, politically based, has now been overtaken by the virtual disappearance of the threat of a Soviet attack, the

French-German imbalance in the nuclear area, a latent issue for some time, is rising to the fore. A major point of contention, aside from the fact that the French nuclear umbrella has never been explicitly extended beyond the sanctuary of France, has been the stocks of Hadès missiles (and also the older Pluton variety)—those tactical weapons of short and medium range ("pre-strategic" weapons, in French terminology) that are supposed to serve as a final warning shot, but of which France possesses hundreds. The sudden uselessness of these weapons, which can land only in Central or Eastern Europe, became evident with the end of the Cold War.

Taking the new situation into account, President Mitterrand announced unilaterally in September 1991 the non-deployment of French pre-strategic weapons.[59] On April 12, 1992, he announced on television the suspension of nuclear testing in the Pacific.[60]

What is more, Mitterrand seems also to have recognized the problem the French strategic nuclear deterrent poses for a European defense identity. He opened the debate on this hitherto taboo subject, although in characteristically vague terms, in the wake of the Maastricht Summit: "Is it possible to conceive of a European [nuclear] doctrine? This question will rapidly become one of the major issues in the construction of a common European defense."[61]

Jacques Delors, president of the European Commission, went even further with the observation that "I cannot be prevented from thinking that if, one day, the European Community has a very strong political union, then why not transfer the nuclear weapon to this political authority?"[62]

It will be difficult for the Germany of the future to accept the nuclear imbalance between itself and France (or, for that matter, between itself and Britain), especially given the fact that a common defense policy was evoked at Maastricht. The closer integration of French and German forces, as the Franco-German brigade mutates into a corps, will stand in stark contrast to France's sanctuary policy in the nuclear domain. Put another way, it would seem in the order of things that if France aspires to the military coleadership of Europe with Germany, it should accept Franco-German integration in all areas of military activity, including nuclear. It cannot be expected, at least in the short term, that France will share its nuclear weapons technology with other European powers. The focus may instead be on control of the stocks of nuclear weapons held by France.

As the unity of Europe proceeds, it seems inevitable that, on the nuclear and political planes, the latter symbolized by France and Great Britain as permanent members of the UN Security Council, the privileged position of these two countries will be more and more contested, especially by Germany. Once the problems of absorbing the former East Germany are overcome, and once Germany has a military force that is independent of NATO command and able to intervene anywhere in the world, it is hardly likely that Germany will accept a military role inferior to that of France or Britain.

CONCLUSION

Taken all together, the Rome and Maastricht Summits and the October (1991) surprise of Kohl and Mitterrand appear to have cleared the way in theory for Europe, over time, to cut off its moorings to America in matters of defense. The United States, for its part, is faced with resolving the future of a defensive alliance whose enemy has, in effect, gone away, or at any rate no longer represents a massive threat. The continued large-scale presence of American forces on the Continent became strategically irrelevant with the end of the Cold War.

The Europeans, on the other hand, are faced with the problem of forging an effective military machine on a continent that is still far from political union and on which the mechanism of a defensive alliance represented by NATO has already been in place for many years. As Catherine Guicherd put it, "The challenge is to combine the effectiveness of military arrangements in the Atlantic Alliance with the development of the European defense identity carried out by the European Union project."[63]

Although the effectiveness of NATO as a military instrument is undeniable, there is an ambiguity surrounding its employment. Despite the fact that NATO has agreed in principle to conduct missions outside of the original NATO zone (starting with the Oslo Summit of May 1992), the latter still remains, in the terms of the Washington Treaty, as the area of operations of NATO. Another fact which casts NATO's employment into doubt is the demonstrable lack of political will to conduct operations as an alliance outside the NATO zone. Equally important, Germany is still prohibited by its own constitution from doing so.[64]

Paradoxically, the European Union has a larger potential defense vocation than NATO. As a *European* entity, the union can legitimately expand into Eastern Europe, whereas NATO can do so only against Russian opposition. This was evident in the "Partnership for Peace" proposal laid out by Secretary of Defense Les Aspin at Travemuende on October 21, 1993: the countries of the North Atlantic Cooperation Council, including Russia, were offered joint exercises leading to "interoperability" but only a vague future prospect of ever becoming full members of NATO.

It follows from the above that a European defense force should be able to intervene more credibly outside NATO's zone of Western Europe. But a European force is not, and may never be, the equivalent of an American-led force in terms of power and unity.

Protecting American security while ceasing to be dominant militarily is at the heart of the United States's post–Cold War transition problem in Europe. Protecting European security while moving toward greater union is the dimension of Europe's transition. A European defense identity, to be credible and politically viable, should have a large measure of autonomy, so that the transfers of power and sovereignty implied in its creation will appear to have been worthwhile. It follows from this that were the relationship of semi-tutelage that NATO has with the WEU to remain unaltered, and were an American SACEUR to remain an immutable principle, it would make hollow the concept of a European defense identity.

Eventually, some form of power sharing in the command of military formations in Europe should be worked out between the United States and the European Union. As the American troop draw-down nears completion, both sides must eventually define what is to be their relationship. This definition cannot logically take the form of a deeper, more integrated defense commitment: the ties between the United States and Europe have been and will inexorably continue to loosen, given the disappearance of the Soviet threat. Whatever the outcome, the emergence of a European defense identity is likely to require, over time, transfers of sovereignty and powers on both sides of the Atlantic.

NOTES

1. Jean Doise and Maurice Vaïsse, *Diplomatie et outil militaire* (Paris: Imprimerie Nationale, 1987), 623.

2. From a seminar conducted by Gates at the Olin Institute, Harvard University, May 1, 1992.

3. "French Dilemmas and Strategies in the New Europe," in *After the Cold War: International Institutions and State Strategies in Europe, 1989–1991*, ed. Joseph Nye, Robert Keohane, and Stanley Hoffmann (Cambridge: Harvard University Press, 1993), 130.

4. Interview with Jacques Andréani, French Ambassador to the United States, June 26, 1992.

5. French Embassy Press Service, Washington, D.C., text of speech of President Mitterrand, 6.

6. Alain Rollat, "Jeu de patience à l'Elysée," *Le Monde*, October 19, 1991, 9.

7. Frédéric Bozo, *La France et l'OTAN* (Paris: Masson, 1991), 195.

8. Ibid., 196.

9. Catherine Guicherd, "A European Defense Identity: Challenge and Opportunity for NATO," *Congressional Research Service Report for Congress*, June 12, 1991, summary page. The European Political Union was the linear successor to (a) the aborted plan to develop a European Political Community alongside the European Defense Community in the 1950s; then (b) the various subsequent plans to develop greater political cohesion, the most prominent of which was the failed Fouchet Plan of the 1960s; and finally (c) the loose, consensus-based mechanism of European Political Cooperation developed in the 1970s (pp. 76–77).

10. The two conferences were eventually held in December 1990.

11. Guicherd, "European Defense Identity," 7.

12. American Embassy telegram no. 4066 to State, July 6, 1990, 2–3.

13. *Le Monde*, July 8–9, 1990, 5.

14. Ibid.

15. Doise and Vaïsse, *Diplomatie et outil militaire*, 649.

16. Less than two weeks after the London Summit, and the image it projected of a more benign and more politically oriented Atlantic alliance, Mikhail Gorbachev gave up

his objections to a united Germany remaining in NATO and promised to withdraw all Soviet troops from eastern Germany by the end of 1994. Guicherd, "European Defense Identity," 7–8.

17. *Le Monde*, July 8–9, 1990, 5.

18. After the withdrawal of two French Armored divisions from Germany, the 3rd in 1991 and the 5th in 1992, there remains only one French division there, the 1st Armored. The latter, together with a German mechanized division, initially were to compose the Franco-German Corps. *Le Monde*, April 16, 1992, 6.

19. See p. 4.

20. See pp. 3–4.

21. Guicherd, "European Defense Identity," 58.

22. Bozo, *La France et l'OTAN*, 188.

23. Guicherd, "European Defense Identity," 14. The WEU action was aided by the fact that the WEU had conducted a minesweeping operation in the Gulf in 1987 during the Iran-Iraq War.

24. The North Atlantic Council (NAC) meets either as a summit or as a ministerial (foreign ministers).

25. *Le Monde*, June 9–10, 1991, 3.

26. American Embassy Copenhagen telegram to State, no. 4244, June 7, 1991, 1.

27. Ibid., 1–2.

28. "Rome Declaration on Peace and Cooperation," NATO Press Service, November 8, 1991, 3.

29. Ibid., 2. A summary of the "core functions" of NATO are: (1) to provide a stable security environment in Europe based on democratic institutions; (2) to serve as a transatlantic forum for allied consultations; (3) to deter and defend any threat of aggression against a NATO state; and (4) to preserve the strategic balance within Europe. NATO Press Communiqué M-1(91)44, June 7, 1991.

30. Bernadette d'Armaillé, *L'Architecture européenne de sécurité* (Paris: CREST, 1991), 114.

31. Interview with the author, June 26, 1992.

32. SACEUR is the acronym for Supreme Allied Commander Europe.

33. Bozo, *La France et l'OTAN*, 185.

34. The defense ministers of the alliance make up the Defense Planning Committee.

35. NATO Press Service, Press Communiqué M-DPC/NPG-1(91) 38, 3.

36. *Le Monde*, May 30, 1991, 6. According to Pentagon officials, as of June 1992 there was already a multinational corps in NATO, the BALTAP, in the Baltic region, composed of one German and one Danish division. Also, though the Rapid Reaction Corps was initially planned at 70,000 men, it has since grown in planning terms to ten divisions, well beyond the span of the one corps headquarters initially envisioned.

37. Bozo, *La France et l'OTAN*, 182.

38. *Le Monde*, October 17, 1991, 4.

39. Ibid.

40. *Le Monde*, October 6–7, 1991, 5.

41. *Financial Times*, October 17, 1991, 5.

42. Maastricht Treaty text published by the European Community, Article D, paragraph 1.

43. This is the text of Article 4 of the revised Brussels Treaty (*United Nations Treaty Series*, vol. 211, 1955, 346).

44. Maastricht Treaty, Article D, paragraph 2.

45. Ibid., paragraph 4.

46. Ibid., paragraph 5.

47. ''Rome Declaration,'' 2.

48. Maastricht Treaty, Article D, paragraph 1.

49. Dominique David, ed., *La Politique de défense de la France: textes et documents* (Paris: Fondation pour les Études de Défense Nationale, 1989), 120.

50. D'Armaillé, *L'Architecture européenne de sécurité*, 47, 54.

51. See p. 188.

52. NATO Press Service, Press Communiqué M-NAC-1(92) 51, 2–3.

53. *Le Monde*, May 24–25, 1992, 3.

54. *Le Monde*, March 12, 1993, 1. As of early 1994, the French status vis-à-vis NATO's Military Committee as a result of this decision remains ambiguous. The French fully participate on operations involving their forces, such as in the Yugoslav case, but they revert to observer status on other matters.

55. *Le Monde*, November 7–8, 1993, 9.

56. *Le Monde*, May 24–25, 1992, 3.

57. Maastricht Treaty, Article D, paragraph 6.

58. *Le Monde*, October 27, 1993, 1.

59. *Le Monde*, September 13, 1991, 3 (press conference of President Mitterrand).

60. Antoine Sanguinetti, ''L'équipement militaire français, trop cher et dépassé,'' *Le Monde diplomatique*, July 1992, 10.

61. *Le Monde*, January 12–13, 1992, 1.

62. Ibid.

63. Guicherd, ''European Defense Identity,'' 62.

64. However, the German Constitutional Court and the Bundestag have allowed the principle that German troops could be stationed in Bosnia and Somalia. *Le Monde*, November 7–8, 1993, 9.

❖ 9 ❖

Epilogue: By Default of Enemies?

The French people seem to have a two-thousand-year advance on the rest
of the human species . . . this sensitive and proud people is truly born for
glory and for virtue. . . . O sublime people! Receive the sacrifice of my
entire being; happy is he who is born in the midst of you! Happier still is
he who can die for your happiness!

Maximilien-Marie Isidore de Robespierre[1]

It is small wonder that, with such a degree of national exaltation present in the
strands of the French conscience, any attempts to denigrate or deny France's
role in the world are met with fierce resistance.

THE UNIQUENESS OF FRENCH NATIONALISM

Unlike in America, where the universalist experiment was coincident with the
founding of the nation, in France the nation long preceded the Revolution and
its message to the world. In the nineteenth century Jules Michelet gave voice
to this spirit of the French nation, transcendent and mystical, hovering some-
where apart from mere Frenchmen: "Frenchmen, whatever your condition,
whatever your class, and whatever your party, keep one thing in mind: you have
only one sure friend on this earth, and that is France."[2]

This personification of the nation—expression of the general will and those
who deem themselves destined to represent it—was carried on into modern
times by Maurice Barrès, Charles Péguy, and others, and it heavily influenced
the actions of Charles de Gaulle.

In France the respect for the state runs very deep. Because the nation is the oldest in Europe, the state has therefore long become the embodiment of the nation. The oft-repeated imperative to "express the French difference" is a reflection, in an oblique way, of an intense nationalism, ingrained over the ages.

Against the backdrop of this centuries-long impregnation, one can arrive at a sense of the sacrosanct quality of the French nation. It is perhaps more difficult to incorporate the notion that, because of this millennial bond between the French nation and the French people, cooperation of any other nation with France can only go so far.

THE "TENSION AROUND THE MESSAGE"

This particularity around the notion of France, around the nation of France, goes largely unheeded in America. As Ernest May has pointed out,[3] whatever the sympathies that individual Americans may entertain for France, the fact is that the United States as a polity has never recognized the special role and mission of France. Thomas Jefferson could well say, "Ask the travelled inhabitant of any nation, in what country on earth would you rather live? Certainly in my own. . . . Which would be your second choice? France."[4]

Such sentiment exists only on a personal level. It does not extend to the polity. From the outset of its experience the American nation has considered France as another part of old Europe, left behind and repudiated; the beginning of the United States as a nation was as a breakaway from Europe. There is an overwhelming sense in the United States that the experiment of a democratic republic has taken place only in the New World, and only in America.

The French, on the other hand, with a highly developed sense of national pride, cultivated for centuries; with the notion of having created the world's best society in which to live, think, and enjoy, and whose benefits can be extended to others, press with insistence their own universalist message. Many observers have noted this "tension around the message" between the French and the Americans.

The great imbalance in the power position between the two countries has not prevented the French from pressing their case. Thus when François Mitterrand, in the wake of the Los Angeles riots of April 1992, rejected "any comparison between France and the American 'conservative society'," [5] he was projecting the thought that the French message to the world was better, especially in terms of social justice and equality. In the reaction that followed (President Bush was said to be "appalled"; others noted that even de Gaulle had not gone so far in his criticism of American society in the wake of the Watts riots in 1965[6]), this point of ideology seems to have been lost.

DIFFERING MEANINGS OF DEMOCRACY

A Latin country, France has a destiny in history of an uncertain constitutional life. The notion of the general will, pervasively a part of French political thought from Rousseau to Robespierre to de Gaulle, where the sum is not equal to all of the democratic parts, has meant in historical terms an invitation to extra-constitutionality in the cloak of a claim of legitimacy. In another sense, social instability in this Latin country is part of the fabric of society. Whereas the United States has had only one constitution, to which amendments are added only rarely, the French have had a dozen since the monarchy was overthrown.

The idea of legitimacy is at the opposite of American thinking: the United States, reacting in a prudential fashion and supporting the government legally in place, was led into major strategic error by the decision, at the end of 1940, to help the regime of Marshal Pétain. Later, during the 1950s, the United States accepted with resignation the idea of supporting the tottering governments of France, it being juridically correct. The United States was never able to envisage in that period the coming to power of General de Gaulle within a legal and democratic framework. It was with surprise that, on the eve of de Gaulle's taking power in 1958, John Foster Dulles solemnly noted, in a telegram to the American Embassy in Paris, that "developments in France which might bring de Gaulle to power by orderly process are so extraordinary that they justify exceptional measures."[7] What made it extraordinary was that de Gaulle was acting in the name of legitimacy and of the general will, and the French people were supporting him; the constitutional framework would follow. In such situations of deep crisis legitimacy becomes more important than legality as viewed in the Anglo-Saxon context.

The coming to power of de Gaulle in 1958 profoundly changed French democracy. The French model began to approach the American model. The coherence the "hidden monarchy" of the Fifth Republic gave to French foreign policy was in happy contrast to the weakness and hesitations of the Third and Fourth. But the unbridled exercise of executive power, without the legislative or, especially, the judicial constraints that prevail in the American system, could at some point provoke a new upheaval in France, a Latin country and as such inclined to solutions of rupture.

Perhaps the central difference between the French and the American political cultures is suggested in the formula of Stanley Hoffmann: that during the French Revolution the "liberal" and "democratic" strands became separated.[8] There was a fault line between liberalism in the European sense—liberties exercised in a mode of laissez-faire capitalism—and democracy, in the sense of an ideal of equality. As Raymond Aron put it, the democrats "laid claim to the people's will [as a means of] suppressing individual freedoms and representative institutions. . . . Too often the defenders of liberties were not democrats."[9] This fault line was at its most acute in the nineteenth century in France, when the two parties, the liberals and the democrats, each claimed to be the valid heirs of the French Revolution. Shortly before the midway point in that century a third claimant appeared: socialism.

One aspect of this split between liberals and democrats has been that democracy in France has come to be imposed by a central government. (Obviously the split occasioned by the Revolution was not the only reason for this, as France was an administratively centralized country long before.) Until the coming to power of de Gaulle and the Fifth Republic in 1958, this central power in "legicentrist" France was exercised by the French National Assembly—except for the periods of the Restoration and the two Bonapartist empires.

The experience in France was unlike that in America, where democracy grew from below, through what was essentially liberalism instilled through a decentralized federal system. These were, and remain, despite growing convergences, two very different means of responding to the central question of the equality of conditions of mankind.[10]

The evolution of this difference in these two republics has meant for France a later acceptance of capitalist methods: the split in France between the liberal and the democratic models has manifested itself in a split over bourgeois virtues, which are less universally accepted than in the United States. In the United States, on the other hand, there has been a late, and grudging, acceptance of state-imposed measures of redistributing wealth.

The paradox that lies in the background of this difference is that the American liberal model of laissez-faire capitalism, in striving to improve itself, has had a socially fluid terrain in which to operate; in France the attempts to impose equalization have taken place against a background of an aristocratic and vertical society. Although the models in both countries have lately begun to reverse themselves, in the twentieth century the United States has been largely a consensus environment, whereas France has been divided against itself in a traditional left-right verbal civil war.

It is interesting in this context to compare the reactions of French and American officials and businessmen to charges from the other side concerning discriminatory business practices. In an America that is largely a government from below, it is not seen as culpable if local interests in Congress impose discriminatory tariffs to protect outmoded industries, as this is not seen as government policy: not only is there not a monolithic center in this American polity deriving its inspiration from Montesquieu, but there is also a large devolution of power to the individual states.

France, on the other hand, has been a government from above going back to the days of Louis XIV's finance minister, Jean-Baptiste Colbert. It is deemed only natural that the state should help its agriculture and its enterprises, especially its numerous public-sector enterprises—all the more so because it is the central government that has traditionally held the initiative in France, not the local authorities (though this is changing somewhat in France with the decentralization laws of the 1980s).

In both countries these discriminatory trade practices, which spring from different sources, probably tend to balance out overall. But because they derive differently, they become grounds for irritations and misunderstandings. In France it is expected that the French intelligence services will help French enterprises with information derived from commercial espionage against American firms, especially those enterprises in France's public sector, given the central role of the state in French society and the sense of nationalism in France, especially in the political class. By contrast, America's government from below has been unable to date, and is unlikely in the future, to solve the challenge of how to help individual American enterprises with economic and commercial intelligence it has received.

THE DENIAL OF FRENCH NATIONAL INTERESTS: THE REASONS

Starting with World War II and continuing throughout the postwar period, the United States, for a variety of reasons, going back principally to the wartime period but also related to the Cold War, systematically refused to give consideration to the national interests of France.

This denial of French national interests manifested itself principally in two ways. The United States first sought to prevent France from exercising a major role in the peace that followed World War II. Later, in the postwar period, the United States denied the French a role in European defense equivalent to that of the British. In particular, the United States sought variously to block or retard the French national nuclear force. Culturally speaking, it was perhaps too large a leap of faith to provide the ultimate weapon to a Latin and Catholic society, as contrasted to an Anglo-Saxon and Protestant one.

The United States tempered this primordial quarrel—primordial because it concerned defense—with the major concession, albeit essentially a political and philosophical one, represented by the Ottawa Declaration of June 1974. The concession was largely political and philosophical because the French had already left the NATO military structure in 1966. France had already taken itself out of the game, with attendant advantages and disadvantages.

Though the United States no longer contested France's role as a nuclear military power—a considerable event in itself—the question of who controlled Europe's defense was never settled to the satisfaction of all parties, least of all France—the one country that has consistently contested U.S. leadership in this area. And far from disappearing, this ambivalence at the heart of the Atlantic alliance reappeared as the Cold War faded away. The question of "who's in charge here" (i.e., in charge of Europe's defense) had become by the early 1990s a renewed issue of contention between France and the United States.

At the beginning of this period of severe misunderstanding, that is, with the defeat of France in 1940, the Roosevelt administration, taking a view that was excessively contemporary or, more broadly speaking, ahistorical, looked upon France as a permanently weakened country. This approach was symbolized by the fact that the American leadership, taking its cue from Roosevelt himself, constantly ridiculed the notion of French "grandeur."

By this ahistorical approach the United States in effect denied the role France had fulfilled in the defense of the West, especially during World War I. The American leadership during World War II, in its majority at least, was unable or unwilling to have the vision of a France that would bring itself out of the abyss of 1940. The French, in contrast to the Americans, have depended *too much* on history, *their* history, and have a hard time accepting the permanence of reality. François Furet has referred to "the national French problem . . . the French, and particularly their elites, have difficulty adjusting the present of the Nation with its past."[11]

The French, and first and foremost General de Gaulle, had every interest in putting 1940 behind him: it was imperative to transcend this shameful event. For de Gaulle, it was necessary to rebuild French morale and to arrange things in such a way that France at the end of the war would not have to pay for its defeat and surrender. "The Republic has never ceased to exist . . . Vichy always was null and void and it remains so," said de Gaulle to Georges Bidault on August 25, 1944, when the latter urged him to declare the restoration of the republic before the Parisian throng.[12]

It is interesting to speculate on the consequences if, as Cordell Hull maintained,[13] the presence of the American Ambassador along with France's "touring government" in June 1940 would have tipped the scales in favor of a continuation of the war and a fallback of the French government to North Africa. In this event the Germans likely would have struck into North Africa, and the result could have been that America, strategically threatened, might have been drawn into the war sooner. Most importantly for France, the scars of its government's June 1940 surrender ("This armistice is dishonorable," General de Gaulle proclaimed[14]) would not have been there.

But events were otherwise. Soon after the surrender the United States characteristically sided with the party in power, with "rump France," and as a consequence it became more or less inevitable that France and the United States would come into conflict over the outcome of the war: the United States, in seemingly wanting France to recognize the fact of its surrender by, in effect, a reduced rank among nations and shorn of its colonies; and France, in wishing to assure for itself a share of the booty of a war it had not, properly speaking, won. France wanted its share to be as equal as possible to that of the full-fledged winners, the United States, the Soviet Union, and Great Britain. For France, it was up to the Germans, largely conquered by countries other than France, to pay for having caused the loss of French grandeur. For France, victory in World War II had been a quasi-proxy victory.

THE EFFECT OF THE "SPECIAL RELATIONSHIP": ITS LESSENING

This almost ineluctable quarrel between the United States and France stemmed also from the fact of an American policy anchored in the "special relationship" with Great Britain—or what Professor Edward N. Saveth termed the conception of an Atlantic civilization as seen in the patrician WASP tradition. According to Saveth, "the so-called Wasp establishment did possess a long view of American foreign policy, even an ideology. Defined by Henry Adams, Theodore Roosevelt, and John Hay, among others, its core was linkage to England in the context of Eurocentrism.''[15]

In this world of Eurocentrism based on ties with Great Britain, there was only a secondary role for France. Nevertheless, as the Cold War began, France, then the "country of the center" (it is no longer), became indispensable to American plans for the defense of Europe. Curiously, the U.S. leadership did not want to accord France special considerations to take this indispensability into account. Instead, France was in effect relegated to the status of a second-zone nation, although in policy statements by Washington, France was continually characterized as a major ally of the United States in Europe. Thus, fundamentally, both from the historical and the geopolitical point of view, the United States neglected to take into account the importance of France.

Even after the recovery of France, and even after France had overtaken Great Britain economically by the start of the 1960s, the United States did not consent to treat France on the same footing as Great Britain, although all three had been allies on a par at the end of World War I. Instead, France had to force its way back into a position of parity with Great Britain. This it did largely through the *"Trente Glorieuses"* (its thirty years of economic recovery, 1950–80) and through its independent nuclear deterrent.

This American foreign policy anchored in the "special relationship" with Great Britain, although still extant, has by now lost some of its emotional content. The generation of the so-called Wise Men,[16] rooted in the Anglo-American tradition and for the most part a product of the East Coast establishment, is no longer around. In its place, as Henry Kissinger forecast some twenty years ago,[17] is a generation that is at the same time more pluralist and less focused on the European world than its predecessor. The increasing ethnic and racial diversity of the United States is reflected, with some cultural lag but inexorably, in the American foreign policy establishment. It is a phenomenon at times refuted by the facts but generally valid: the establishment that directs American foreign policy is more diversified than before.

America's increasing ethnic and racial diversity should serve over time to lessen the impact of the Anglo-American relationship such as it is perceived by Europe and particularly by France. The more America's diversity is manifested and represented, the less America will be perceived by France as part of a monolithic Anglo-Saxon bloc competing with and threatening French interests, as so often has been the case in the past.

THE "ABSENT POPULATION"

In the French-American emotional context there has been nothing comparable to the affinity between the two great Anglo-Saxon countries: the American-British relationship is "family." Apart from the fact that it was a long-ago event, French aid to the American Revolution does not count for much, and for two reasons. First, in the United States there is no emotional charge to accompany it. Not only was there no substantial French immigration to cultivate the myth, there was even a negative past, as pointed out by Jean-Baptiste Duroselle: the ancient rivalry in the New World between French and English colonists (the Americans naturally and geographically being the heirs of the latter).[18]

Second, in France, the aid given to the American Revolution is in a sense "non-legitimate," by the fact that it was launched by the monarchy of Louis XVI. The public commemorations of this assistance, in anniversaries and other French-American festivals, are devoid of real emotional substance and characterized by a rather empty and forced sentimentality.

This is not to say that there does not exist an affinity between the United States and France. Although they are two very contrasting countries, they are, importantly, two countries of democracy. Apart from Great Britain, emotionally and historically tied to the United States, there is no other great country in Europe that is comparable with the United States in this respect. Germany, despite its reemerging power, has always had, at least until recently, an uncertain or provisional relationship with democratic principles. Italy, although comparable with France on the economic plane, is of a different order in political and military terms. France and America are the two premier republics of the Western world.

But even this almost unique systemic affinity between the two great Western republics born out of revolutions did not count for much in the tense atmosphere of the Cold War period. It was rather toward Germany that the United States fixed its attention. Quickly transformed into a major strategic asset, the Federal Republic became the favorite child of the United States. And the Germans reciprocated. There was an extraordinary current of sympathy, at least until recently, toward the great ally from across the Atlantic. Moreover, for Germany, this relationship was the means par excellence for assuring its security and for finding its place again in the world. And it was not just a matter of mutual strategic interest. As has been noted earlier, there were internal and affective reasons to explain the honeymoon between Germans and Americans, which contrasted with the sourness of French-American relations: the presence of a strong German culture in the United States, more or less related to the Anglo-Saxon culture.

In the case of France, a Latin country of a very different culture with a Catholic, not a Protestant base, there was the added disadvantage of not being a country of emigration. A large mass of French origin does not, properly speaking, exist in the United States. There is not per se a German bloc, but there are vast numbers of people of German origin, some localized here and there but most melted into the population as a whole. The prejudice of the average American against this "absent population" (that is, the French) is very marked. Other peoples of Latin origin strongly represented in the United States, such as the Italians and the Spanish-speaking populations, perforce do not encounter the same incomprehension as this "absent population." Because it was not a country of emigration, France, of all the great countries of Europe, remains the one that is fundamentally the most apart from the United States. They are, in a certain sense, strangers in a common Western house.

It is striking to recall the debate that raged in the United States in the 1930s over foreign policy: the German community provided a dedicated, or at least sympathetic, mass behind the isolationists ("America Firsters"), and the interventionists were largely pro-British internationalists. There was no comparable group advocating the mutual interests of France and the United States.

It is also interesting to reflect on the sudden and irrational swings of opinion against the French in the United States, notably over the French refusal to allow American overflights for the raid against Libya in 1986. Could this issue have produced such intensity, indeed could it have developed at all, with any other European country except France?

THE GATHERING FRENCH REACTION

Despite all the disadvantages France faced at the end of World War II, its weakness was overcome in time, thanks largely to the quality of its élites and their vision of a policy of independence. Fundamentally, France was obsessed by independence because she had lost it in 1940. For the French, independence came to be focused on a policy of nuclear independence. Nuclear weapons and independence went together. France's *Defense White Paper* of 1972, which has remained the bible of the Gaullist-inspired French policy of national nuclear independence, noted that "if the nuclear strategic force is the instrument of nuclear deterrence, it is the will to national independence that is the foundation of it."[19]

As the development of the French nuclear weapons program began to take shape, it became clear that this would allow France to achieve a rank among nations greater than was her due on the basis of population and resources. This activity had begun before de Gaulle's return to power, but it became essentially a Gaullist program, with a highly political objective: to obtain for France nuclear hegemony on the continent of Western Europe. This program turned out to be a brilliant success—until now at least. Since its nuclear weapons became operational toward the end of the 1960s, France has remained the sole nuclear power on the continent of Western Europe.

The French policy of nuclear independence was constantly contested by the United States until Nixon and Kissinger arrived on the scene at the end of the 1960s and broke with the demons of the past. France in turn drew closer to the military organization of NATO. This was only partly due to the tradition of independence of the French military from the French government. There had to be a modicum of political cover for the France-NATO military rapprochement, as symbolized in the Lemnitzer-Ailleret accords of 1967 and its sequels. However, this rapprochement remained low-key. Even the significant step of placing the French element in the Euro-Corps under NATO command in a crisis[20] was accompanied by disclaimers that France was planning to return to the NATO military structure. Until now at least their wartime and postwar experience appears to have traumatized the French against placing their defense outside of their own control.

Together with the thrust toward nuclear independence, the other aspect of French strategic policy in the long term was to aspire to the leadership of Europe and, in so doing, make a statement of France's independence and rank. This aspiration was to be met by France's nuclear (and economic) power, supported by the economically most powerful country in Europe: Germany. The end of the division of Germany transformed the terms of this calculation. Reunified Germany has become much more important than France economically. However, by a time-lag that parallels the United States–Europe duality, France remains more important in strategic and military terms, largely from the fact of its nuclear weapons (and also because of its permanent seat on the UN Security Council). Although with the reunification of Germany, France is no longer its equal, France has something Germany does not: nuclear weapons. As for Italy, another non-nuclear power, it cannot be compared with France in political and military terms, though it is its equal in economic terms.

It was due in no small part to its policy of nuclear independence that France regained its prewar parity with Great Britain: France in effect recovered its rank of 1918. Indeed, a thread running through this account from the 1940s to the present is the restoration of France's status as a great European power. This fact notwithstanding, the end of the Cold War marked the end of that exceptional period when France, generally supported by a truncated Germany, could well aspire to be the most important power on the continent of Western Europe. With the reunification of Germany this is no longer the case, all the more so with the end of the Cold War, and the deemphasis on nuclear weapons.

THE STRUGGLE FOR THE HEART OF GERMANY

The country that most opposed the hegemonic drive of the United States during the postwar period was France, which wanted to respond to the "injury" inflicted on it by the United States and at the same time recover its rank among the great nations of Europe. In order to reclaim this rank, France, as noted above, carried out a dual policy aimed at acquiring a nuclear hegemony over the continent of Western Europe and becoming the locomotive of Europe in tandem with West Germany.

What Frédéric Bozo has characterized as France's forty-year-long goal of a "European strategic identity"[21] could only be accomplished by maintaining and strengthening the Franco-German alliance, France being essentially unable to carry out a policy in this framework by herself. What developed, then, with the return of de Gaulle to power in 1958 and the meeting between him and Adenauer in September of that year, was that France and the United States began competing for the favors of Germany. In order for France to feel strong enough to challenge her powerful transatlantic partner, she needed either the support, or at least a benign attitude on the part of Germany. In this struggle for the heart of Germany the French have had only a partial success, at least until now.

The French-American rivalry for the friendship of Germany—which has been going on more or less continually since 1958—lies within the larger problem of the relationship between the United States and Europe. The military domination of the United States over the Continent has begun to diminish, if only because of the withdrawal of thousands of American troops from Europe, a process that is almost certain to accelerate. In turn, the leadership of France over the continent of Western Europe, which lessened gradually during the 1970s and the 1980s, is now diminishing more sharply with the reunification of Germany. France, having already made major economic concessions to Germany, will be forced to make concessions in other areas; France cannot maintain its leading rank on the Continent outside the framework of the Franco-German alliance. Whether this alliance can hold firm remains the central question for France's European policy in the coming years. Conversely, a central question for America's European policy in the near future is whether, as the heretofore hegemonic power in Western Europe, it should help the Franco-German alliance to endure and prosper.

THE SUBSUMING OF FRANCE'S NATIONAL AMBITIONS

Having traditionally (since 1789) sought the role of preeminence in the propagation of universalist messages, it is not surprising that France should want to restate this preeminence at a moment when the composition of Europe is profoundly and rapidly changing. The French have been in the lead in this redefinition of Europe—to the point where France has given itself the job of transforming national ambition into European ambition. Whether the new Europe turns out to be satisfactory for France's ambition is being called sharply into question with the Euro-pessimism that set in after the Maastricht Conference and the deepening recession in Europe. Still, it appears that some form of European unity will eventually emerge, and France, despite various neo-Gaullist, leftist, and corporatist pressures, will be a leading part of it. But France's European outcome, and indeed European unity, still turns largely on the durability of the Franco-German alliance. Such durability is far from certain.

Often in the past specificity for France has been a rationale for going it alone, against difficult odds. The French sense of national pride finds it very difficult to face the prospect of playing with a losing hand. The French, more than most, prefer not to be outnumbered, because they so often are. They fought against the introduction of other than economic subjects in the G7 meetings because they were outnumbered by Anglo-Saxons—even the Japanese being considered, in this forum, as Anglo-Saxons. More recently, the French enthusiasm for the Conference on Security and Cooperation in Europe (CSCE), originally welcomed because it broke the model of two blocs facing each other (as in the

Mutual and Balanced Force Reduction talks), has waned as the American attitude has grown more favorable. The CSCE's very inclusionism ("from Vancouver east to Vladivostok") now works for U.S. (and German) purposes at the end of the Cold War and not as it did earlier for French ones. The EC on the other hand, with at its core the Franco-German alliance, has been the perfect arena for the exercise of French influence.

THE LOOSENING OF AMERICA'S CONTROL

The United States is in a position of economic decline relative to the European Community and Japan. The European Community, on the other hand, has seen its economic importance to Eastern Europe and the former Soviet Union grow sharply. Politically, the end of Western Europe in tutelage, as was generally though increasingly less the case during the bipolar era that existed from 1947 to 1989, has arrived; but the mentalities conditioned by this tutelage situation have not caught up with this fact.

The United States is the world's only military superpower, but it is riven with deep economic and social difficulties, not as serious, to be sure, as those of the former Soviet Union but nevertheless deep-seated. The time would seem to be at hand for the United States to scale back its foreign commitments (as it has had to do in the case of Yugoslavia) and at the same time stop trying to command Europe's defense at a time when such command is becoming unnecessary.

Whether or not NATO gradually disappears or transforms itself by means of a new treaty with the EC, the United States will have to make adjustments in its old habits and attitudes. It will have to alter its sense of gigantism, of tutelage over Europe. As the year 2000 approaches, it will be necessary for the United States to recognize that it is an economic power smaller than Europe on the world scene. The old habit of dominance—in its most egregious aspects symbolized by the term coined by Senator William Fulbright, "the arrogance of power"—will have to be shed by a nation economically in the throes of adjustment if not decline and militarily in withdrawal from Europe. As noted in the previous chapter, the collapse of the Soviet Union in 1991 brought about the breakup of two imperia in Europe, not just one. For all the bows toward NATO in the Maastricht Treaty, the death knell of this "other" empire was sounded in the declaration announcing a defense entity for Europe.

On the level of the relations of states, it seems inevitable that the United States will eventually have to accept some form of institutional relationship with the European Union. There already is a framework for such a relationship embodied in the U.S.–EC declaration of November 1990, which the "Europeanists" point to while contending that the United States pays only lip service to it. The essence of this framework is that relations between the United States and the EC are to take place with the EC as a whole. This would not be exclusively between an EC representative and a U.S. representative, however: in some situations representatives of all the EC countries as well as the commission, would take part in meetings.

For the United States to accept dealing with the European Union essentially as a collectivity would go a long way toward easing the friction that has existed between itself and France for the last forty-some years. However, some sort of balance would have to be worked out between the "Europeanists," led by France, seeking true independence, and the United States, seeking to avoid isolation and a fallback to the Western Hemisphere. Indeed, multiple and alternate frameworks do exist for transatlantic consultations (the UN, CSCE, GATT, NATO, the North Atlantic Cooperation Council, and the G7), and they should be maintained as the new U.S.–European Union relationship works itself out.

In sum, the United States, as it becomes relatively more excluded from Europe by the strengthening of European unity and the virtual disappearance of the Soviet threat, will inevitably find itself less important in Europe's calculations. It will have to adjust to this status as a power that is less relevant (and certainly less dominant) than it has been in Europe heretofore.

THE FRENCH-AMERICAN DIALOGUE

A new and different chapter has emerged in the old quarrel between France and the United States for the leadership and defense of Europe. Now is essentially the first time since the great misunderstanding began in 1940 that both countries are largely free from the constraints of the wartime period and the Cold War that followed.

The end of the Cold War is certain to produce a new calculus in French-American relations, if only from the fact of the disappearance of the threat from the former Soviet monolith. This calls into question the integrated NATO military command and America's control over the use of NATO's conventional and nuclear weapons—the single greatest source of tension between America and France for the past forty years. However, as was pointed out in the preceding chapter, the issue of America's command over Europe's defense remains to be resolved definitively.

There will certainly be tensions between America and France, and indeed new tensions have arisen with the end of the Cold War, but it is important to bear in mind the possibility of new compromises, as both countries enter a period of relative decline. The worldwide power of the American imperium will become weaker as its relative economic position diminishes and as Europe's integration proceeds. And the privileged position the oldest nation in Europe enjoyed in the Gaullist era and its aftermath will inexorably be adjusted downward.

In the new dialogue between America and Europe, in which the most difficult scene will likely be with France, it is well to bear in mind the experience of the past. In part it has been a question of French abstractionism and American pragmatism having a hard time getting through to each other. For the French, it is in the order of things to find the philosophical framework first, to establish a vision of things, before entering into practical matters. For the Americans, it is necessary first and foremost to be practical and to do first what is possible.

The difficulty in communications can be summed up in the American perspective by the following recurring formula: the French are "duplicitous." Sometimes this turns out to be a question of the French not wanting, for their own reasons, to engage in a frank dialogue. The American view of an alliance, in which there is a frank exchange between partners, may not be the same as that of the French. In an alliance that has never been to their liking, because it is essentially on the United States's terms, the French may adopt an attitude that is polite but constrained and defensive; on other occasions, and of course depending on the individuals, the French pattern is to be confrontational and aggressive, partly perhaps out of the French feeling generally that they give in too easily to foreigners.

The apparent duplicitousness may also reflect a deep French feeling about the sanctity of the state and of *raison d'etat*. French puzzlement over the gravity Americans attached to Watergate is a testimony thereto. To an extent far greater than the more open "children of Europe" from across the Atlantic, the French are used to a tradition of secrecy in affairs of state. The only gradual lifting of the veil, fifty years later, of the Vichy government's active participation in crimes against the Jews is a reminder thereof, in a particularly grim register.

Additionally, the apparent duplicitousness is a reflection of the fact that the United States in many respects is *the* adversary. The United States, as superpower, now carries the mantle of the hereditary rivalry between France and Britain—a rivalry that was interrupted by the seventy-five-year torment Germany visited on France, but which is now considered a thing of the past. Germany and France are now attached by continental adjacency and by France's solicitations of Germany for many years. And the forty-year interlude of the threat from Russia has suddenly, almost mysteriously, gone away.

The British, in French eyes, show greater comprehension of Europe's problems with America than the Americans. They are closer, virtually (though not quite) a part of Europe, and in the view of French officials understand Europe's problems better. The British, not the Americans, first suggested in October 1991 that forces under WEU direction could intervene in areas outside the zone of NATO's defensive alliance.[22] It was British Defense Minister Malcolm Rifkind who stated on May 14, 1992, that the WEU "should have available to it a variety of forces and capabilities" and that "the Franco-German Corps may be one of these." (To be sure, Rifkind added in the next breath, "There may also be many others."[23])

The difficulty of communication can be summed up in the French perspective by the *lack* of communication. "They had nothing to say," was the comment of a French official after discussions in early 1992 with American interlocutors on the subject of Europe's defense. American leadership seemed to have no vision of the future of Europe, no framework in mind as to the future of the alliance or a new political direction in the aftermath of the Cold War. Indeed, American officials had no precise idea of what the eventual American troop level in Europe might be: sometimes the figure of 150,000 was mentioned, sometimes 100,000, and sometimes 50,000. Their main aim, unstated, appeared to be the very practical one of how to maintain American military control in Europe.

Too often in the past, America has seen dialogue with France as an act of ratification of its wishes; a dialogue that is necessary but not ultimately one that will deter the outwardly "collegial" decisions of the imperium. This mind-set characteristically takes the form of refusing to heed signs or of not listening. The essential has been that a dialogue took place, and that it appeared to be relatively harmonious. In January 1965 Ambassador Bohlen made reference to "the amicable nature of the conversations the Secretary [of State Dean Rusk] had in Paris in December on the subject [of the MLF and the ANF] with General de Gaulle and with Couve de Murville."[24] Rusk himself described de Gaulle in the first of these two meetings as "cordial and relaxed" and in the second as "courteous and even affable throughout [the] discussion,"[25] even though it was clear that the two sides were heading toward a very serious impasse. (Obviously, it was of little import to de Gaulle whether the Americans saw his mood as benign or not.) American pragmatism is such that often an agreement is perceived to have been reached with the French when it has been a question only of favorable atmosphere or of abstraction of language.

By contrast, sometimes the American language is so lacking in abstraction that the French call it "naïve." The Americans, on the other hand, as when Secretary of State James A. Baker, on May 11, 1992, demanded of French Foreign Minister Roland Dumas, "Are you for us or against us?"[26] would simply call it "blunt." For the Americans, it is difficult to understand, much less accept, the French rejection of multinationalism in a revised NATO force structure and yet support it for a European Corps. The answer from the French point of view is that the former hinders the development of a united Europe and the latter helps it.

BY DEFAULT OF ENEMIES?

It is often ignored—perhaps because it is easier to do so—that there exists between France and the United States a past laden with bad memories. In the final analysis history cannot be denied; the rancors of the past cannot be swept away easily. And when new disputes arise, as with the end of the Cold War, this troublesome past has to be taken into account; it cannot be expected that these "transatlantic antagonisms"[27] will disappear. Each new American administration, which thinks it has corrected past errors in the policy toward France, learns to its chagrin that new problems crop up or old ones reappear. The memories have remained: in particular, the denigration of the Free French movement by the Roosevelt administration during World War II, and later the rejection by

Washington of the French *force de frappe*. The wounds are still there, although the causes have largely been corrected.

Does this mean that, by "default of enemies," France is destined to become "Enemy No. 1" of the United States, to paraphrase the title of an article by Thierry de Montbrial?[28] Unthinkable and not very likely, as Americans and Frenchmen generally walk toward the brink and, having looked at it, step back, often at summit meetings. And yet, with the disappearance of the Soviet threat, the wraps are off, and therefore the situation bears watching. Both sides (but more particularly the French) have motives of revenge: the French for having been held in check all these years by the "nuclear consensus" of the West, and the Americans for having to endure Gaullist barbs and the French "difference" for decades.

It remains to be seen whether the state of "reciprocal cordial distrust" between America and France will last in perpetuity, or whether there will be a softening of the conflicts that have arisen because of competing ambitions of the two sides, ambitions that inexorably will have to be scaled down. In turn these two countries which are carriers of universal messages to the other peoples of the world, and which are the two premier republics of the West, could be led to a greater mutual understanding. Perhaps most to be borne in mind by both sides, as these two countries confront each other at the approach of the twenty-first century, is that each does indeed carry a universal message born out of revolutions, and that these messages, while not wholly irreconcilable, are nonetheless very different.

Each side, therefore, should recognize the nature and validity of the other's message.

Relations between the United States and France are only a part, albeit a defining part, of relations between America and Europe. These relations are at a moment as decisive as in 1947, when the Truman administration committed itself to the rescue of Europe—politically, economically, and militarily.

Is it the case, as Henry Kissinger put it, that "France should abandon its relentless effort to set up a European defense structure outside NATO" and that "the European Community should encourage a larger political role for the United States within its deliberations"?[29] Is it justified that America should act as though it is the greatest European power and therefore by right be accorded a voice in Europe's councils? Or is America so far away that such consultation would be self-defeating for an integrated Europe? Put another way, is European unity a fact that America is unable or unwilling to grasp? Can one agree with Ambassador Jacques Andréani that statements such as Ambassador Jeane Kirkpatrick's ("France is advocating free trade—but only within the European Community"[30]) reflect an unwillingness to recognize the fact that Europe in itself has become a new economic entity?[31] Conversely, can one agree with Ambassador Kirkpatrick that "although they do not say so outright, they [the French] would like the whole of Europe to have the same relationship with NATO that France has had since 1967. They believe that NATO and the United States should have no significant role in Europe's future unless Europe becomes the object of a major, and unexpected, attack from some unsuspected source."[32]

Is it sufficient to argue, as some European officials have done, that there will be no hegemonic power in Europe because it will be unified and hence no danger to the United States? Or should the United States, as the so-called "Wolfowitz report" is supposed to have advocated, "dissuade possible rivals from aspiring to a larger regional or global role," or more specifically "prevent the emergence of a system of an exclusively European security system which could destabilize NATO"?[33]

Most fundamentally, should the United States "encourage an expanding and more cohesive European Community to play an increasing political, economic and military role," as Stanley Hoffmann has recommended?[34] Or should the United States, in a comparison pointed up by Jean-François Deniau, act toward the Franco-German alliance in the manner of Rome ("this law of the Roman Senate, applied during six centuries, and which forbade any alliance between two allies of Rome")?[35] The weight of wisdom would seem to be with the thesis of Stanley Hoffmann, which recognizes the limits of American power, and against the "Roman" precedent.

The words of Henry Kissinger on European unity, a stated ideal of the United States ever since 1947, ring prophetically from their moment of origin nearly thirty years ago:

[A] European sense of identity can no longer be nourished by fear of the U.S.S.R. [Therefore] a united Europe is likely to insist on a specifically European view of world affairs—which is another way of saying it will challenge American hegemony in Atlantic policy. This may well be a price worth paying for European unity; but American policy has suffered from an unwillingness to recognize that there is a price to be paid.[36]

NOTES

1. Robespierre, *Discours et rapports à la Convention* (Paris: Union Générale d'Editions, 1965), 248–49 (on the relation between religious and moral ideas and republican principles, and on national holidays; speech delivered to the Convention on May 7, 1794).

2. Jules Michelet, *Le Peuple* (Paris: Flammarion, Édition Champ Historique, 1974), 75.

3. Interview with the author, June 22, 1992.

4. Burton Stevenson, ed., *The Home Book of Quotations*, 10th ed. (New York: Dodd Mead, 1967), 719 (taken from Thomas Jefferson, *Writings* [Washington, D.C.: Thomas Jefferson Memorial Association of the United States, 1907], 159).

5. *Le Monde*, May 29, 1992, 1.

6. Ibid.

7. Dwight D. Eisenhower Presidential Library (DDEL), White House Office File, Office of the Staff Secretary, Box 3, Department of State, May–August 1958: Message from Dulles to Herter, May 29, 1958.

8. From a seminar given by Professor Hoffmann, Harvard University, spring 1992, entitled, "French Political Thought."

9. Raymond Aron, *Essai sur les libertés* (Paris: Calmann-Lévy, 1965), 17.

10. See pp. 10–11.

11. *Le Monde*, May 19, 1992, 2.

12. Jean Lacouture, *De Gaulle: The Rebel 1890–1944*, trans. Patrick O'Brian (New York: Simon and Schuster, 1990), 575.

13. According to Hull, Ambassador Bullitt, instead of remaining in Paris between June 10 and 17, should have followed the French government in its peregrinations: "This decision, in my opinion, was unfortunate. It deprived Bullitt of all contact with the French Government between June 10, when it left Paris, and June 17, when it asked for an armistice. Had Bullitt, with his unequaled contacts with the leaders of the French Government, been able to represent us during those historic days, it is possible, if not probable, that the Government would have taken the fleet, gone to North Africa, and continued the fight from there." Cordell Hull, *The Memoirs of Cordell Hull* (New York: Macmillan, 1948), 1:789.

14. Charles de Gaulle, *Discours et Messages* (Geneva: Editions Edito-Service, 1970), 1:11 (radio broadcast from London, June 26, 1940, addressed to Marshal Pétain).

15. Edward N. Saveth, "Suicide of an Elite?" *Commentary*, August 1991, 46.

16. Cf. Walter Isaacson and Evan Thomas, *The Wise Men* (New York: Simon and Schuster, 1986).

17. "We often told ourselves that our generation could be the last to concentrate on European problems. Those who followed might be more interested in other parts of the world." Interview with the author, November 7, 1991. See also p. 158.

18. Jean-Baptiste Duroselle, *France and the United States: From the Beginnings to the Present*, trans. Derek Coltman (Chicago: University of Chicago Press, 1978), 1. See also p. 15.

19. *Livre Blanc sur la Défense Nationale* (Paris: CREST, 1972), 14.

20. See p. 189.

21. See p. 179.

22. See p. 187.

23. Speech to the Center for Defense Studies, King's College, London (British Information Services, New York, 11).

24. Lyndon Baines Johnson Presidential Library (LBJL), National Security File, Committee on Nuclear Proliferation, Box 5, France: American Embassy Paris telegram 3798, January 5, 1965, section 1, 5. (N.B., ANF stands for Atlantic Nuclear Force.)

25. LBJL, NSF, France, Box 24, MLF cables: Secto 26 of December 16, 1964 and Secto 12 of December 14, 1964, from Paris.

26. *New York Times*, July 2, 1992, A10. According to the *Times*, the remark is contained in an official French transcript of a meeting in Washington on May 11, 1992, between Secretary Baker and Foreign Minister Dumas.

27. The phrase is Alfred Grosser's. See p. 3.

28. "La France est-elle 'l'ennemi numéro 1' des Etats-Unis?" *Le Figaro*, June 16, 1992, 3. In this article, de Montbrial noted, "The *Washington Post* went so far as to describe us as the 'Number One Enemy' of America."

29. "The Atlantic Alliance Needs Renewal in a Changed World," *Los Angeles Times*, March 1, 1992, M2.

30. *Los Angeles Times*, June 21, 1992, M7.

31. Interview with the author.

32. *Los Angeles Times*, June 21, 1992, M7.

33. Paul Marie de la Gorce, "Washington et la maîtrise du monde," *Le Monde Diplomatique*, April 1992, 14–15. (N.B., though the report, never published in toto, was prepared under the supervision of Under Secretary of Defense Paul Wolfowitz, it is not established whether the latter had reviewed the document, which was obtained by the *New York Times*. After the *Times* published extracts on March 8, 1992, and at least in part because of the stir it caused, the report was revised.)

34. *The New York Times*, June 21, 1992, section 4, 5.

35. Text dated June 20, 1966, p. 18, addressed by Mr. Deniau to French Foreign Minister Maurice Couve de Murville.

36. Henry A. Kissinger, *The Troubled Partnership* (New York: McGraw Hill, 1965), 40.

Selected Bibliography

BOOKS

Acheson, Dean. *Present at the Creation: My Years in the State Department.* New York: W. W. Norton, 1969.

Aglion, Raoul. *De Gaulle et Roosevelt: La France Libre aux Etats-Unis.* Paris: Plon, 1984.

Alphand, Hervé. *L'étonnement d'être: journal, 1939–1973.* Paris: Fayard, 1977.

Aron, Raymond, and Daniel Lerner, eds. *La querelle de la C.E.D.* Paris: Armand Colin, 1956.

Attali, Jacques. *Lignes d'horizon.* Paris: Fayard, 1990.

Auriol, Vincent. *Journal du Septennat, 1947–1954.* Paris: Armand Colin, 1974.

Azéma, Jean-Pierre. *De Munich à la libération, 1938–1944.* Paris: Seuil, 1979.

———. *1940, l'année terrible.* Paris: Seuil, 1990.

Ball, George W. *The Past Has Another Pattern: Memoirs.* New York: W. W. Norton, 1982.

Bell, Coral. *Survey of International Affairs 1954.* London: Oxford University Press, 1957.

Borne, Dominique, and Henri Dubief. *La crise des années 30: 1929–1938.* Paris: Seuil, 1989.

Bozo, Frédéric. *La France et l'OTAN: De la guerre froide au nouvel ordre européen.* Paris: Masson, 1991.

Bundy, McGeorge. *Danger and Survival: Choices about the Bomb in the First Fifty Years.* New York: Vintage Books, 1990.

Calvocoressi, Peter. *Survey of International Affairs 1947–1948.* London: Oxford University Press, 1952.

Carpentier, Jean, and François Lebrun, eds. *Histoire de France.* Paris: Seuil, 1987.

Chatelain, Jean. *La Nouvelle Constitution et le régime politique de la France.* Paris: Editions Berger-Levrault, 1959.

Chautemps, Camille. *Cahiers secrets de l'armistice: 1939–1940.* Paris: Plon, 1963.

Coutau-Begarie, Hervé. *Darlan*. Paris: Fayard, 1989.

Debré, Michel. *Trois républiques pour la France: Mémoires*. 3 vols. Paris: Albin Michel, 1988.

Doise, Jean, and Maurice Vaïsse. *Diplomatie et outil militaire: politique étrangère de la France, 1871–1969*. Paris: Imprimerie Nationale, 1987.

Duguit, L., H. Monnier, and R. Bonnard. *Les Constitutions et les principales lois politiques de la France depuis 1789*. Paris: Librairie Générale de Droit et de Jurisprudence, 1952.

Duroselle, Jean-Baptiste. *La France et les Etats-Unis: des origines à nos jours*. Paris: Seuil, 1976.

———. *France and the United States: From the Beginnings to the Present*, trans. Derek Coltman. Chicago: University of Chicago Press, 1978.

Eisenhower, Dwight D. *The Papers of Dwight David Eisenhower*. Edited by Alfred D. Chandler, Jr. Baltimore: Johns Hopkins University Press, 1970–.

Elgey, Georgette. *Histoire de la IVe République*. Vol. 1, *La République des illusions, 1945–1951*. Paris: Fayard, 1965.

Ferro, Marc. *Pétain*. Paris: Fayard, 1987.

Flohic, François. *Souvenirs d'Outre-Gaulle*. Paris: Plon, 1979.

Fontaine, André. *Histoire de la guerre froide*. Vol. 1, *De la Révolution d'Octobre à la Guerre de Corée 1917–1950*. Paris: Fayard, 1965.

———. *Un seul lit pour deux rêves: Histoire de la "détente," 1962–1981*. Paris: Fayard, 1982.

Funk, Arthur Layton. *Charles de Gaulle: The Crucial Years, 1943–1944*. Norman: University of Oklahoma Press, 1959.

Furet, François, Jacques Juillard, and Pierre Rosanvallon. *La République du Centre: La fin de l'exception française*. Paris: Calmann-Lévy, 1988.

Galante, Pierre. *Le Général*. Paris: Presses de la Cité, 1968 (cassette version).

Gaulle, Charles de. *Mémoires de Guerre*. 3 vols. Paris: Plon, 1955, 1956, 1959.

———. *The Complete War Memoirs of Charles de Gaulle*. 3 vols. New York: Simon and Schuster, 1964.

———. *Discours et Messages*. 7 vols. Geneva: Editions Edito-Service, 1970.

———. *Lettres Notes et Carnets*. 12 vols. Paris: Plon, 1981.

Giscard d'Estaing, Valéry. *Le Pouvoir et la vie*. Vol. 2, *L'affrontement*. Paris: Editions Compagnie 12, 1991.

Godechot, Jacques, ed. *Les Constitutions de la France depuis 1789*. Paris: Garnier-Flammarion, 1970.

Goldschmidt, Bertrand. *Le complexe atomique: histoire politique de l'énergie nucléaire*. Paris: Fayard, 1980.

———. *Pionniers de l'atome*. Paris: Stock, 1987.

Grosser, Alfred. *Les Occidentaux: les pays d'Europe et les Etats-Unis depuis la guerre*. Paris: Fayard, 1978.

———. *The Western Alliance*. New York: Continuum, 1980.

———. *Affaires extérieures: la politique de la France, 1944–1984*. Paris: Flammarion, 1989.

Hoffmann, Stanley. *Decline or Renewal? France since the 1930s*. New York: Viking, 1974.

Horne, Alastair. *A Savage War of Peace: Algeria 1954–1962*. Hong Kong: Elisabeth Sifton Books–Penguin Books, 1977.

Hull, Cordell. *The Memoirs of Cordell Hull.* New York: Macmillan, 1948.

Hurstfield, Julian G. *America and the French Nation, 1939–1945.* Chapel Hill: University of North Carolina Press, 1986.

Jobert, Michel. *Mémoires d'avenir.* Paris: Grasset, 1974.

———. *L'autre regard.* Paris: Grasset, 1976.

Johnson, Lyndon Baines. *The Vantage Point: Perspectives of the Presidency, 1963–1969.* New York: Holt, Rinehart and Winston, 1971.

Kissinger, Henry A. *The Troubled Partnership: A Reappraisal of the Atlantic Alliance.* New York: McGraw-Hill, 1965.

———. *Years of Upheaval.* Boston: Little, Brown, 1982.

Lacouture, Jean. *Léon Blum.* Paris: Seuil, 1977.

———. *Pierre Mendès-France.* Paris: Seuil, 1981.

———. *De Gaulle.* 3 vols. Paris: Seuil, 1984, 1985, 1986.

———. *De Gaulle.* 2 vols., trans. Alan Sheridan. New York: Simon and Schuster, 1991, 1992.

Lacroix-Riz, Annie. *Le choix de Marianne: les relations franco-américaines, 1944–1948.* Paris: Messidor/Éditions Sociales, 1985.

Laloy, Jean. *Yalta: hier, aujourd'hui, demain.* Paris: Robert Laffont, 1988.

———. *Yalta: Yesterday, Today, Tomorrow,* trans. William R. Tyler. New York: Harper and Row, 1988.

Langer, William L. *Our Vichy Gamble.* New York: Knopf, 1947.

———. *An Encyclopedia of World History.* Boston: Houghton Mifflin, 1972.

McGeehan, Robert. *The German Rearmament Question.* Urbana: University of Illinois Press, 1971.

Maillard, Pierre. *De Gaulle et l'Allemagne: le rêve inachevé.* Paris: Plon, 1990.

Mélandri, Pierre. *Les Etats-Unis face à l'unification de l'Europe, 1945–1954.* Paris: Pedone, 1980.

———. *Une incertaine alliance: les Etats-Unis et l'Europe, 1973–1983.* Paris: Publications de la Sorbonne, 1988.

Monnet, Jean. *Mémoires.* Paris: Fayard, 1976.

———. *Memoirs.* Garden City, N.Y.: Doubleday, 1978.

Murphy, Robert D. *Diplomat among Warriors.* Garden City, N.Y.: Doubleday, 1964.

Neustadt, Richard E. *Alliance Politics.* New York: Columbia University Press, 1970.

Perse, Saint-John. *Oeuvres Complètes.* Paris: Gallimard, 1972.

Rimbaud, Christiane. *L'affaire du Massilia.* Paris: Seuil, 1984.

Rioux, Jean-Pierre. *La Guerre d'Algérie et les Français.* Paris: Fayard, 1990.

Roosevelt, Elliott, and James Brough. *A Rendezvous with Destiny: The Roosevelts of the White House.* New York: Putnam, 1975.

Rouanet, Pierre. *Mendès-France au pouvoir, 1954–1955.* Paris: Robert Laffont, 1965.

Rousso, Henri. *Le syndrome de Vichy: 1944–198-.* Paris: Seuil, 1987.

Sherwood, Robert E. *Roosevelt and Hopkins: An Intimate History.* New York: Harper, 1948.

Spaak, Paul-Henri. *Combats Inachevés.* Vol. 1, *de l'Indépendance à l'Alliance.* Paris: Fayard, 1969.

Tournoux, Jean-Raymond. *Secrets d'Etat.* Paris: Plon, 1960.

Truman, Harry S. *Memoirs.* 2 vols. Garden City, N.Y.: Doubleday, 1956.

Ullman, Richard H. *Securing Europe.* Princeton, N.J.: Princeton University Press, 1991.

Vaïsse, Maurice. *Les relations internationales depuis 1945.* Paris: Armand Colin, 1990.

Wall, Irwin. *L'influence américaine sur la politique française, 1945–1954*. Paris: Balland, 1989.
Welles, Sumner. *The Time for Decision*. New York: Harper and Brothers, 1944.

ARTICLES

Ambrose, Stephen E. "Le Grand Charles." *New York Times Book Review*, November 11, 1990, 1, 8.
Barbier, Collette. "Les négotiations franco-germano-italiennes vue de l'établissement d'une coopération militaire nucléaire au cours des années 1956–1958." *Revue d'Histoire Diplomatique*, no. 104 (1990): 81–113.
Bozo, Frédéric, and Jérôme Paolini. "Trois Allemagnes, deux Europes et la France." *Politique Etrangère* 1 (1990): 119–38.
Buchan, Alastair. "The Multilateral Force: An Historical Perspective." *Adelphi Papers* (London: Institute for Strategic Studies), no. 13 (October 1964).
Burr, William. "Marshall Planners and the Politics of Empire." *Diplomatic History* 15, no. 4 (Fall 1991): 495–522.
DePorte, Anton W. "De Gaulle's Europe: Playing the Russian Card." *French Politics and Society* 8, no. 4 (Fall 1990): 26–40.
Duval, Marcel. "Elaboration et developpement du concept français de dissuasion." *Relations Internationales*, no. 59 (Fall 1989): 371–83.
Emerson, William R. "Roosevelt and de Gaulle." *The View from Hyde Park*, Winter 1989, 8.
Fromkin, David. "Eyeless in Suez." *The New Republic*, July 29, 1991, 39–42.
Hoffmann, Stanley. "The Man Who Would Be France." *The New Republic*, December 17, 1990, 29–36.
Jouve, Edmond, and Maurice Couve de Murville. "Mémorandum de 1958 sur l'O.T.A.N." *Espoir*, no. 15 (June 1976): 2–14.
Katz, Milton. "The Marshall Plan after Twenty Years." *The Foreign Service Journal*, June 1967, 1–6.
Leroy, Jacques Guillaume. "Le petit homme, la France et l'Europe." *Contrepoint*, no. 15 (1974): 69–83.
Mélandri, Pierre, and Frédéric Bozo. "La France devant l'opinion américaine: le retour de de Gaulle début 1958–printemps 1959." *Relations Internationales*, no. 58 (Summer 1989): 195–215.
Rouche, Geneviève. "Le Quai d'Orsay face au Problème de la Souveraineté Allemande." *Revue d'Histoire Diplomatique*, no. 104 (1990): 37–55.
Saveth, Edward N. "Suicide of an Elite?" *Commentary*, August 1991, 44–47.
Soutou, Georges-Henri. "The French Military Program for Nuclear Energy, 1945–1981." *Nuclear History Program Occasional Paper* (College Park: Center for International Security Studies, University of Maryland), no. 3 (1989).
Ullman, Richard H. "The Covert French Connection." *Foreign Policy*, no. 75 (Summer 1989): 3–33.
Vaïsse, Maurice. "Aux origines du mémorandum de septembre 1958." *Relations Internationales*, no. 58 (Summer 1989): 253–68.
———. "Autour des Accords Chaban-Strauss 1956–1958." *Revue d'Histoire Diplomatique*, no. 104 (1990): 77–80.

Yost, David S. "France and Conventional Defense in Central Europe." *European American Institute for Security Research*, no. 7 (Spring 1984).

PARTS OF COLLECTED WORKS

L'Aventure de la bombe: De Gaulle et la dissuasion nucléaire (1958–1969). Colloquium organized by the University of Franche Comté and the Institut Charles-de-Gaulle, Paris, September 27–29, 1984. Paris: Plon, Collection Espoir, 1985.
Bator, Francis M. "The Politics of Alliance: The United States and Western Europe." In *Agenda for the Nation*, edited by Kermit Gordon. Washington, D.C.: The Brookings Institution, 1968.
De Gaulle et la Nation face aux problèmes de défense (1945–1946). Colloquium organized by the Institut d'Histoire du Temps Présent and the Institut Charles-de-Gaulle, Paris, October 21–22, 1982. Paris: Plon, Collection Espoir, 1983.
Vaïsse, Maurice. "France and the Suez Crisis." In *Suez 1956: The Crisis and Its Consequences*, edited by William Roger Louis and Roger Owen. Oxford: Clarendon Press, 1989.

UNPUBLISHED REPORTS

Barbier, Colette. "La Force Multilaterale." 1990. Institut d'Histoire des Relations Internationales Contemporaines (IHRIC), Paris.
Girault, René. "La France et les Autres: Les Enjeux de la Modernisation." In *La France en voie de modernisation 1944–52.* Colloquium organized by the Fondation Nationale des Sciences Politiques, Paris, December 4–5, 1981. Fondation Nationale des Sciences Politiques.
Neustadt, Richard E. "The Skybolt Affair: A Report to President Kennedy." November 15, 1963. John F. Kennedy School of Government, Harvard University.

UNPUBLISHED MATERIAL IN LIBRARY COLLECTIONS

Archives of the Quai d'Orsay, Paris: Series B, America, 1944–1952, United States, Atomic Issues, August 10, 1945–August 9, 1949, and Interim Aid to France, 1947–1948.
Dwight D. Eisenhower Presidential Library, Abilene, Kans.: White House Central File; White House Office File, Office of the Staff Secretary, and Office of the Special Assistant for National Security Affairs; Ann Whitman File; Dulles-Herter Papers; Lauris Norstad Papers.
Fletcher School of Law and Diplomacy, Medford, Mass.: Oral History Interviews of François de Rose and Pierre Gallois.
Franklin D. Roosevelt Presidential Library, Hyde Park, N.Y.: President's Secretary's File; Office File; Map Room File on France (FOF); Harry Hopkins Papers.
Harry S. Truman Presidential Library, Independence, Mo.: President's Secretary's File; Official File; Psychological Strategy Board File; Papers of Dean Acheson; Papers of John W. Snyder; Papers of Matthew J. Connelly; Office Files of the Assistant

Secretary of State for Economic Affairs; Oral History Interviews on the Marshall Plan of Robert Marjolin, Raymond Aron, and Etienne Hirsch.
Hoover Institution on War, Revolution and Peace, Stanford, Calif.: Papers of Robert D. Murphy.
John F. Kennedy Presidential Library, Boston, Mass.: National Security File; President's Official File; Oral History Interviews of Theodore C. Sorenson, Walt W. Rostow, Lyman Lemnitzer, Roswell L. Gilpatric, Maurice Couve de Murville, Hyman G. Rickover, Dean Acheson, Charles E. Bohlen, William R. Tyler, Adam Yarmolinsky, and Peter Thornycroft.
Lyndon Baines Johnson Presidential Library, Austin, Tex.: National Security File; Papers of the President—Confidential File; Papers of Francis M. Bator.
National Archives, Washington, D.C.: Office of Strategic Services, Foreign Nationalities Branch Files, 1942–1945, French.
Naval Historical Archives, Washington, D.C.: Papers of Captain Tracy B. Kittredge.
Nixon Presidential Materials Staff, Alexandria, Va.: White House Central Files Subject File.

PUBLISHED OFFICIAL MATERIAL

Documents diplomatiques français. Paris: Ministère des Affaires Etrangères, Commission de Publication des Documents Français. 1954–56.
Foreign Relations of the United States. Washington, D.C.: United States Government Printing Office. 1940–57.
Livre Blanc sur la Défense Nationale. Paris: CREST, 1972.

INTERVIEWS WITH THE AUTHOR

Aglion, Raoul, November 22, 1990.
Andréani, Jacques, June 26, 1992.
Ball, George W., May 3, 1991.
Bissel, Richard, April 23, 1991.
Bowie, Robert, December 17, 1990.
DePorte, Anton, February 3, 1991.
Dillon, Douglas, October 25, 1990.
Gordon, Lincoln, April 11, 1991.
Hoffmann, Stanley, September 20, 1991.
Jobert, Michel, November 22, 1990.
Katz, Milton, March 6, 1991.
Kissinger, Henry A., November 7, 1991.
Liddy, John, April 26, 1991.
May, Ernest R., December 11, 1991, June 22, 1992.
Neustadt, Richard E., December 18, 1991.
Reinstein, Jacques, April 26, 1991.

Rodman, Peter M., January 17, 1991.

Rose, François de, November 21, 1990.

Sonnenfeldt, Helmut, December 17, 1990.

Welles, Benjamin, January 15, 1991.

Yost, David S., September 3, 1990.

Index

About the Author

CHARLES G. COGAN (Doctor of Public Administration, Harvard University) is a Visiting Scholar, John M. Olin Institute for Strategic Studies, Center for International Affairs at Harvard University. After a stint in journalism and service as a Signal Corps officer during the Korean War, Dr. Cogan joined the CIA, where he spent 37 years, 23 of them on assignments overseas.